Yale Studies in English

Benjamin Christie Nangle, Editor

Volume 151

COLERIDGE

AS RELIGIOUS THINKER

BY JAMES D. BOULGER

New Haven, YALE UNIVERSITY PRESS, 1961

Published with aid from the foundation
established in memory of Philip Hamilton
McMillan of the class of 1894, Yale College

TO MY

Mother and Father

ACKNOWLEDGMENTS

This study of Coleridge's religious thought began as an undergraduate essay at Holy Cross College under the direction of Professor Francis Drumm. It expanded at Yale University with the aid of Professors Frederick A. Pottle and Cleanth Brooks to include much of the present material. The present form of the essay was not conceived, however, until I had studied, under the kind direction of Professor Kathleen Coburn, the unpublished Coleridge Notebooks and other works at the University of Toronto. I owe a special debt of gratitude to these four friends and Coleridgeans for their scholarly and personal interest in my work.

I am indebted to many studies of Coleridge's thought; these are cited in the footnotes. Here I will mention my two favorite books: John Muirhead's *Coleridge as Philosopher* and I. A. Richards' *Coleridge on Imagination,* which have influenced my thinking in an all-pervasive way. My book attempts to complement these studies in the somewhat neglected area of Coleridge's religious thought.

In preparing this book I have received help in many areas from colleagues at Yale University. Professor Robert L. Calhoun of the Yale Divinity School and Professors Brand Blanshard and John Smith of the Department of Philosophy advised me on several problems. In its original form the book was a doctoral dissertation submitted to Yale University. The readers were Professors Charles Feidelson, Jr., William K. Wimsatt, Jr., and Cleanth Brooks, who made helpful suggestions for revision. To Dwight Culler,

Benjamin C. Nangle, David Horne, and Frederick A.
Pottle, readers of the book in its present form, I owe
special debts of gratitude for exacting criticisms of the
context and style.

The Bollingen Foundation, publishers of *The Notebooks of S. T. Coleridge,* have kindly allowed me to quote
material from Coleridge's as yet unpublished notebooks.
My thanks are also due the staff of Victoria College Library, Victoria College, Toronto University, and also
Professor Kathleen Coburn for assistance on many occasions in working with the photograph notebooks and
other unpublished Coleridge manuscripts.

Publication has been substantially assisted by the Fund
for Young Scholars of Yale University.

Finally there is my wife, who as typist, editor, and con-
sultant has had more than the usual share of drudgery in
the preparation of this book.

                                                    J. D. B.

New Haven
February 1961

CONTENTS

CUE TITLES

Biog. Lit.	*Biographia Literaria* (1817), ed. J. Shawcross, 2 vols. Oxford, 1907.
Letters	*Letters of Samuel Taylor Coleridge,* ed. E. H. Coleridge, 2 vols. London, Heinemann, 1895.
Log. & Learn.	*Coleridge on Logic and Learning,* ed. Alice D. Snyder, New Haven, Yale Univ. Press, 1929.
New Letters	*The Letters of Samuel Taylor Coleridge,* ed. E. L. Griggs, 2 vols. Oxford, Clarendon, 1956.
Phil. Lect.	*The Philosophical Lectures of Samuel Taylor Coleridge,* ed. Kathleen Coburn, London, Pilot, 1949.
Unpub. Let.	*The Unpublished Letters of Samuel Taylor Coleridge,* ed. E. L. Griggs, 2 vols. New Haven, Yale Univ. Press, 1933.
Works	*The Complete Works of Samuel Taylor Coleridge,* ed. G. T. Shedd, 7 vols. New York, Harper, 1853.
Aids	Vol. 1, *Aids to Reflection,* 1825.
Church and State	Vol. 6, *On the Constitution of the Church and State,* 1830.
Confessions	Vol. 5, *Confessions of an Inquiring Spirit,* 1840.
The Friend	Vol. 2, *The Friend,* 1818.

CHAPTER 1

AIDS TO REFLECTION

"All the products of the mere *reflective* faculty partook of DEATH."

Coleridge occupied a good part of his later life commenting on religious matters and writing theological tracts. The Bard of *Lyrical Ballads* became the seer of Highgate, producing *Aids to Reflection, Confessions of an Inquiring Spirit, Essay on Faith,* and filling many unpublished Notebooks with important religious musings. As might be expected by students of Coleridge's other endeavors, the theological writings are not organized or shaped in such a way as to merit the title "Coleridge's theology." Coleridge was not a Hegel. But his speculations are insights and gropings toward a wider and more vital theology than was held by the dogmatic creeds, in and out of the Church of England, in his day. They are fragmentary, but we are invited by their brilliance.

To appreciate this brilliance, however, one must understand the idealistic premise within which Coleridge worked, and sense the significance of the historical and traditional aspects of his work. For instance, the relationship between his speculations and the Anglican orthodoxy which we meet in *Aids to Reflection* is very complex. Coleridge was not merely a speculator and a spectator, but an

1

individual energetically acted upon by a living tradition of Reformation theology.

As a speculator, rebelling against the Orthodoxy of his time, Coleridge was responsible in some degree for the restoration of intellectual stature in the religious thinking of the Anglican Church. The assumptions and methods of eighteenth-century rationalism which still gripped the contemporary clergy were attacked in his writings and discarded in favor of a more idealistic, intuitive system. In a general sense, his basic religious ideas stem from the Platonic tradition of the seventeenth-century Cambridge Platonists as it was modified and altered by contact with German transcendental philosophy. This is a commonly known generalization but one which by itself leads only to confusion, and to a misunderstanding of Coleridge. The problem is that Coleridge mentioned seventeenth-century and German sources so many times and in such different contexts that the influence of each upon his thinking has become the subject of controversy. In the following pages this controversy must necessarily be explored, not for the sake of once again reviewing old material, but in the hope of finding a fresher and more rewarding viewpoint than has yet been found for examining the sources of Coleridge's idealism.

Much more interesting than speculation upon this controversy, from our modern point of view, is a conviction which gradually impressed itself upon me during the early stages of preparation for this book: that the idealistic mode of thought, which grew with Coleridge's distinction between reason and understanding, reflects the peculiar nature of the religious problems themselves, and cannot be isolated by mere definition. While it seems, surely, that the whole subject of Coleridge's religious thinking must have as a starting point the idealistic premise of "reason vs. understanding," the fact remains that this premise is largely conditioned by the religious problems which Coleridge undertook to solve. Hence a thorough student must acquaint himself with eighteenth- and early nineteenth-century religious background. The rich store of unfavorable allusion to contemporaries, especially notable in *Aids,* is significant in accounting for the complexity and seeming incongruity in many of Coleridge's religious opinions. It is immediately clear, for instance, that he could not accept the rigid orthodoxy of the "High Church" party, the overemotionalism of contemporary "Methodists and Enthusiasts," or the shallow rationalism inherited by the school theologians from the eighteenth century. His arguments for idealism are largely dictated by these negative interests. To balance the forces of emotional evangelicalism and rigid orthodoxy he advanced interpretations of orthodox doctrines which might take into account the emotions and will, without swamping the intellect and the rational elements in religion in a deluge of sentiment. Such a combination would have been sheer contradiction in the two existing modes of religious thought, either the decayed eighteenth-century rationalism or the debile scholasticism still persisting in Anglican theology. Hence there is an important practical reason why the Kantian philosophy and the Platonic tradition of the seventeenth century function so prominently in Coleridge's religious thinking. His success in making this combination more than a confused and useless garble is a matter we must decide for ourselves.

In *Aids* Coleridge first tried to present, combining "idealism" with contemporary Anglican theology, a lively, viable form of Christian orthodoxy to replace the moribund product of the early nineteenth century. An insight into the nature of this orthodoxy, which was based upon the philosophical and historical factors suggested thus far, is the goal of the following chapters. And one must look

beyond *Aids* itself to the late Notebooks and other unpublished works to deal fully with the philosophical and
historical problems.

The search for this vital orthodoxy was in a very real
sense pragmatic—that is, based upon a deep personal need
in Coleridge, the man and poet, as we also shall try to show.
Those who know and love Coleridge will not expect to
find in either the prose or poetry a logical, coherent system; rather, they will expect to struggle with a complex,
paradoxical, and sometimes contradictory mode, fashioned
to cope with doctrines which are themselves paradoxical,
and, in the strict sense, beyond the confines of rationalism
and logic. To a very legitimate degree this idealistic mode
owes its peculiarities to the nature of the subject under
investigation.

Aids to Reflection, which was destined to become Coleridge's most influential contribution to nineteenth-century
thought, was met by lack of enthusiasm when it came
from the press in 1825.[1] Jeffrey and the other popular
reviewers had given Coleridge up for lost after the *Biographia Literaria* in 1817, and greeted his next produc-
tions with uniform silence. *Aids to Reflection,* except for
a notice of publication, was not mentioned by any of the
leading reviews of the day. This conspiracy of silence in-

1. The *Aids to Reflection* of 1825 passed through three editions (1825,
1831, 1836). The 1839 edition of H. N. Coleridge was reissued in 1843
and 1848. Derwent Coleridge edited it in 1854 and 1856. There was also
Thomas Fenby's edition, 1873, and the Bohn Library edition, 1884. In
addition, there were numerous American editions. *Aids to Reflection* ap-
peared in the *Complete Works of Samuel Taylor Coleridge,* edited by
Shedd in 1853, reissued in 1854, 1860, 1863, 1868, and reprinted in 1884.
The enormous influence of this book is mentioned in Vernon Storr's *The
Development of English Theology in the Nineteenth Century* (London,
1913), pp. 317–37; in John Tulloch's *Movements of Religious Thought in
Britain during the Nineteenth Century* (New York, 1885), pp. 8–9; and in
René Wellek's *Kant in England* (Princeton, 1931), p. 124.

cluded—besides the *Edinburgh Review—The Gentle-
man's Magazine, The Eclectic Review, The Quarterly*
the London Magazine.

that Coleridge's
emphasis upon a new approach to more fundamental
theological problems than were interesting his contemporaries, stood little chance of being successful.

Aids to Reflection was a challenge to an age which was
tired of religious controversies. In its negative emphasis it
is an attack upon the principle of latitudinarianism that
passed as the dominant religious mode of the time. A close
look at the book uncovers the pattern of early nineteenth-
century religious thought, as it is reflected in the numerous allusions Coleridge made to his contemporaries and
their religious ideas.

It is not an easy book to read or to understand. Polemic
and cross-purpose in organization account for the zig-zag
movement of the thought, and for the seeming inconsistency in the form. We get the feeling, first of all, that Coleridge believed himself to be out of touch with his own
time; he is the proverbial unheeded prophet flinging his
challenge to one and all. This obsession with the role of
ignored seer accounts for the great amount of digression
which at times almost disrupts the continuity of his positive religious thought.

Any book which indulges in frequent personal asides
must obviously have a clear and intricate over-all plan to
prevent the dissipation of energy in essentially secondary
areas. Unfortunately for *Aids to Reflection,* its two structural principles of organization are intricate without being

clear. Coleridge's division into Introductory, Prudential, Moral and Religious, and Spiritual aphorisms, unintentionally belies the importance and number of the religious issues considered; nor does it coordinate the numerous allusions to contemporary religious figures and problems.

The work opens with some introductory aphorisms which give the distinction between Prudential, Moral, and Spiritual Religion. This tripartite division is related in the closing aphorism to Coleridge's favorite distinction:

> It may be an additional aid to reflection, to distinguish the three kinds severally, according to the faculty to which each corresponds, the part of our human nature which is more particularly its organ. Thus: the prudential corresponds to the sense and the understanding; the moral to the heart and the conscience; the spiritual to the will and the reason . . .[2]

The moral and prudential aphorisms then appear. A number of the moral aphorisms, we might observe, could easily have been called aphorisms of spiritual religion; such is the looseness of Coleridge's organization, which he admits himself in reference to one aphorism (p. 170). A very short section, "Elements of Religious Philosophy," precedes the Aphorisms of Spiritual Religion. These "Elements" are very obscure, and without knowledge of Coleridge's religious writings as a whole a reader would not perceive the connection between them and the practical doctrines handled in the Aphorisms of Spiritual Religion. These form the longest, final, and most important section of *Aids*. On the surface this entire structure seems quite arbitrary, external, and rambling.

Even less does our knowledge of Coleridge's original intention help in the question of structure. Two letters indicate what the original plan had been. In the first he

2. *Aids*, p. 134.

tentatively

Murray:

> Briefly, th
> cause I stro
> bishop Leigh
> (better) Life
> and critical intro
> make not only a
> VOLUME . . .[3]

A second letter clarifies t   ..ewhat:

> Now the Volume, I ha.e prepared, will be best de-
> scribed to you by the proposed Table—

> Aids to Reflection: or Beauties and Characteristics
> of Archbishop Leighton, extracted from his various
> Writings, and arranged on a principle of connection
> under the three Heads, of 1. Philosophical and Miscel-
> laneous. 2. Moral and Prudential. 3. Spiritual—with
> a Life of Leighton and a critique on his writings, and
> opinions—with Notes throughout by the Editor.[4]

The "Life of Leighton" was never written; other seventeenth-century divines, such as More and Taylor, made
their way into the Volume, and, most significantly, the
editor's "Notes" dwarfed all the rest in space and importance in the final version. What began as an objective commentary upon Leighton became one of Coleridge's major
performances, equaled in length and sustained interest
only by the *Biographia Literaria. Aids, Biographia,* and
"The Rime of the Ancient Mariner" have the same casual
origin.

Is there, then, any organization in the baffling arrange-

3. Jan. 18, 1822; *Letters, 2,* 717.
4. Aug. 8, 1823; *Unpub. Let., 1,* 315.

ment which resulted from the merger of the "Beauties of Leighton" with the "Moral, Prudential, and Spiritual aphorisms"? If there is, it is certainly not a schematic but an ideational principle, and only corresponds occasionally with the putative structures. For another intended principle, the famous Coleridgean distinction between the reason and the understanding appears in Aphorism VIII. Then it promptly gets lost in the maze of distinctions in later sections. Thereafter, it seems, it becomes the task of the reader to sense the presence of the understanding in the author's negative arguments, and the presence of the author's reason in the positive arguments. Following this procedure is admittedly difficult but rewarding. The general rule is as follows: The reason is the organ of "spiritual religion," while the understanding, when used alone, issues in the decayed theology and philosophy of the late eighteenth and early nineteenth centuries.

The validity of this distinction between the reason and the understanding is a controversial matter; also, Coleridge's use of the reason in discussing religious questions has never really been explored. Yet one aspect of the definition, that the understanding should be equated with decayed philosophy and theology, offers no great difficulties. In many parts of *Aids to Reflection* Coleridge is using the word "understanding" not in any precise philosophical sense but as a convenient symbol under which to class whatever he considered to be narrow in religion and false in philosophy. If we look upon this symbol as symptomatic of a negative, polemical stance, the purpose of certain sections of *Aids* becomes clear. Actually, everything he attacked in eighteenth-century religious rationalism has been duly recorded in the histories of philosophy in much the same terms.[5] The negative criticism is interesting to

5. Storr, *Development of English Theology in the Nineteenth Century*, pp. 317–36, has a section crediting Coleridge as a critic of the age. In

the extent that it provides clues for finding what the sensitive areas and important interests in Coleridge's theological position really were.

His probing into rationalism and orthodoxy is not done systematically in *Aids*. Many people and many ideas, representing the most divergent points of view, are harshly treated. The only common denominator is his constant insistence that the errors were products of the understanding. It is also important to note that the method in this attack can be found in all Coleridge's other late works, such as the *Philosophical Lectures* and *Theological Notes*. In fact, the attacks on contemporary rationalism in these other late works can quite properly be considered with the negative message in *Aids* as related chapters in the case Coleridge was preparing against his age. Thus it is important to realize that the principle of organization in *Aids* is ideational rather than schematic. Coleridge attacks the rationalism of the understanding at the beginning, middle, and end, in footnotes, and even in the midst of discussions of his own positive beliefs. Our immediate object will be to gather together the most illuminating criticisms of the understanding as they appear in *Aids* and other late writings. A significant clue to Coleridge's religious temper and interest is the fact that his chief targets, Evidence-writing, Socinianism, and rational theology, were the three forces most corruptive of Anglican Orthodoxy during the first two decades of the nineteenth century.

By 1825 the spate of Evidence-writing, which had begun in the late eighteenth century in refutation of Hume's essay on Miracles,[6] had ceased to have any great impor-

---

Otto Pfleiderer's *The Development of Theology in Germany since Kant and Its Progress in Great Britain*, trans. J. F. Smith (London, 1890), pp. 308–11, Coleridge is praised for his pioneer work in the field.

6. For a general idea of the number of refutations that Hume's denial of miracles received in the late eighteenth century see John Hunt's *Re-*

tance for the issues of the day. Still it continued with un-
abated flow, in the endowed lectures at Oxford, and in
other works of individual divines. Coleridge, in a spirited
burst characteristic of *Aids,* reveals his undisguised contempt for this kind of writing and points out its futility
for his time:

> Hence, I more than fear the prevailing taste for books
> of natural theology, physico-theology, demonstrations
> of God from Nature, evidences of Christianity, and
> the like. Evidences of Christianity! I am weary of the
> word. Make a man feel the want of it; rouse him, if
> you can, to the self-knowledge of his need for it; and
> you may safely trust it to its own Evidence,—remem-
> bering only the express declaration of Christ himself:
> *No man cometh to me, unless the Father leadeth him.*[7]

Not only is Evidence-writing a useless enterprise; its
mode of presenting Christianity in some kind of rational
demonstration is erroneous. Coleridge urged that such
demonstrations are the product of scientific rather than
religious enthusiasms, and served no useful purpose. The
blindly orthodox considered them unnecessary, and the
philosophically minded doubted the premise upon which
they are based. Yet such studies had replaced true religious
interest in the late eighteenth and early nineteenth centuries.

Along with works on "Miracles" and "external evidence," Coleridge gave short shrift to their scholastic
counterpart, religious writing which "demonstrated" the
teleological argument as the basis for natural theology.

---

ligious Thought in England (London, 1873), *3,* 210–21. His summary of
the refutations opens (p. 210): "No writer on miracles omits to notice
Hume. To refute him has been the ambition of every Christian apologist
for the last hundred years . . ."

7. *Aids,* p. 363.

Like the Evidence-writing, the rational approach led away from true religious and ethical beliefs. But there was also a deeper reason for Coleridge's attacks upon natural theology, a reason occasioned by his interest in contemporary philosophy. He realized, as did few others in England at that time, that Hume's skeptical remarks on causality had not been answered successfully by any English philosopher in the tradition of Locke. This is brought out quite clearly in the *Philosophical Lectures* of 1818:

> If you doubt [this], just refer to the beginning of Hume's essay on *Cause and Effect;* you will find immediately the channels made on Locke's opinions. Everywhere it is (*argued*), you have no real truth, but what is derived from your senses. It is in vain to talk of your ideas of reflection, for what are they? They must have been originally in our senses or there is no ground for them.[8]

Despite these shortcomings, the writers of natural theologies, raised in the tradition of Lockean epistemology, remained blind to the necessity of revamping the entire philosophical structure supporting their religious thinking. Coleridge helped, with his famous distinction between the reason and the understanding, and with his knowledge of German critical philosophy and seventeenth-century divinity to provide that basis in *Aids to Reflection* and other religious works. He hoped in his later writings to bring about a revolution in the way of knowing religious truth. Little wonder that he disagreed with his contemporaries, and even less that his writings were unintelligible and unacceptable to the greater part of his audience.

Coleridge, for special reasons, took notice of the growth of Socinianism in the late eighteenth and early nineteenth centuries, but by the time of his writing *Aids to Reflection*

8. *Phil. Lect.,* p. 381.

he tended to dismiss it as a serious interpretation of Christianity, and saw its growth and persistence as an indication of dangerous laxity among the supposedly orthodox rationalists, especially those who followed Dr. Paley:

> I can, however, perfectly well understand, the readiness of those divines in *hoc Paleii dictum ore pleno jurare, qui nihil aliud in toto Evangelio invenire posse profitentur.* The most unqualified admiration of this superlative passage I find perfectly in character for those, who while Socinianism and Ultra-Socinianism, are spreading like the roots of an elm . . . can yet congratulate themselves with Dr. Paley, in his book on the Evidences, that the rent has not reached the foundation . . .[9]

Since he had experienced an early period of belief in materialism and Socinianism himself, he was sensitive to its dangers for the true religious spirit.

It is well known to scholars that before 1801–02 Coleridge's chief speculative interests were philosophical materialism and religious Unitarianism. By falling under these influences early in life he showed himself to have been a child of the late eighteenth century. To those for whom the traditional kind of rationalism and orthodoxy were dead, these were alternatives to skepticism and atheism. He and many other young men in his generation entertained these speculations that Dr. Priestley and David Hartley had brought into vogue.

The most widely known passage on mechanism in Coleridge is that in the letter to Southey dated December 11, 1794,[1] and there are numerous other letters in the same vein.[2] The most extended passage occurs in the first book

9. *Aids*, pp. 323–24.

1. *Letters, I,* 113.

2. *Letters, I,* 105, Nov. 6, 1794, to George Coleridge; *Unpub. Let., I,* 32, Jan. 1795, to George Dyer; *Unpub. Let., I,* 50–51, May, 1795, to John Thelwall.

of the *Biographia Literaria*, chapters 5-8, where an elaborate attack is made upon Hartley and his school.[3] The same ground is again covered in chapter 13 [4] of the *Philosophical Lectures* of 1818. His career as a mechanist has also been charted in many books and articles in recent times.[5] The mechanistic period ended before his serious religious thinking began, and was in form too scientific to have much influence upon the later theological studies. But there was one area in which the theory continued to be important for him, to awaken in him the most violent annoyance, and that was in its connection with Socinianism and Unitarianism. In attacking Unitarianism and mechanism with such violence in *Aids* and elsewhere, he exhibited a *mea culpa* attitude not unlike that of anticommunists who were fellow travelers in the 1930's. Coleridge had at one time favored the connection between philosophical mechanism and religious Socinianism, and was influenced by the theological speculations of Joseph Priestley, who became the target of numerous Coleridgean attacks in later days. Priestley had worked out the philosophical basis for Socinianism in the mechanistic theories of David Hartley.[6]

3. *Biog. Lit.*, *1*, chaps. 5-8.
4. *Phil. Lect.*, pp. 339-67.
5. Solomon Gingerich, *Essays in the Romantic Poets* (New York, 1922), chap. 2. R. F. Brinkley, "Coleridge on Locke," *Studies in Philology*, 46 (1949), 521-43. H. N. Fairchild, "Hartley, Pistorius and Coleridge," *PMLA*, 42 (1947), 1010-22.
6. In 1775 Priestley had republished a portion of Hartley's famous *Observations on Man* (1749), leaving out some of the crudities of the mechanical theory and adding some essays of his own. While most of these essays are concerned with refinements of Hartley's theory of association, at some points he boldly states the implications of the materialistic theory for doctrinal Christianity. And not content with letting these implications speak for themselves, Priestley published in 1782 his *History of the Corruptions of Christianity*, in which a decidedly Socinian view of Christianity is upheld. Needless to say, this stirred up a great deal of agitation among the orthodox and the Christian rationalists, and Bishop Horsley, who shares with Paley the honor of being the foremost champion of the

But as early as 1796 Coleridge was questioning the
soundness of Priestley's scheme in a letter to the Reverend
John Edwards, a liberal clergyman at Cambridge:

> How is it that Dr. Priestley is not an atheist? He as-
> serts in three different places that God not only *does,*
> but *is* everything—But if God be everything, every-
> thing is God: which is all the Atheists assert. An eat-
> ing, drinking, lustful God with no unity of *conscious-
> ness*—these appear to me the unavoidable Inferences
> from his philosophy—Has not Dr. Priestley forgotten
> that Incomprehensibility is as necessary an attribute
> of the First Cause as Love, or Power, or Intelligence.[7]

We know from a much later source, his *Table Talk,* that
Coleridge attributed his return to Christianity, at least in
part, to just such a *reductio* of Priestley as is sketched out
above.[8] In his later opinion semimaterialism was a half-
measure which owed its seeming denial of atheism to a

Church in his day, indulged in a series of controversial works with
Priestley which lasted through the decade. Also, the materialistic premise,
that man is entirely corporeal and must rely upon an external revelation
for any guarantee of immortality, rekindled the fires of the Evidence-
writers and tended more than the controversy with Hume on miracles
to make external evidence for Christianity the major interest in the
thinking of Christians as well as Socinians. Most students of intellectual
history now agree that Horsley had the better of Priestley in the historical argument on the nature of the belief of the first Christians
regarding the divinity of Christ, even though neither writer had
great command of the principles of historical criticism. Further,
from the philosophical point of view it is equally evident how inconsistent the materialistic-Socinian hypothesis of Priestley really was. But
this was not evident from 1790 until 1825, years when Socinian materialism had a large following among the intelligentsia in and out of the
Church.

7. *Unpub. Let., 1,* 49, March 20, 1796, to Rev. John Edwards.
8. *Table Talk,* p. 517. Entry for June 23, 1834: "I think Priestley must
be considered the author of modern Unitarianism. I owe, under God, my
return to the faith, to my having gone much further than the Unitarians,
and so having come round to the other side."

specious Socinianism, and yet could not deny an atheistic premise. During his mature period, from 1817 until his death, he attacked Priestley's materialism, his Socinianism, as attempts to undermine the Establishment. In the *Philosophical Lectures* he carries the battle into the enemy camp, pointing out that Priestley's materialistic scheme of mental processes clearly explained nothing.[9] In his attack on *A Barrister's Hints,* itself an attack on Methodism, he alluded to Priestley's denial of free will and its consequences.[1] And of course there are the attacks in *Aids to Reflection,*[2] which are mainly aimed at exposing the dangers of Priestley's system to orthodox believers.

The strategy in many parts of *Aids to Reflection,* and in much of his criticism of contemporary divinity, whenever the subject was more congenial than Evidence-writing or teleology, was often merely to point out the inherent weakness in the logical and philosophical method of the author. For even more prevalent than benighted Evidence-writing and tracts on natural theology were books on theological subjects handled in an inept rationalistic way. The force and number of attacks Coleridge made upon inept rationalism is impressive. He was more interested in correcting the process of religious thinking in general than in changing the orthodox view of particular doctrines. In

9. *Phil. Lect.,* p. 352.
1. *Lit. Rem.,* pp. 471, 476.
2. *Aids,* pp. 238, 331, and esp. 361: "The law and the lawgiver are identified. God (says Dr. Priestley) not only does, but is everything. *Jupiter est quodcunque vides.* And thus a system, which commenced by excluding all life and immanent activity from the visible universe, and evacuating the natural world of all nature, ended by substituting the Deity, and reducing the Creator to a mere *anima mundi:* a scheme that has no advantage over Spinosism but its inconsistency, which does indeed make it suit a certain order of intellects, who, like the *pleuronectae* (or flat fish) in ichthyology which have both eyes on the same side, never see but half of a subject at one time, and forgetting the one before they get to the other are sure not to detect any inconsistency between them."

a marginal note to Philip Skelton's *Deism Revealed,* he makes a point that is extremely important in all his religious thinking—that religious subjects must be treated in a special way:

> That there is a sophism here, every one must feel in the very fact of being *non-plus'd* without being convinced. The sophism consists in the instance being *haud ejusdem generis* (ἔλεγχος μεταβάσεως εἰς ἄλλο γένος) and what the allogeneity is between the assurance of the being of Madrid or Constantinople, and the belief of the fact of the resurrection of Christ, I have shown elsewhere.[3]

The following comment on Oxlee's *Origin of Arianism Disclosed* (1701) reveals another important orientation in Coleridge's religious ideas:

> I am so far from agreeing with Mr. Oxlee on these points, that I not only doubt whether before the Captivity any fair proof of the existence of Angels, in the present sense, can be produced from the inspired Scriptures,—but think also that a strong argument for the divinity of Christ, and for His presence to the patriarchs and under the Law, rests on the contrary, namely, that the Seraphim were images no less symbolical than the Cherubim. Surely it is not presuming too much of a Clergyman of the Church of England to expect that he would measure the importance of a theological tenet by its bearings on our moral and *spiritual* duties, by its practical tendencies.[4]

This might seem at first glance to place Coleridge with the antitheological, "pure morality" school of divinity. But this is certainly not so. By including the word "spiritual"

3. *Lit. Rem.,* p. 440.
4. Ibid., p. 461.

in his comment he incorporated as important doctrines all the major and universal dogmas of Christianity, and made them legitimate, even mandatory, subjects of speculation and of systematized thinking. He did intend to restrain the more fanciful and trivial theological speculations, examples of which are found in abundance in Oxlee and others.

Coleridge evokes the distinction between the reason and the understanding again and again in his criticism of contemporary divinity. In his view the wide ignorance of true religious reasoning caused much muddled and erroneous thinking. On page 375 of Davidson's *Discourses on Prophecy*, he wrote, "If I needed proof of the immense importance of Ideas, and how little it is understood, the following discourse would supply it." And he ruefully acknowledged to himself that his would-be disciple, Edward Irving, had not been able to hold the distinction clearly in mind: "I cannot forbear expressing my regret that Mr. Irving has not adhered to the clear and distinct exposition of the understanding, *genere et gradu*, given in the Aids to Reflection." [5] These comments run to considerable length, and provide interesting material for study of Coleridge's own dialectic. What strikes us at the moment is the consistency and sweep of his condemnation of the methodology and interests of contemporary theology.

About this theology he was right. Others now recognize that the theology in the Church of England in the first two decades of the nineteenth century was not characterized by bold or clear thinking. With those segments of the clergy whose theological thinking was stagnant Coleridge had very little to do, except when he deplored the dull tendency to keep the letter of the law, which vitiated spiritual religion.[6] He dismissed the anti-intel-

5. Ibid., pp. 508–9, 514.
6. *Confessions*, p. 595.

lectual movement of the Hutchinsonians, a late eighteenth-century reaction to rationalism, "as the dotage of a few weak-minded individuals." [7] And although he defended the Methodists against an unfair attack in his notes on *A Barrister's Hints*,[8] there are many places in his writings where a careful distinction is made between his spiritual religion and theirs. A distinction between enthusiasm and fanaticism, based upon the root meanings of the words, was a convenient means by which he defended feelings and at the same time decried the Evangelical party in and out of the Church:

> Enthusiasm is the absorption of the individual in the object contemplated from the vividness or intensity of his conceptions and convictions: fanaticism is heat, or accumulation and direction, of feeling acquired by contagion, and relying on the sympathy of sect or confederacy: intense sensation with confused or dim conceptions. Hence the fanatic can exist only in a crowd, from inward weakness anxious for outward confirmation; and, therefore, an eager proselyter and intolerant. The enthusiast, on the contrary, is a solitary, who lives in a world of his own peopling, and for that cause is disinclined to outward action . . . Enthusiasts, ἐνθουσιασταὶ, from ἔνθεος, οἶς, ὁ θεὸς ἔνεοτι, or possibly from ἐν θυσίαις, those who, in sacrifice to, or at, the altar of truth or falsehood, are possessed by a spirit or influence mightier than their own individuality.

7. Ibid., p. 600.
8. *Lit. Rem.*, pp. 464–503. These "Notes on a Barrister's Hints" refer to *Hints to the Public and to the Legislature on the Nature and Effect of Evangelical Preaching*, 4th ed. 1808. Coleridge here takes the side of the Methodists against the unjust assertions of the barrister; yet at no point does his own spiritual religion become confused with the so-called "enthusiasm" of the early Methodists. The difference between him and them lies in his unwillingness to surrender the intellectual faculties entirely to the emotional.

Fanatici—qui circum fana favorem mutuo contrahunt et afflant—those who in the same conventicle, or before the same shrine, relique or image, heat and ferment by co-ascervation.[9]

The very fact that the Evangelical party in the Church was anti-intellectual [1] and the High Church party narrowly dogmatic precluded the possibility of any intellectual stimulation in those quarters. The intellectual activity in the Church, with a few happy exceptions such as Archbishop Magee of Dublin was centered upon the universities, whose leading teachers were also clergymen. Through the Bampton Lectures, founded in 1780 at Oxford,[2] and the Boyle Lectures, which had been continued from the early eighteenth century,[3] and also through the activities of scattered groups of clergymen who gathered at such places as Oriel College, a small but disorganized class of intellectually alive men struggled to revamp the orthodoxy of the day. It is this class toward which Coleridge directed his *Aids to Reflection, Confessions of an Inquiring Spirit,* and *An Essay on Faith,* and from this class he chose targets for particular attacks on the blind spots in its rationalism. Some of his targets are prominent figures, such as Arch-

9. Ibid., pp. 529–30.

1. For a treatment of the general characteristics of Evangelical and Orthodox thinking in the early nineteenth century see Storr, *Development of English Theology in the Nineteenth Century,* chaps. 4–5; Tulloch, *Movements of Religious Thought in Britain during the Nineteenth Century,* chaps. 1–2; and J. H. Overton, *The English Church in the Nineteenth Century* (London, 1894), chaps. 2–4.

2. The Bampton Lectures, delivered at Oxford every Easter, are the richest source of background material for the religious thought of the late eighteenth and early nineteenth centuries. They were founded by the will of John Bampton in 1780 and became the center for discussion of the chief religious problems of the time.

3. The Boyle Lectures, famous in the early eighteenth century during the deistic controversy, had fallen into decline by 1800. Van Mildert revived the interest in them by publishing his lectures on Evidences of Christianity in 1800–04.

deacon Paley and Edward Irving. Others, for instance
Robinson and Davidson, would now be forgotten except
for mention in textbooks of church history, had not
Coleridge taken note of them. The writings of these men
had produced the extremely rationalistic religious climate
of opinion in the Church in the early nineteenth century.
Coleridge struggled against this opinion with much
sharper weapons than he used against Socinians, Evidence-
writers, and other "outsiders."

These religious thinkers, from Coleridge's point of view,
were arguing about the wrong material in the wrong way.
In this class must be placed most of the Bampton and Boyle
lecturers on the Evidences of Christianity and natural
theology, as well as many an individual divine. The
progenitor of all this activity was William Paley, the arch-
enemy Coleridge appointed for himself.

Even if Coleridge had not stated his opposition to Paley
on so many occasions and in such a sweeping manner, it
would be obvious to anyone reading the works of each on
similar subjects that here were two men who would never
agree. Paley's name is associated with almost every kind of
religious writing which Coleridge held in abhorrence.
His *Evidences of Christianity* (1794) is a classic on the subject which placed the external, historical importance of
the proofs for Christianity uppermost in the public mind.
The *Principles of Moral and Political Philosophy* (1785)
became the dominant textbook at Cambridge during the
early nineteenth century, [4] and also served as a convenient

---

4. For proof of this we have the evidence of William Whewell, professor
of Ethics at Cambridge, who said in his *Lectures on the History of the
Moral Philosophy in England* (London, 1852), p. 166, speaking of his
predecessors in the Chair: "Perhaps we may add, that they were not
unwilling to join with Paley in rejecting all the more profound investigations into the foundations of moral principles, as useless metaphysical
subtleties or empty declamations." And further, p. 179: "Having thus
considered the Moral and Political Philosophy of Paley, and its reception,

point of reference for all the rationalists who wished to separate ethics from religion. In 1802 he produced *Natural Theology*, which was for the early nineteenth century a painstaking study of organization in bodily structure. The scientific interest was nevertheless subordinated to a religious interest in reinforcing by induction the old teleological arguments which adduced the existence and purposes of God from examples of "design" in the universe. In all these works Paley displays a strong rationalistic temperament, a keen dislike for "mystical or spiritual or internal evidence for religion," and the desire to find universally valid demonstrations for his propositions.

Paley was a product of the time in which he lived—the late eighteenth century. The matter and manner of his work were directed entirely toward the rationalistic mind. Today, he is regarded as minor, with a second-rate mind. Yet the influence he wielded in his own time and in the early nineteenth century was enormous.[5] Those who would take issue with rationalism in religion, like Cole-

---

I have very few words to add. The doctrine of Paley was accepted, as we have seen, in this University, and among the moralists of the English Church in general. It might seem that there is something congenial to the mental habits of Englishmen in a philosophy of this kind, which, assuming peremptorily an ultimate point of analysis, receives with some impatience all endeavors to analyse further."

5. John H. Overton, *The English Church in the Nineteenth Century*, while admitting Paley's limitations (p. 165)—"It is rather too much the tendency of the present day to depreciate Paley . . ."—has this to say in defense of his popularity, a statement which is no doubt true, but indicates the temper with which Coleridge had to deal (p. 166): "He was simply a plain, common-sense Englishman, not at all likely to commend himself to the mystical mind of a man like S. T. Coleridge, fresh from the study of the great German writers. 'The watchmaker's scheme of prudence' seemed to Coleridge groveling and inadequate. The majority of Englishmen, however, were not Coleridges, but plain, common-place people, and the arguments which Paley uses are just of the sort that would come home to them, and his plain, downright, lucid style, without any rhapsody or superfluous ornament, is just the style to suit them."

ridge in England and Erskine in Scotland, were forced to recognize Paley's influence on the popular thinking of the time. Coleridge's attacks on him were largely directed at the dominant mode of eighteenth-century thought, which Paley so aptly and conveniently symbolized. This mode still held sway in the universities, in the journals, and among the leading clergymen in 1825. *Aids to Reflection* was intended to subvert it.

It is important to stress the motives which called for such a concentrated attack on Paley in the *Aids*. Paley became a forceful illustration for the entire negative part of Coleridge's work, which was a criticism of the decadent rationalism of the day. The popularity and continued hold of Paley's work upon the public galled Coleridge: it was an indication that the eighteenth-century assumptions and errors had not been successfully dispelled. The Deistic controversy, the precise rationalism of Butler, even the keen arguments of Hume and Berkeley were forgotten outside of the study and the school, but Paley's work, which enshrined the sacred principles of rationalism in their most banal form, lived on to lull the religious community of the day into a sense of satisfaction that "the rent had not reached the foundation."

Long before his period of great interest in religious matters, Coleridge had attacked Paley's scheme of morality in *The Friend*. At one point he classed Paley with the mechanistic philosophers of the eighteenth century:

> And truly, if I had exerted my subtlety and invention in persuading myself and others that we are but living machines, and that, as one of the late followers of Hobbes and Hartley has expressed the system, the assassin and his dagger are equally fit objects of moral esteem and abhorrence; or if with a writer of wider influence and higher authority [Paley], I had reduced

all virtue to a selfish prudence eked out by superstition,—for, assuredly, a creed which takes its central
point in conscious selfishness, whatever be the forms
or names that act on the selfish passion, a ghost or a
constable, can have but a distant relationship to that
religion, which places its essence in our loving our
neighbor as ourselves, and God above all . . .[6]

Later in the same work, in announcing his new mode of
thought, he begins appropriately enough with an attack
on Paley's thought, after doing justice to his character and
the style of his writings:

> Much and often have I suffered from having ventured
> to avow my doubts concerning the truth of certain
> opinions, which had been sanctified in the minds of
> my hearers by the authority of some reigning great
> name; even though, in addition to my own reasons,
> I had all the greatest names from the Reformation
> to the Revolution on my side. I could not, therefore,
> summon courage, without some previous pioneering,
> to declare publicly, that the principles of morality
> taught in the present work will be in direct opposi-
> tion to the system of the late Dr. Paley.[7]

In *Aids to Reflection, Notes Theological and Political,*
and later religious works, the attacks on Paley become
more specific and violent; this one, from the *Aids,* will
indicate how clearly Paley came to stand in Coleridge's
mind for all that was both unphilosophical and irreligious:

> But on this very account I believe myself bound in
> conscience to throw the whole force of my intellect
> in the way of this [Paley's] triumphal car, on which
> the tutelary genius of modern idolatry is borne, even

6. *The Friend,* pp. 102–3.
7. Ibid., p. 285.

at the risk of being crushed under the wheels. I have
at this moment before my eyes the eighteenth of his
Posthumous Discourses: the amount of which is
briefly this,—that all the words and passages in the
New Testament which express and contain the peculiar doctrines of Christianity, the paramount objects of the Christian Revelation, all those which
speak so strongly of the value, benefit, and efficacy of
the death of Christ, assuredly mean something: but
what they mean, nobody, it seems, can tell! [8]

That Paley's theology should be carried in a triumphal
car indicated for Coleridge that philosophy was bankrupt
and religion in a dangerous position. Paleyism was cor-
rupting the spirit of Christianity in the English Church
even while the Orthodox adhered to the letter of the law.
It was obvious to Coleridge that new philosophical tools
had to be fashioned in order to preserve the spiritual
meaning in the Christian dogmas. But first William Paley,
and the shallow position on which his rationalism rested,
had to be exposed before the complacency of even more
liberal elements in the Church could be shaken.

From our viewpoint in the twentieth century the ex-
posure of Paley and his rationalism does not seem very
remarkable. We have long been aware of the limitations
in the development of thinking in the Enlightenment, and
smile at the assumption that all problems, of any nature
whatever, might easily be solved by an exercise of the
pure reason. Through the scholarship and insight of such
modern philosophers as Ernst Cassirer, whose *Philosophy of
the Enlightenment* is a model for the study of eighteenth-
century thought,[9] it is now easy to trace the main line

8. *Aids*, p. 364.
9. See Ernst Cassirer's *The Philosophy of the Enlightenment*, Princeton,
1951; and Basil Willey's *The Eighteenth Century Background*, London,
1940.

of development from Descartes and Locke to Berkeley, Hume, and Kant. But at the time that these events in the history of modern thought were taking place, and in Coleridge's own day, the significance and main line of this revolution in thought was unclear. The very existence of Paleyism as a major force in the early nineteenth century attests to it. Coleridge, largely through his knowledge of German philosophy and his own early experience as a disciple of Hartley,[1] was more aware of the basic problem involved in contemporary rationalism than most men in England, and certainly more so than any of the religious leaders. These leaders did not see the problems, and deferred to the authority of Paley, so that the bankruptcy in philosophy led to a similar situation in religious thinking. From the point of view of religious thought and trends, the full flowering of Paleyism in the early nineteenth century should be our major interest, as it was that of *Aids to Reflection*. But its roots lie deep in the eighteenth century, where, ultimately, English rationalism had been nourished. This requires us to make a summary investigation of Coleridge's attitude toward that eighteenth-century philosophy.

It is not my intention to trace the development of Coleridge's philosophical views as he passed from Hartleyan materialism through Platonism, to German idealism. That has been done with various degrees of success in the past.[2] What is of chief interest for us is Coleridge's

1. The history of Coleridge's early adherence to the materialistic doctrines of Hartley and his conversion to idealism around 1800 can be traced in his letters—from that to Southey in 1794, in which he announced himself a complete materialist, until he advised Poole in 1801 that he had "extricated the notions of space and time." Also, the chapters on materialism in the *Biographia Literaria, 1*, chaps. 5-9, contain his repudiation of materialistic principles.

2. See Gingerich, *Essays in the Romantic Poets*, chap. 2; and H. N. Fairchild, *Religious Trends in English Poetry* (New York, 1949), *3*, 263-328. Gingerich has overestimated the pull of mechanistic philosophy on

degree of awareness of the important religious trends in eighteenth-century philosophy. There are several rich sources for getting at this awareness, most notably the *Philosophical Lectures* of 1818 and the annotations he made in the margins of the works of numerous eighteenth-century theologians. Upon these sources I shall draw freely, in order to point out how accurately Coleridge had diagnosed the limitations and difficulties in eighteenth-century thought, knowledge of which has become commonplace in our time.

The quotation from the *Philosophical Lectures* (above, p. 11) makes it evident that Coleridge had put his finger on the chief weakness in eighteenth-century rationalism in England. This was its epistemological basis in the philosophy of Locke, with its famous *nihil est in intellectu sed quod fuerit primo in sensu*, the *tabula rasa*. Coleridge further criticized this basis, in the same lectures, in a more specific way: "Now Leibnitz first opposed Lockean philosophy as then understood in the simplest manner in which it could be opposed. Mr. Locke's followers had repeated 'there is nothing in the mind which was not before in the senses.' Leibnitz added [*praeter ipsum intellectum*]—except the mind itself . . ." [3]

But the English rationalists of the early eighteenth century had accepted Locke's premises without question, and had proceeded on that basis to reduce all problems to the level of the reasonable understanding. The heyday of this kind of rationalism occurred during the Deistic controversy, when both the Deists and their Christian adversaries employed reason to prove or disprove the Articles of Faith. This long controversy rests at peace now in the Boyle Lec-

---

Coleridge's thinking as a whole. Fairchild, while admitting his conversion to some kind of religious idealism, refuses to admit that Coleridge's religion could really be called Christianity.

3. *Phil. Lect.*, p. 383.

tures, and in the writings of Chubb, Morgan, Tindal, Toland, Bishop Butler, Lord Bolingbroke, and War-burton.[4] It is, of course, very important in the history of religious thought, although much less so, except as a symptom of confusion, in philosophy. Coleridge estimated its significance quite accurately in the *Philosophical Lectures:*

> I wish to give a striking instance of what the human reason, of itself, I will not say *could* arrive at but I speak more safely of what it ever *did* arrive at; for there is not a more frequent delusion, or one that it was more fashionable about a hundred years ago, in the time of the Chubbs and Morgans, more frequently to bring forward—what they called "natural" proofs of religion, the object of which was to shew the inutility of Christianity, that it was of no value; and it is astonishing with what coolness they proceed[ed] to give demonstrative proofs, which no man could reject, of the being and attributes of God and a future state.[5]

This kind of rationalism spent itself in meaningless controversies, and was closed out by the appearance of Henry Dodwell's *Christianity Not Based on Argument* in 1743.[6]

4. For a résumé of the works of each of the leading deists and their Christian adversaries see John Orr, *English Deism: Its Roots and Fruits,* Grand Rapids, 1934. A more penetrating investigation of the issues in this controversy can be found in Maynard Mack's Yale dissertation of 1936, "The Intellectual Background of Alexander Pope's *Essay on Man.*"

5. *Phil. Lect.,* p. 126.

6. Henry Dodwell, *Christianity Not Founded on Argument and the True Principle of the Gospel-Evidence Assigned,* 3d ed. London, 1746. Coming at the end of the fruitless deistic controversy, Dodwell's blows at pure reason were well timed. His concern was to prove "that Reason, as the intellectual Faculty, could not possibly, both from its own Nature and that of Religion, be the Principle intended by God to lead us into a true Faith" (p. 7). He aimed his blows particularly at the rationalistic divines who used pure reason as a weapon for religion: "What they mean by inviting us to dispute upon religious Subjects, shall appear at

The attack on the value of rationalism in that ironical little piece was followed by the Methodist revival, and overnight the Deistic controversy died. This left the field to the Christian rationalists, who held it, defining religion by demonstration, until the arrival of Hume. His attack on miracles, the evidences of Christianity, and causality dictated the turn of religious rationalism for the remainder of the century.[7] The emphasis from this point on was to be external evidence rather than a priori demonstration. Paley's brand of rationalism arose as an answer to Hume, as did the Scotch philosophy of Common Sense, the antirationalistic movements in the Church, and the Mechanist philosophers who were influenced by Hume in their attempt to push sensationalism to its logical conclusions.

So it is little to be wondered that Coleridge opposed Paleyism in religion and philosophy, rising as it did on the

---

last to imply no more than this, that we are to dispute for, not against them" (p. 95). Although written in an ironic manner that grossly overestimated the cleavage between revelation, faith, and reason, this treatise was valuable in reasserting for its day some of the same points Coleridge emphasized in *Aids to Reflection*.

7. Hume published his *Treatise on Human Nature* in 1738, but as he said, "it fell dead-born from the press." In 1741 he began to publish his *Essays*, followed by the famous *Enquiry Concerning Human Understanding* (1748), in which the attack on miracles occurs, and which attracted the notice of contemporary divines. *Dialogues Concerning Natural Religion* was published in 1777, after his death. The refutations of his assertions began in his own day and continued into that of Coleridge. Among the divines who attacked his religious views were William Adams, chaplain to the Bishop of Llandaff; George Campbell in *Dissertation on Miracles;* John Douglas, Bishop of Salisbury, in *The Criterion;* Warburton in *Remarks on Hume's Natural History of Religion;* John Leland in *View of the Deistic Writers;* and finally Paley in *Evidences of Christianity.* There is no doubt that Hume's skeptical position on causality baffled his contemporaries' attempts to disprove it, and that his miracle- and Evidence-writing, more open to question, produced this spate of confutation which succeeded in a short time in focusing the attention of most Christian apologists on the historical aspects of Christianity

collapsed structure of "Lockean rationalism." For through his own early experiences as a "mechanist" and a "rationalist," and through his knowledge of the work of the German philosopher Kant, he was able to see its inherent weaknesses, as few other Englishmen could. As long as the English philosophers and theologians adhered to Locke's psychology and epistemology, Hume's conclusion was inevitable and irrefutable. The numerous refutations of Hume which the rationalists produced in defense of their system were either beside the point, or cut the ground from under their own position. Coleridge saw this clearly:

> Mr. Hume—no one will suspect me of being an advocate of Mr. Hume's opinions, but I most assuredly do think that he was attacked in a very illogical not to say unhandsome manner both by Priestley and Oswald, and I grieve to say for the beauty of the book in other respects, by Beattie. It was a book that honoured Beattie from the display of genius and eloquence which shot through and through as it were with a good heart and sincere piety, but notwithstanding that, Mr. Hume had some right to say it was a great big lie in octavo as far as it referred to him; for it went on the ground that Hume did not believe there was any connection of cause and effect that man could act by, whereas it was a proud challenge to your proud dogmatists who conceived all things to be the influence of their reason, and particularly those (as was the case with ninety-nine out of a hundred for whom he wrote) compleat [Lockeans] who held that all knowledge was derived *from* the senses and that there was no reality *in* the senses, and he cut the matter short by calling on them to prove that the ideas of cause and effect have any reality at all.[8]

8. *Phil. Lect.*, pp. 202–3.

Paley himself, along with a host of other noted religious thinkers of the day, had exercized their pens in efforts to refute Hume, and without success. Only Hume's *Essay on Miracles* had been countered in a telling way.[9] Since Hume had not been successfully refuted, the rationalists and dogmatists shouted him down, and after a while ignored his position. From our vantage point, as from Coleridge's, Hume was the terminal point of the English rationalism which had begun with the Restoration. And even though the religious and philosophical interests did not recognize or admit this conclusion, their works reflected it.

The rationalism which dominated the Church from 1780 until 1825 was not the bold speculative kind of the eighteenth century. No great advance in theological or historical scholarship was made. From the viewpoint of original thinking it was a dull period,[1] weakening interest in speculative theology with the kind of common denominator sought by Paley to minimize the importance of specific doctrines.[2] Explaining away the mysteries of Scrip-

9. Campbell showed that Hume had begged the question in the discussion of miracles by defining a miracle as a phenomenon contrary to nature. All the other refutations followed along the same line. Since the question of miracles rested upon belief in a Supreme Being, the whole controversy soon took a new turn, after Hume's arbitrary definition of a miracle had been discarded.

1. Sir Leslie Stephen, *History of English Thought in the Eighteenth Century* (2 vols. London, 1881), *1*, 372: "The most conspicuous literary phenomenon in the latter half of the eighteenth century in England is the strange decline of speculative energy. Theology was paralysed. The deists railed no longer; and the orthodox were lapped in drowsy indifference. They boasted of the victory won by their predecessors; but were content on occasion to recapitulate the cut and dried formula of refutation or to summarize the labours of the earlier inquiries. The one divine of brilliant ability was Paley; and Paley's theology escapes, if indeed it escapes, from decay, only because it is frozen. His writing is as clear and as cold as ice."

2. C. J. Abbey and J. H. Overton, *The English Church in the Eighteenth Century* (London, 1878), *1*, 511: "Archbishop Secker, in his Charge of 1758, complains bitterly of the teaching of mere virtue and natural

ture, or reducing them to the level of common sense, became the order of the day. Coleridge attacked the reasoning of many of these writers, but singled out Paley for his popularity and importance. An amusing incident from Coleridge's youth will also help to suggest his interest in Paley. It is in a letter from the young Coleridge to the mother of his early sweetheart, Mary Ann Evans. The letter is conciliatory, of course, and the young Hartleyan materialist could think of no better way of winning the good graces of the older woman than the following: "I have inclosed a little work of that great and good man Archdeacon Paley; it is entitled *Motives of Contentment*, addressed to the poorer part of our fellow men. The twelfth page I particularly admire, and the twentieth. The reasoning has been some service to *me*, who am of the race of the Grumbletonians." [3]

We can imagine how much consolation Coleridge received from the facile arguments of Paley addressed to the poor! The important point is that in his dealing with a conventionally orthodox person of that day, he would have chosen Paley. Whatever secret contempt he might have held for the man and his work, it is obvious that he realized the power and influence of Paley's work among the people. It is not surprising, then, to find Coleridge attacking Paley with great zeal, once he had earnestly accepted

---

religion, and urges his clergy to dwell more on the doctrine of the Trinity, on Christ's sacrifice, and on sanctification by the spirit. Bishop Horsley, in his Charge of 1790, says that matters in this respect were better than they were thirty years before, when he first entered the ministry, but still he felt it necessary to prove the fallacy of supposing that the peculiar doctrines of the Trinity, Incarnation, Expiation, Intercession, and Communion with the Holy Spirit are above the reach of the common people. These two writers have been quoted because, as they did not belong to that party to whom the Church is mainly indebted for again bringing the distinctive doctrines of Christianity into prominence, they will not be suspected of over-stating the case."

3. *Letters, 1,* 47, Feb. 5, 1793, to Mrs. Evans.

the orthodox position as valid. He came to recognize in Paley's work a lukewarm Christianity, one which had a vitiating influence upon those who took religion seriously. Paley's *Principles of Moral and Political Philosophy* was written in 1785, the *Evidences of Christianity* in 1794, and *Natural Theology* in 1802. He lived until 1805, thus spanning the old and new centuries, which his fellow workers and followers helped him to dominate from 1780 to 1825. His own works approximate a system to a greater extent than do those of his followers, who generally confined themselves to work on one or another of the three great subjects of religious interest at the time—Evidence-writing, natural theology, and ethical systems. It might not be far-fetched to consider Paley's works as the *Summa Theologica* of his era.

The ethical ideas of Paley, known as the principles of the general consequence and of utility, which Coleridge attacked in *The Friend* and in *Aids to Reflection,* did not receive the universal approbation in church circles accorded to the *Evidences of Christianity* and the *Natural Theology.* They were widely received, to be sure, and *Principles of Moral and Political Philosophy* became the standard text at Cambridge, but it was for the time too Latitudinarian and rationalistic for the Orthodox. The position might be justified in terms of the purely external Christianity advocated in the *Evidences,* and so be consistent from Paley's point of view, but it could not be accepted by the Orthodox, who understood the implications of Christian theology. Paley's pleasure principle was dangerously close to the assumptions of deism and natural religion. What it meant for the Christian sense of personal sin is obvious enough: "It is the utility of any moral rule which alone constitutes the obligation of it." [4]

4. William Paley, *The Principles of Moral and Political Philosophy* in *The Works of William Paley* (Boston, 1811), *3, 70.*

Coleridge was concerned with the principle of utility, which Paley established to replace the fiction of the "moral sense." Chapter 5 of Paley's *Principles* is an elaborate attack on the innate moral sense, or conscience, which was basic for Christian morality. As usual, Paley is precise and blunt, damning the moral sense as a meaningless term.[5] That the essentially hedonistic ethics with which he replaced it did not cause great stir except for a few philosophically minded individuals indicates the dormant state of the church theologians at the time. The inconsistency in separating ethics from religion seemed to bother few people, least of all Paley himself.

With the *Evidences of Christianity* and the *Natural Theology*, Paley was on firmer ground with the Orthodox of the time, even though the philosophical and theological implications of some of his positions were ominous. He handled Hume's tract against miracles in the usual way,[6] without facing squarely Hume's objections against the "argument from design." All the controversialists against Hume insisted that he begged the question by calling a miracle an inconsistency in the order of nature: If God created the laws of nature He might alter them. But Hume countered that this proof rested on a false "argument from design." Thus the "miracle" controversy had a metaphysical basis, though the ostensible issues were of a historic kind.

Paley's interpretation of Christ's mission left much to be desired from a theological point of view. As an announcement of rewards and punishments sanctioned by Divine Authority and proved by miracles, Christ's mission was reduced to meaninglessness, and Christianity itself became merely an appendage of natural religion. This is probably what Paley believed. But numerous other Evi-

5. Paley, *The Principles of Moral and Political Philosophy*, p. 36.
6. Paley, *Evidences of Christianity*, in *Works*, 2, 14.

dence-writers, hardened in the tradition of finding external proofs for Christianity, still sincerely held the orthodox theological system in all its implications. They did not seem to be able to perceive, in hailing Paley and his emphasis on external evidence, that the doctrines of original sin, the atonement, and the resurrection had been de-emphasized to the point that Priestley's Socinianism or Unitarianism must necessarily follow. That is why the more perceptive Coleridge often linked the names Paley and Priestley together, and why he believed that "the rent had reached the foundation."

Natural Theology was the most celebrated, though least significant ultimately, of Paley's works. It is an elaborate display of examples of the argument from design, probably the last truly great example of the eighteenth-century "divine architect" theory of the Universe.

Based upon Locke's empirical method, it is of course vitiated by Hume's arguments on causality, while modern criticisms of the "cosmological argument" in general date it definitely as a period piece. Yet its popularity artificially stimulated the dying rationalism, kept it alive into the first third of the nineteenth century, and lulled the intellectual classes in the Anglican Church with the feeling that religion was firmly based on sound metaphysics and science. Few realized, as did Coleridge, that a new metaphysics must soon be found to cope with the findings of a much less static and docile science than that which Paley incorporated into the *Natural Theology*.

Coleridge's case against Evidence-writing, Socinianism, religious rationalism, and Paley's philosophy is ultimately based on his indictment of Locke's "understanding," which he defines pejoratively. Our presentation of his case against religious rationalism and, ultimately, Lockean philosophy should conclude by repeating the earlier observation that the validity of this criticism does not stand or fall with the peculiar brand of Idealism he established in his own thinking. That is why his criticisms, in *Aids* and other works, of all kinds of eighteenth-century religious thought have been considered without previous investigation into the technical meaning of the "understanding" in his system. Perhaps the prosaic nature of much of the thinking he criticized might help us to understand his need for a more intuitive, emotional way of viewing the religious problem.

This review of the religion of the "understanding" criticized in *Aids* and other works has given an indication of the major contemporary influences which stimulated Coleridge to become a religious writer. And perhaps it has brought some sense of immediacy to those readers who are puzzled or bored with Coleridge's numerous digressions into contemporary divinity, citation of obscure divines, and protracted debate of seemingly dead issues. We have seen that Coleridge fulfilled—in his own characteristic way—the structural principle of *Aids* given in Aphorism VIII. Evidence-writing, Socinianism, religious rationalism and the merely moral preoccupation of Paley and others were in Coleridge's eyes the religion of understanding. Moreover we have not ignored the voices of Paley, Priestley, Horsley, Mant, Magee, Erskine, Irving, unheard by scholars who think Coleridge framed his distinction between reason and understanding under the influence only of German or Platonic sources.

But what of the so-called "reason" mentioned in Aphorism XXXII of *Aids to Reflection?* This reason bears the same relation to the positive side of Coleridge's religious thinking as does the understanding to the negative. In the strict sense it is not a structural principle of *Aids* but provides a clue to the method of reasoning in the book. And it is not adequately defined in *Aids to Reflection,* which, as a practical and pragmatic work, assumes certain a priori definitions. Happily it is possible, without taking the a priori road, to give an example of Coleridge's reason at work. The aphorism on justifying faith shows Coleridge the man as well as the thinker, and introduces us to the contemporary religious controversy which first led him to make *Aids* a positive and personal contribution to religious thought.

CHAPTER 2

STEADFAST BY FAITH

When Coleridge entered the three-hundred-year-old controversy on the meaning of Justification by Faith, most important of the Thirty-nine Articles, the death rattle of the contemporary phase of the argument between Calvinists and Arminians could already be heard. He was nevertheless eager to join Bishop Tomline, Richard Mant, Richard Lawrence, and Richard Whately [1] in upholding the "original" meaning of the article for the Anglican Church, to attack the Arminian and extreme Calvinist positions, and to work out a "middle way" of his own which he called "pure Lutheranism." To do all these things Coleridge was forced to cope with a complex historical and theological problem.

From the historical point of view, the burst of argument in the early nineteenth century, which excited Coleridge at the time of *Aids to Reflection,* was merely another cycle in the perennial dispute between Calvinistic and Arminian

---

1. Bishop George Tomline, *Refutation of Calvinism,* 1811; Richard Lawrence, *An Attempt to Illustrate Those Articles of the Church of England, Which the Calvinists Improperly Consider as Calvinistical,* Bampton Lecture, 1804, 3d ed. Oxford, 1838; Richard Mant, *An Appeal to the Gospel or An Inquiry into the Justice of the Charge—That the Gospel Is not Preached by the National Clergy,* Bampton Lecture, 1812, 3d ed. Oxford, 1812; Richard Whately, *Essays on Some of the Difficulties in the Writings of St. Paul,* 3d ed. London, 1833.

interpreters of the spirit of the Thirty-nine Articles, a dispute reflected in the wording of some of the Articles. In the sixteenth century the Articles had been cautiously phrased, in the conservative spirit of Elizabeth I, to prevent any faction in the Church of that time from gaining complete ascendency in a land which had been torn by religious strife for years.[2] Yet controversy between "High" churchmen and "Calvinists" flourished throughout the seventeenth century. The issue was further complicated by the introduction of the theological system of Arminius [3] from Holland in the early seventeenth century. Arminianism was a modified Calvinism, closely related to pre-Reformation scholasticism in many respects, and was accepted by High churchmen during the reigns of the Stuarts [4] in preference to the violent Calvinism of the Puritans. After the Glorious Revolution of 1688 moderate churchmen seemed to agree that Arminian theology was

2. The Thirty-nine Articles were settled in final form in 1571. An attempt was made to give the Lambeth Articles of 1595 a Calvinist basis, but this was rejected by the majority in the Church. John D. Tulloch in *Rational Theology and Christian Philosophy in England in the Seventeenth Century* (London, 1862), *1*, 42, characterizes the Elizabethan spirit in this way: "The theology of these Articles is conciliatory and moderate. The great question of predestination, round which the theological thought of the Reformation everywhere circulated, is handled in a strictly Scriptural manner without argument, or any attempt to draw out the divine fact in its negative as well as its positive side. The same thing may be said of the definitions in the Tenth, Eleventh, and Twelfth Articles on Free Will, Justification, and Good Works."

3. Arminius (James Hermann or Hermensen, 1560–1609) launched an attack upon the pure Calvinism of the Dutch Confessions. His views were condemned at the Synod of Dort in 1618 but continued to be influential, especially in England, where the rigorous Calvinistic doctrines had never been fully accepted. Modifying the Calvinist rigorism on predestination, Arminius advanced interpretations of Original Sin, grace, and justifying faith which were, in the eyes of his contemporaries, dangerously similar to the scholastic doctrines of the pre-Reformation era. In these interpretations man's free will, works, and sacramental efficacy are given large scope.

4. See *Lit. Rem.*, p. 195, for Coleridge's view of the Stuarts and the Arminianism which they encouraged.

a happy compromise between the virulent Puritanism of the Commonwealth and the Catholicism of James II. Both the strict Calvinistic and High Church interpretations of the Articles remained out of favor. This lethargic compromise managed to survive the rationalistic early eighteenth century, since acute thinkers were more interested in deism and Evidence-writing than in theological controversy at that time. But the specifically doctrinal issues were revived by the Methodists, whose spirited and successful preaching to the people in the late eighteenth century put the Establishment on the defensive. Thus the evangelical movement [5] within the Church arose to combat the success of Methodism by reviving the older interpretations preached by the Methodists but officially ignored by the conservative members of the High Church party.[6] This controversy within the Church

5. In Overton's *The English Church in the Nineteenth Century*, pp. 51–109, there is a very penetrating and just assessment of the strong and weak points in Evangelicalism. The author recognizes the spiritual force which the Evangelicals brought into the Church (p. 51): "Regarded purely as a spiritual force, the Evangelicals were undoubtedly the strongest party in the Church during the first thirty years of the nineteenth century." Their missionary and anti-slavery work is also commended. But the old faults of the Methodists whom they emulated—anti-intellectualism and a narrow puritan morality—were carried over into the Anglican Church, until by 1825 Evangelicalism had ceased to be a force that might help the Church face the problems of the new century.

6. The immediate cause of the nineteenth-century dispute was not faith vs. works or predestination vs. free will, the usual forms in which the Arminian-Calvinist dispute manifested itself. It was infant baptism, which had been a custom in the Church over the centuries. According to the Arminian High Church doctrine on Original Sin, baptism was adequate for justification. This the Methodists, Evangelicals, and Low Church clergy denied, insisting with the Eleventh Article that only justifying faith might save: "Wherefore, that we are justified by faith only, is a most wholesome doctrine, and very full of comfort, as more largely expressed in the homily of justification." The moderates on both sides wished to retain the custom of infant baptism without denying the article on justifying faith. The dispute ultimately led to a re-examination of all the issues disputed by the Arminians and Calvinists, such as Original Sin,

reached its peak in the early nineteenth century when both Evangelicals and High churchmen solidified their positions and seemed to be moving apart at a rapid rate. It became a question of some importance whether the Thirty-nine Articles were flexible enough to hold both groups in the Church. Appeal to history was of course futile, and evidence of this futility can be found in the contradictory statements of Mant, Lawrence, and other contemporary traditionalists. The vagaries of English ecclesiastical history seemed to offer fare for almost any position or claim, while affording proof for none. The attractions of this controversy, especially with regard to the doctrine of Justification by Faith, were in no small way responsible for Coleridge's interest in writing *Aids to Reflection.*

This doctrine of Justification by Faith, the center of the early nineteenth-century controversy, had always presented a challenge to theologians and continued to be in Coleridge's day a subtle and thorny problem in both Catholic and Protestant thinking. Justification is the term by which all major divisions of the Christian Church signify the renewal of fallen man, his liberation from the effects of original sin. This justification, not in any way merited by men, was achieved by means of the condign sacrifice of Christ for mankind. In the pre-Reformation view, as presented by St. Augustine and modified by various Scholastics, man's redemption from original sin was effected and symbolized by the sacrament of baptism, and justification, strictly speaking, was the state of restoration into God's favor which followed baptism. But God's favor, despite the continuing faith of the justified individual, might be lost. Original justification itself could not ensure continued fellowship with God in the face of actual sin. As

---

free will, predestination, and grace. Many of the points considered by Coleridge in *Aids* were hot issues in this dispute.

man grows, so does his inclination to commit sin. Thus the Catholic system of penance and good works exists to assure the renewal of justification. One can see the relationship between God and man envisioned by Scholastic thinkers as a legal one, the primary purpose of which was to ensure obedience to the moral law and the sanctification of each individual Christian.

Luther interpreted the Pauline texts on justification in a different way. Man, in his view, could be saved only by personal justification, brought about by his faith in the righteousness and achievement of Christ. The legal and moral relationship of medieval Catholicism became subordinated to the religious sonship of believer in Christ. Man was *justus et peccator.* Justification then was viewed as a personal religious relationship between man and God against which sin had no power. Man, potentially sinful by virtue of the power of concupiscence, and actually through his own deeds, was simultaneously justified by means of his faith in Christ. This doctrine of justification, following the historical development of Protestantism in the sixteenth and seventeenth centuries, assumed three specific forms—the "high" Calvinist, the "moderate" Calvinist (which Coleridge called "pure Lutheranism"), and Arminian. All three views were influential in the development of doctrine in the Church of England.

To understand exactly what the Lutheran or moderate position on justification implied, it is necessary also to know something about other positions. Luther had shifted the focus of Christian doctrine from moral perfection to religious fellowship based upon faith. Calvin and his followers drew several far-reaching inferences from this doctrine. Since faith was the all-important thing, it seemed dangerous to them to hold that man merited or earned this saving faith; it must come from a decree of God. Hence the will cannot be free, and individuals must be predestined to salvation or damnation according to God's plan for them. The Arminians found this strict Calvinism repugnant, and opposed predestination with a new form of the doctrine of merit, which restored the free will and the possibility of universal salvation. In practice the Arminian doctrine tended to restore the Catholic idea of legal and moral relationship between God and man, and, especially in England where there was sympathetic High Church feeling in the seventeenth century, it restored to favor the Catholic practices of works and penance. Now the loose or moderate form of Calvinism, which had been adopted as a compromise in the sixteenth century, followed the spirit of Luther himself by insisting upon justification as a personal and continuous victory for the individual, while rejecting the Calvinistic deductions of election, predestination, and, at worst, antinomianism. Scholastic theologians in the Established Church were often forced into a dualism of speculative Calvinism and practical Arminianism in their attempts to defend the Church's Article.

Some early nineteenth-century thinkers attempted to reconcile this dualism. Significant contributions were made by John Henry Newman and the little-known Thomas Erskine. Coleridge undertook a defense of the Lutheran meaning of justification in the *Aids,* which appeared three years after Erskine's *An Essay on Faith* and preceded Newman's *Lectures on Justification* by thirteen years. In spirit, and to a degree in method and specific results, the writings of these three contemporaries are remarkably similar. Each attempted to revitalize the idea of dogma and doctrine in a way that would be meaningful for a new age. Their efforts can be construed as a counterforce to the dead, rationalistic eighteenth-century orthodoxy hanging on in the thinking of early nineteenth-century divines of all shades of persuasion.

Yet there are significant differences between the rationalistic mystic Erskine, the voluntarist traditionalist Coleridge, and the emotive rationalist Newman. In noticing the contrasts in the thinking of the three on justifying faith, perhaps the reader will have a close view of Coleridge's higher reason at work, and judge for himself its value in comparison to the thought of two other perceptive theologians. Erskine's attack on orthodox rationalism was radical, Coleridge's energetic, Newman's cautious and conservative.

Thomas Erskine of Linlathen (1788–1870) was by profession a lawyer, by vocation a semi-hermit, given to asceticism and search for mystical experience. Hence he was not committed to any Church, nor did he attach any importance to the prevailing philosophy and theology of the day. He was of the generation of Jeffrey, Scott, and Thomas Brown, and with them he felt the impact of German philosophy and of Romanticism. But his capacity to absorb the new spirit was far greater than that of the others, probably because the cast of his mind had been less permanently influenced by training in eighteenth-century tradition. We should not wonder at his anticipations of Coleridge's views, or feel the need to discover a direct relationship between the two. Once given the similarities of their mentalities and interests and the identical influences under which each fell, the general tendency of their writings to assume the same tone, and sometimes attitude, follows without difficulty.

Erskine's one great principle, which he illustrated in a variety of ways in his religious writings, is that both the truth and the power of Christianity have to be tested primarily by subjective means. This struck a blow at the "external evidence" writers of contemporary rationalism, the Mants and Lawrences with their Bampton Lectures, and undercut the Orthodoxy that held the essence of Christianity to be in forms and beliefs per se. The efficacy and validity of Revelation must be tested by its correspondence and analogy with the moral nature of man.[7] Christianity, in this view, not only gives to man moral feeling, but this feeling itself, or the sense of congruity between the Revelation and the moral feeling, resulting from regeneration of the will and the moral faculties, provides the greatest proof of the validity of Christianity. It is therefore not surprising to find in *The Essay on Faith* a general derogation of the reasoning process in the establishment of faith and an insistence that real assent or faith is moral assent, accompanied by very definite emotions and an active compliance of the will. One of Coleridge's favorite divines, Archbishop Leighton, the divine in whom *Aids to Reflection* had its source, is cited by Erskine to support his position on these matters.[8]

7. Thomas Erskine, *Remarks on the Internal Evidence for the Truth of Revealed Religion*, 3d American from 5th Edinburgh ed. (Boston, 1853), pp. 16–17: "This sense of moral obligation, then, which is the standard to which reason instructs man to adjust his system of natural religion, continues to be the test by which we ought to try all pretensions to divine revelations. This, then, is the first reasonable test of the truth of a religion, that it should coincide with the *moral* constitution of the human mind . . . The second test, then, of the truth of a religion is, that it should coincide with the physical constitution of the human mind."

8. Thomas Erskine, *An Essay on Faith* (Edinburgh, 1822), pp. 17–18: "The science of the human mind requires this reflex exertion, because its object is to examine and discover the laws according to which the mind acts, or is acted upon; but Christianity requires no such act, because its object is not to discover the laws according to which the mind is impressed, but actually to make impression on the mind, by presenting to it, objects fitted and destined for this purpose by Him who made the mind, and fixed its laws." P. 39: "Of course then we do not understand nor believe a moral action, whilst we do not enter into its spirit, and meaning . . . through the excitement of the corresponding susceptibilities of our own minds. In morals, we really know only what we feel." Pp. 43–44: "This is evidently a moral intention, and the object presented to our view for the accomplishment of it is a moral object, even the character of God; the impression therefore on our minds must correspond to this object, that is to say, it must be a moral impression, otherwise we do not understand it, and therefore cannot believe it." P. 52: "It is

The similarity between Coleridge and Erskine is shown by their emphasis on certain doctrinal positions. The importance of emotional, subjective assent in his method led Erskine to place great importance on justifying faith and on the doctrine of the atonement.[9] Both Coleridge and Erskine rejected Arminianism. In the light of these similarities we should carefully evaluate Coleridge's leanings toward Calvinistic positions in doctrines such as justifying faith, in which the emotions play a great role.

Erskine and Coleridge reached the same conclusions on the meaning of justifying faith and the atonement, each leaning heavily on the emotional and volitional basis of these doctrines. But the lengths to which the subjective emotional basis for faith was carried in Erskine exceeded Coleridge's more cautious statements in some significant points. For Erskine, subjective spirit almost seems to create its own doctrines, giving to them autonomous validity independent of objective historical Revelation. This gives

---

therefore evident, that unless we see joy in the substance of the message, we do not understand it as God meant it, and therefore cannot believe it." P. 84: "There is an aphorism quoted by that holy and heavenly minded man Archbishop Leighton, but from what author I do not recollect, which, under the form of a paradox, contains most sober and valuable counsel: 'If you would have much faith, love much; and if you would have much love, believe much.'"

9. Ibid., p. 31: "In order to the believing of the Gospel, it is necessary that the plan of justification by faith should be understood; because this is the prominent feature of the Gospel, and because the benefits bestowed by the Gospel, are communicated to the soul through the knowledge of this doctrine." P. 112: "The pardon has been proclaimed simply, in order that the power and influence of sin may be overcome; we are therefore falsifying the record, and undoing its purpose, if we teach men to cast off their sins as a preparatory work previous to believing, and in order that they may accept of the pardon." P. 123: "The doctrine of the atonement is the great spiritual mould from which the living form of the Christian character is to derive its features. Could we closely and accurately fill out and follow this mould in all its lineaments, though we had never heard of the precepts, our hearts would present an exact tally or counterpart to them."

him kinship with Schleiermacher, with whom, by the way, he was associated by the Tractarians.[1] Coleridge was wary of this purely emotional basis for religious thinking and wished to avoid the charge of enthusiasm cast upon the Methodists, or of mysticism leveled at Erskine and Schleiermacher. In his attitude toward the Methodists and in his criticisms of Edward Irving, his own and Erskine's disciple, we find some hints on this very slippery point in Coleridge's theory—that is, the precise nature of his commitment to the emotional element in religion.

Edward Irving, the divine influenced by both Coleridge and Erskine, is the connecting link between the English and Scottish religious awakenings. During the early 1820's he frequently visited Coleridge. Irving was a preacher of some force and not primarily a thinker. With him "spiritual religion" tended to lapse into extreme emotionalism, a pitfall Coleridge always decried in his works.

In his discussion of Irving's translation of "Ben Ezra" [2]

1. Erskine was attacked in *Tracts for the Times*, No. 73 (1838), by John Henry Newman, for his rationalism and emotionalism. This attack the Tractarians might also have applied to Coleridge (p. 13): "Striking indeed is the contrast presented to this view of the Gospel [*the Orthodox*], by the popular theology of the day! That theology is as follows:—that the Atonement is the chief doctrine of the Gospel;—again, that it is chiefly to be regarded, not as a wonder in heaven, and in its relation to the attributes of God and the unseen world, but in its experienced effects on our minds, in the change it effects where it is believed."

2. "Ben Ezra," *The Coming of Messiah in Glory and Majesty*, trans. Edward Irving with Introduction, 1827. Beside censuring Irving for not observing his distinction between reason and understanding, Coleridge goes on to observe (*Lit. Rem.*, p. 513): "It may not be amiss that I should leave a record in my own hand, how far, in what sense, and under what conditions, I agree with my friend, Edward Irving, respecting the second coming of the Son of Man. I. How far? First, instead of the full and entire conviction, the positive assurance, which Mr. Irving entertains, I —even in those points in which my judgment most coincides with his, —profess only to regard them as probable, and to vindicate them as nowise inconsistent with orthodoxy. They may be believed, and they may

Coleridge takes pains to censure Irving's emotionalism. Closely related to this is his fear that Irving had relapsed into a peculiar fanaticism and abandoned sound doctrine. A sharply rationalistic spirit appears in his annoyance with Irving's extravagances in explication of certain texts, and several times he marshals Kant and Archbishop Leighton against Irving.[3] Now these explicit censures of Irving's almost prophetic strain, generalized to the necessary degree, give us the clue to the difference between Coleridge on the one hand, and Irving and Erskine on the other. All three stressed the internal evidence of the spirit and the function of the will in deciding religious truths, and agreed that some form of Redemption in the individual is the only practical starting point for Christianity. But fear of this very enthusiasm led Coleridge to fuller sympathy and understanding for orthodox positions, while his native rationalistic bent urged him to seek a basis for his insights into the value of emotion in religious experience outside the emotion itself. Hence the doctrine of ideas and the concept of the higher reason.

The attack upon Irving's emotionalism is closely paralleled by others on enthusiasm and Methodism. From the excerpt quoted above (pp. 18–19), we know there was one kind of enthusiasm which Coleridge included in his rationale of the higher reason.[4] These criticisms of evangel-

---

be doubted, *salva Catholica fide.* Further, from these points I exclude all prognostications of time and event; the mode, the persons, the places, of the accomplishment; and I decisively protest against all parts of Mr. Irving's and of Lacunza's scheme grounded on the books of Daniel or the Apocalypse, interpreted as either of the two, Irving or Lacunza, understands them."

3. *Lit. Rem.,* p. 521: "O Edward Irving! Edward Irving! by what fascination could your spirit be drawn away from passages like this [II Thes. 2:1–10] to guess and dream over the rhapsodies of the Apocalypse?" See p. 518, on the Epistles of St. Peter; p. 521, on the Apocalypse and Daniel; pp. 514–15, for reference to Kant and Leighton.

4. *Lay Sermon I,* pp. 432–33.

ical zeal help us to make the distinction between his enthusiasm and the popular kind.

The disdain with which Coleridge alluded to the "pietistic school" of Schleiermacher [5] is characteristic of an entire set of attitudes which he established toward the evangelical movement. The Hutchinsonians, in *Confessions of an Inquiring Spirit* and the Methodists in a note to *A Barrister's Hints* received the same supercilious treatment. This last treatise is revealing, for everywhere in it Coleridge defends the Methodists against the unjust charges of the rationalistic, Socinian barrister on theoretical grounds. But when the barrister accuses the Methodists of ignoring Scripture in their reliance upon excitement produced by Sermons, he exclaimed, "Excellent and just. In this way are the Methodists to be attacked: even as the Papists were by Baxter, not from their doctrines, but from their practices, and the Spirit of their Sect." [6] An obvious relationship exists between this attitude toward Methodistic practices and Coleridge's distinction between fanaticism and enthusiasm. Thus one distinguishing point of his enthusiasm appears to be that it functions as an internal attitude toward doctrine, more open to the charge of mysticism than ordinary religious zeal. He was peculiarly sensitive to possible criticism on the counts of enthusiasm and mysticism,[7] as we know from *Aids to Reflection,* where he mentions William Law, who also appears in the *Biographia* as one who helped keep Coleridge's emotions alive during the lean years of speculation:

5. See marginalia to Tenneman's *History of Philosophy* in *Blackwood's Magazine, 131* (1882), 125.
6. *Lit. Rem.*, p. 472.
7. *Aids*, p. 350: "There is nothing new in all this. (As if novelty were any merit in questions of Revealed Religion!) It is Mysticism all taken out of William Law, after he had lost his senses, in brooding over the visions of a delirious German cobbler Jacob Böhme."

The feeling of gratitude, which I cherish towards
these men [George Fox, Jacob Behmen, and William
Law] has caused me to digress further than I had
foreseen or proposed; but to have passed them over
in an historical sketch of my literary life and opinions,
would have seemed to me like the denial of a debt,
the concealment of a boon. For the writings of these
mystics acted in no slight degree to prevent my mind
from being imprisoned within the outline of any
single dogmatic system. They contributed to keep
alive the *heart* in the *head;* gave me an indistinct, yet
stirring and working presentment, that all the products of the mere *reflective* faculty partook of DEATH,
and were as the rattling twigs and sprays in winter,
into which a sap was yet to be propelled from some
root to which I had not penetrated, if they were to
afford my soul either food or shelter.[8]

"All the products of the mere *reflective* faculty partook
of DEATH." Here is Coleridge trying to maintain a balance
between intellect, will, and emotion in religious thinking,
diffident of establishing a monism of the understanding,
and severely critical of other monisms based upon one of
the three. The question of his consistency in this is difficult
to decide.

The emotional element in Coleridge's development of
the religious "ideas" of the higher reason must particularly
be taken into account with regard to the doctrine of
Justification by Faith. It is not the whole story, to be sure,
for the understanding and volition also play equally important roles in his evolving conception of justification.
Nevertheless, emotional commitment is the precipitating
factor. The choices for the early nineteenth-century An-

8. *Biog. Lit. 1,* 98.

glican become clear in a review of contemporary opinion. Justification by Faith could be defended along the lines of high Calvinism, in a logical fashion which denied free will, implied predestination, and disregarded the moral feelings. The denial of free will and individual moral feelings was seemingly avoided by Arminianism, but this theoretical Arminianism tended toward the old Catholic doctrine of merit, and many honest men like Whately and Hampden could avoid merit only by adopting a dualism of theoretical Calvinism and practical Arminianism. Forthright Arminians such as John Wesley in the preceding century had solved the problem by moving into Methodism, and were followed in the nineteenth century by the equally forthright Oxford Movement thinkers, pushing Arminianism in the direction of Catholicism. And while mystics like Erskine held to a modified Calvinism, they did not care to justify it on rational grounds. It was this modified Calvinism which Coleridge defended in the marginalia to controversial works and in *Aids*, and to which he attached the title "pure Lutheranism." He attempted to free this doctrine from the charges of emotionalism and anti-intellectualism, which were always leveled against it. His method of exposition is less theoretical and doctrinaire than that of Erskine, but also stands in contrast to Newman's defense of the High Church doctrine.

The divergence between Coleridge and Newman is essentially that between Protestant and Catholic thinking. It is not merely a matter of disagreement in doctrinal technicalities; the opposing views on Justification by Faith, for instance, indicate a chasm rather than a rent in basic attitudes toward Christian doctrine. In 1834, when Newman wrote *Lectures on Justification,* he was still an Anglican, yet even then he exhibited a kind of thinking basically Scholastic and Catholic. To make this contrast in method clear let us discuss first the doctrine as it appears in Newman's *Lectures,* and then collect Coleridge's numerous commentaries and his position in the *Aids.* As the doctrine of the Established Church, Newman prefers the position of the High Church Arminians on justification and baptism—unsatisfactorily argued earlier by Lawrence, Whately, and Mant—to the Calvinistic scheme. He considered pure Lutheran doctrine, so dear to Coleridge, illogical and therefore not worthy of serious consideration.[9] But he also finds, as is quite evident, that the Arminian scheme is a half-way measure between strict Calvinism and strict Catholicism: "They escape from the strict definition, they pitch their tent in the very middle of their route, dread to go forward, and burn at the notion of going back" (p. 298); "What indeed can be expected but arbitrary distinctions and unreal subtleties in the conformation of a theology, which has a flaw in its leading principle" (p. 299). To his mind a Calvinistic or Catholic interpretation is preferable to the popular doctrine of justification, because Calvinistic and Catholic interpretations are at least logical: "Either notion is intelligible, whichever is the more adviseable; but what is not at all intelligible is the notion of the Protestant schools, which makes it neither the one nor the other" (p. 296). It was necessary for Newman to make a choice, which was, as it happened, the Catholic position. He does not shrink from the consequences this choice had for traditional Protestant doctrine: "The Sacraments are the immediate, faith is the secondary, subordinate, or representative instrument of justification" (p. 257). Nor did he shrink from implicitly denying the wording of the Eleventh Article: "Faith, then, considered as an instrument, is always secondary to the Sacraments" (p. 262). Baptism justified, not faith: "It would seem, then, that Luther's doctrine, now so popular,

9. John Henry Newman, *Lectures on Justification* (2d ed. Oxford, 1840), pp. 276–77.

that justifying faith is trust, comes first, justifies by itself
and then gives birth to all graces, is not tenable; such a
faith cannot be, and if it could, would not justify" (p. 291).
What Newman has done is clear enough. Analyzing the
implications in the idea that faith alone saves, as opposed
to those in the notion that justification is by sacramental
baptism, and finding it impossible logically to hold both
at once, he chose that which seemed to him true—baptism
and works—and subordinated the other.

This process is scholastic, using reason to make clear
the meaning of a revelation, resolving the difficulties by
logic. It is what Whately used and shrank from at the same
time, and what Coleridge called proceeding by means of
the understanding alone. It was inherited by Protestantism
in Calvinistic dogmatics from the medieval tradition, and
soon overwhelmed the more volatile though pure Protestantism of Luther.

A further point can be made which is essential to the
difference between Newman and Coleridge. The logic
here does not infuse the doctrine in any way but merely
establishes the coherent pattern of one viewpoint toward
it, once that pattern has been accepted. The strict chain
of deduction is drawn from ideas of dogma and Scripture.
When speaking of these ideas—the mystery, for instance,
of justification itself—Newman has to have recourse to less
logical terminology, taking advantage of his conception of
symbols as supersensible ideas received by means of language: "In consequence it is a *symbol* of the nature and
mode of our justification, or of its *history*" (p. 276). In another place (p. 268) he describes the mystery of justification in terms strikingly similar to Coleridge's wording of
the Secondary Imagination:

> While we reserve then to Baptism our new birth,
> and to the Eucharist the hidden springs of the new

life, and to Love what may be called its *plastic* power, and to Obedience its being the atmosphere in which faith breaths, still the divinely appointed or (in other words) the mysterious virtue of Faith remains. It alone *coalesces* with the Sacraments, brings them into effect, dissolves, (as it were) what is outward and material in them, and through them unites the soul to God.

This, we see, is an imaginative way to present the doctrine beyond the point where logical inference can go. On this level the Catholic no less than the Arminian or Calvinist doctrine is a mystery, a given fact revealed in the words of Scripture. But in Newman's usage the imagination, conceived in terms of realist epistemology, is not creating the symbol, and merely functions as a receptacle for Revelation. He is still consistent with his earlier views on revealed religion and subjective rationalism, another important concept of which may be mentioned.[1] What is revealed must be received by man as *given,* as a symbol, yet nevertheless upon this *given* logical inferences can be constructed.

Newman employed reason in the traditional way, to make clear the meaning of a revelation; he would not, like Coleridge, call it the "understanding" and be content to show that in the matter of justification, for instance, it could merely arrive at opposed conclusions, the Catholic and Calvinist, from equally admissible premises. Accept-

1. *Tracts for the Times,* No. 73, p. 53: "I will conclude by summing up in one sentence, which must be pardoned me, if in appearance harsh, what the foregoing discussion is intended to show. There is a widely spread, through variously admitted School of doctrine among us, within and without the Church, which intends and professes peculiar piety as directing its attention to the *heart itself,* not to any thing external to us, whether creed, actions, or ritual. I do not hesitate to assert that this doctrine is really a specious form of trusting man rather than God, that it is in its nature Rationalistic, and that it tends to Socinianism."

ing the fact of mystery, he wished as much coherence and
logical sequence as possible in his doctrines. He used the
idea of symbol, imagination, and the illative sense to help
accept and describe the fact of mystery in revelation and
never, as Coleridge at one time seemed to be doing, exalted
the human imagination to the degree of a creative power, a
participation in the Divine. This was no doubt what Newman had in mind in his oft-quoted criticism of Coleridge
in "Status of Anglicanism":

> And while history in prose and verse was thus made
> the instrument of Church feelings and opinions [by
> Scott], a philosophical basis for the same was under
> formation in England by a very original thinker [Cole-
> ridge], who, *while he indulged a liberty of speculation*
> *which no Christian can tolerate, and advanced con-*
> *clusions which were often heathen rather than Chris-*
> *tian,* yet after all instilled a higher philosophy into
> inquiring minds, than they had hitherto been ac-
> customed to accept.[2]

And Newman was right in some respects. Coleridge was
forced to adopt a more orthodox attitude toward mystery
and objective truth after 1818, yet one that was not merely
a return to acceptance of the scheme within which Newman and the other contemporary thinkers always worked.
This attitude invoked the understanding, the will, and the
emotions simultaneously in considering the substance and
truth of any doctrine. Such an attitude would have puzzled
Newman. It may be helpful to recall Coleridge's favorite
distinction between the intuition of Platonists and the
logic of Aristotelians.[3] Remembering, then, where he

2. Newman, "The Prospects of the Anglican Church" (1838), in his
Essays Critical and Historical (London, 1897), p. 268. (Italics mine.)
3. *Log. & Learn.,* p. 125. In discussing his "idea" Coleridge says: "For
considered as *Logic* it is irrefragable: as Philosophy it will be exempt
from opposition and cease to be questioned only when the Soul of Aristotle

placed himself, and Newman's own admission in *Grammar of Assent*, "And as to the intellectual position from which I have contemplated the subject, Aristotle has been my master," [4] we have a just way to distinguish the emotional and intellectual interests of each.

It is now possible to examine Coleridge's own conclusions on justification as opposed to Newman's and Erskine's. He considered the subject from both the objective and the subjective points of view—that is, as an historical doctrine derived from the New Testament and enshrined in the Thirty-nine Articles, and as a personal commitment of the individual will and feelings.

His emphasis on the historical, objective "pole" in religion distinguished his doctrine from that of Erskine; the quality of the emotional experience divides him from the enthusiasts; yet this very emotional element, the proper subjective held in synthesis with the objective, sets his doctrine apart from contemporary orthodox patterns established by Mant or Whately and carried to a logical conclusion by Newman.

Coleridge begins his account of justification from the historical side, stating in *Aids* that redemption, in the wording of the Articles and in all other Protestant declarations, implied personal justification. Justification is complete, anti-Arminian, and by faith, not by baptism and good works: "a Christian can not speak or think as if his redemption by the blood, and his justification by the righteousness of Christ alone, were future or contingent events, but must say and think, I have been redeemed, I am justified" (p. 303 n.). Coleridge wars on historic grounds against the Arminian view of tentative justification and works, first by asserting that Arminian doctrines

---

shall have become one with the Soul of Plato, when the Men of *Talent* shall have all passed into the Men of *Genius* or the Men of Genius have all sunk into men of Talent."

4. *A Grammar of Assent* (New York, 1947), p. 327.

were not introduced into the Anglican Church until the
Revolution of 1660:

> No impartial person, competently acquainted with
> the history of the Reformation, and the works of the
> earlier Protestant divines at home and abroad, even
> to the close of Elizabeth's reign, will deny that the
> doctrines of Calvin on redemption and the natural
> state of fallen man, are in all essential points the same
> as those of Luther, Zuinglius, and the first Reformers
> collectively. These doctrines have, however, since the
> re-establishment of the Episcopal Church at the re-
> turn of Charles II, been as generally exchanged for
> what is commonly entitled Arminianism.
>
> [pp. 207–8]

Taking this position in opposition to the historical
polemics of Mant and Tomline, and satisfied that it was
the correct situation in history, Coleridge launches into
an explanation and a defense of it. The explanation is a
lengthy and rather spirited assertion of the principle that
this justification, in the original sense of doctrinal
Protestantism, is by faith. The essential part of the passage
runs as follows:

> *Steadfast by faith.* This is absolutely necessary for re-
> sistance to the evil principle. There is no standing out
> without some firm ground to stand on: and this faith
> alone supplies. By faith in the love of Christ the power
> of God becomes ours. The Apostle says not—steadfast
> by your own resolutions and purposes; but—*steadfast
> by faith.* Nor yet steadfast in your will, but steadfast
> in the faith.   [p. 302]

This is Coleridge's explanation of his belief, which is consistent with the wording of the Eleventh Article. It is also
his transition from the historical issue to the subjective,

emotional proof, for in the following defense there is a decided shift in the emphasis. His assent to a commentary of Luther's on Justification by Faith in the marginalia to *Table Talk* shows the personal interest, which is basically the acceptance of the traditional Protestant position on account of its subjective truth as well as objective historical validity.[5]

In Coleridge's subjective, emotional proof two elements can be distinguished. First is the personal commitment to the doctrine as a necessity for his own life. In this commitment his doctrine cannot rightly be distinguished from the enthusiasm of Methodists or mystics, for it is a purely empirical assent without rationale. He expresses it boldly and honestly in comments on Luther's *Table Talk:*

> Only cling to Christ, and do thy best . . . O what a miserable despairing wretch should I become, if I believed the doctrines of Bishop Jeremy Taylor in his Treatise on Repentance, or those I heard preached by Dr. ———; if I gave up the faith, that the life of Christ would precipitate the remaining dregs of sin in the crisis of death, and that I shall rise in purer capacity of Christ; blind to be irradiated by his light; empty to be possessed by his fulness, naked of merit to be clothed with his righteousness![6]

5. *Lit. Rem.*, pp. 282–83.
6. Ibid., p. 287. Here is another illustration of Coleridge's reaction to Luther's words on Justification, *Lit. Rem.*, p. 289. Luther's statement runs as follows: "And I, my loving Brentius, to the end I may better understand this case, do use to think in this manner, namely, as if in my heart were no quality or virtue at all, which is called faith, and love (as the Sophists so speak and dream thereof), but I set all on Christ, and say, my *formalis justitia*, that is, my sure, my constant and complete righteousness (in which is no want nor failing, but is, as before God it ought to be) is Christ my Lord and Savior." Coleridge assents with vigor and assurance: "Aye! this, this is indeed to the purpose. In this doctrine my soul can find rest. I hope to be saved by faith, not by my faith, but by the faith of Christ in me."

But he recognized the dangers of this approach, and another comment on Luther attests to his perplexity:

> I will here record my experience. Even when I meet with the doctrine of regeneration and faith and free grace simply announced "So it is!" then I believe; my heart leaps forth to welcome it. But as soon as an explanation or reason is added, such explanations, namely, the reasonings as I have anywhere met with, then my heart leaps back again, recoils, and I exclaim, Nay! Nay! but not so.[7]

It was about this time that the conception of the "higher reason," the doctrine of obscure ideas, came into play, providing the second and distinguishing element in Coleridge's subjective assent to a given doctrine. This element creates a dividing line between his emotionalism and that of the enthusiasts, although, inasmuch as his view was a kind of rationale, it also differs from the orthodox rationalism of Newman and Coleridge's other contemporaries.

This defense of the emotional commitment consisted of two major elements, the negative, or the attack upon the absurdities arising in any strictly logical scheme of the understanding, and the positive, which was the insistence that opposites, or even seeming contradictories, might be held in fusion by the entire existential being in its emotional, volitional, and intellectual aspects functioning as a unit. What Coleridge tried to show was that it is more rational, considering the peculiar nature of religious belief and dogma, to accept the emotional basis with its contraries than to work out a logical system containing all the implications in a given revelation.

As might have been anticipated, the negative aspect of this dialectic of the subjective came forth in criticism of the logic in the Arminian scheme as a system based upon

7. Ibid., pp. 290–91.

the "understanding" alone. In the *Aids* appears an elaborate *reductio* of the Arminian and Catholic systems of Justification by Works, tentative redemption, and retributive justice.[8] This argument would never convince a Newman that the doctrine of Justification by Faith is more logical than the one attacked. But that was not Coleridge's purpose. In his usual way he merely pointed out the limitations of the understanding in judging this question, thereby hoping to undercut the orthodox rationalists' reliance upon logic. Several comments affixed to the works of the Arminian Jeremy Taylor, particularly his treatment of repentance, make this strategy evident. First heartless (and fallacious) logic is exposed in favor of spiritual truth:

> Taylor himself was infested with the Spirit of Casuistry, by which saving Faith is placed in the understanding, and the Moral Act in the outward Deed. How infinitely safer is the *Lutheran* Doctrine, "God can not be mocked." Neither will Truth, as a mere conviction of the Understanding, save, nor Error condemn. To *love* Truth sincerely is spiritually to *have* truth.[9]

In Tillotson the face of Arminianism looked out fuller and Christianity is represented as a mere arbitrary Contrivance of God—yet one without reason. Let not the surpassing Eloquence of Taylor dazzle you, nor his scholastic retiary versatility of Logic illaqueate your good sense! Above all, do not dwell too much on the apparent Absurdity or Horror of the Dogma he opposes; but examine what he puts in it's place . . .[1]

8. *Aids*, pp. 306–17.
9. *Coleridge on the Seventeenth Century*, ed. Roberta F. Brinkeley (Durham, N.C., 1955), p. 284.
1. Ibid., p. 290.

Since the logic of the understanding is to be discounted, it is only necessary, Coleridge felt, to find which scheme represents the moral and emotional nature of man, and obviously this is Justification by Faith:

> But, confining my remarks exclusively to the doctrines and the practical deductions from them, I could never read Bishop Taylor's Tract on the doctrine and practice of Repentance, without being tempted to characterize high Calvinism as (comparatively) a lamb in wolf's skin, and strict Arminianism as approaching to the reverse . . . And it is so marvellous, such a hungry dry corrosive Scheme of a Monacho-manichaean Ethics in so rich, so genial, so tender a Soul as Bishop Taylor's! That he should have strangled the philosophy of Love by the parasite method of rank weeds, the Logic of Casuistry . . .[2]

The doctrine of Justification by Faith, then, is more suitable to the moral feelings than the casuistry of the Scholastics and Arminians, but this is not enough; Coleridge is forced to bring forth some positive element in his own defense, to provide some rationale against the charges of absurdity raised by Taylor or Newman, and recognized by himself in the pure Lutheran doctrine.

In answer to the Arminian and Catholic attacks on Justification by Faith as an absurdity, Coleridge took his stance in the following proposition: "But surely, the more rational inference would be, that the faith, which is to save the whole man, must have its roots and justifying grounds in the very depths of our being." [3] Very depths means, of course, the moral, emotional, and intellectual nature of man. Thus he must show that the Lutheran doctrine is an improvement over the Arminian and Catholic from three

2. Ibid., p. 266.
3. *Aids*, p. 304.

aspects. The emotional he takes for granted, as is evidenced by the commentaries on Taylor's Arminian scheme as dry, "the wolf in sheep's clothing." The possibility that certain men might have emotional natures to which a scheme of retributive justice and works would appeal does not seem to have occurred to him. This assumption of a common psychological nature in man poses a largely unanswered question. But, by going along with the position that Justification by Faith is more emotionally satisfying than Arminianism, we shall watch Coleridge handle the moral and intellectual difficulties in the doctrine.

The moral difficulty was clear and also easy to handle. Coleridge followed Luther's own attacks on Antinomianism in dealing with it. To the charge that Justification by Faith produces in the individual a sense of freedom to sin, Coleridge replied:

> A Christian's conscience, methinks, ought to be a *Janus bifrons,*—a Gospel-face retrospective, and smiling through penitent tears on the sins of the past, and a Moses-face looking forward in frown and menace, frightening the harlot will into a holy abortion of sins conceived but not yet born, perchance not yet quickened. The fanatic Antinomian reverses this; for the past he requires all the horrors of remorse and despair, till the moment of assurance; thenceforward, he may do what he likes, for he can not sin.[4]

A moment of reflection will tell us that in any given instance the relative positions of the forward and backward halves of the Janus face will most likely be determined by the emotional nature of the individual, and thus that a complete answer to the moral problem awaits some solution of the emotional. Coleridge seems to recognize this variety in emotional response in his answer to the second

4. *Lit. Rem.,* p. 280.

Arminian charge—that the Lutheran doctrine breeds profligacy among the ignorant—when he takes this precaution in assenting to Luther's own word on this doctrine: "All in this page is true, and necessary to be preached. But O! what need is there of holy prudence to preach it aright, that is, at right times to the right ears!" [5] But the problem of emotional disparity was not faced fully by Coleridge in his treatment of the doctrine, probably because he was so intensely committed to one position himself. The volitional issue here, it seems safe to say, is settled fairly enough if the emotional premise of Coleridge himself is assumed. But what Coleridge says has been fairly traditional in Lutheran apologetics. His comments on the intellectual difficulties are more interesting and original.

The Arminian attack on Justification by Faith, on intellectual grounds, as exemplified in Newman, dwelt upon its logical absurdity. Coleridge countered by pointing out that Arminianism could not be strictly logical, and we have seen Newman resorting to imaginative language when faced with the basic mystery. Coleridge's own positive position was plain enough, and consisted in making the most of the logical difficulties themselves. If logic could not finally remove the mystery, why not grasp and hold on to it at a more basic psychological level, the emotional, in the first place? Ignorance of the logical difficulties is not suggested as a remedy, and Coleridge is acutely aware, in some of the notes on Luther's doctrines, of the

5. Ibid., p. 289. Here are Luther's words: "Yea, one may say again, we sin without ceasing, and where sin is, there the holy Spirit is not: therefore we are not holy, because the holy Spirit is not in us, who maketh holy. *Answer* (John xvi. 14.) Now where Christ is, there is the Holy Spirit, The text saith plainly, *The Holy Ghost shall glorify me.* Now Christ is in the faithful (although they have and feel sins, do confess the same, and with sorrow of heart do complain thereover): therefore sins do not separate Christ from those that believe."

metaphysical problems involving the will, free grace, and
so forth, which arise in any abstract consideration of Justification by Faith.[6] But his own final position is to accept
these seeming contradictories as mysteries arising out of
dualism and one's merely analogous understanding of religious truth, expressed many times in the form of paradox:

> Without faith there is no power of repentance: with-
> out a commencing repentance no power to faith: and
> that it is a power of the will either to repent or to
> have faith in the Gospel sense of the words, is itself a
> consequence of the redemption of mankind, a free
> gift of the Redeemer: the guilt of its rejection, the
> refusing to avail ourselves of the power, being all that
> we can consider as exclusively attributable to our own
> act.[7]

Now this is not a rationalistic explanation of Justification by Faith. But as an answer to Christian rationalists it
is a very powerful reminder that their logical systems and
practices merely gloss over the mystery, which Coleridge
was willing to accept, holding a dualistic metaphysics
somewhat more modified than their own. Christianity was
a life rather than a speculation, for the orthodox as well
as for Coleridge, but they wished to make it into an orderly life. He wished to face the mysteries, the "ideas," on
a level where the contradictions could not be glossed over,
and thus the reconciliation is possible only through accepting emotional tension and intellectual paradox. Throughout his religious thinking there is constant recognition of
the IT IS, but always and necessarily in relation to an I AM.
For Coleridge Kantian idealism, not the monisms of Schelling or Hegel, had struck deep, modifying completely his

6. Ibid., pp. 281, 288.
7. *Aids*, p. 307.

conceptions of the old Christian dualism held in his day by orthodox rationalists. His method of reasoning to a position on Justification by Faith exposes a very original and complex attitude toward reason and its relation to religious experience.

CHAPTER 3

THE HIGHER REASON

The ubiquitous distinction between the reason and the understanding in Coleridge's religious writings seems at first glance to bear the same relation to his attitudes in philosophy and religion as does the equally famous distinction between fancy and imagination for poetics and literary theory. Standing as it does at the threshold of every important discussion of philosophical and religious questions in his writings, it is little wonder that this distinction has been taken as the key to all his thought.

For one thing, Coleridge's manipulation of the reason and the understanding has been looked upon often enough as an indication of the conflict in his religious thinking between the head and the heart. And there is a certain amount of justice in this view, stemming as it does from the frequency with which Coleridge altered the distinction in terms of various religious experiences and propositions. Yet it does not appear to me, in the ultimate sense, that Coleridge's positive religious position can be interpreted in the light of this formal distinction, even though, as he used it, the distinction served as a convenient means to make negative criticisms on the age. As we saw, he distinguished "rationalism" from religious thought, classed all types of contemporary religious thinking as rationalism of the understanding, and attacked the most diverse groups in this way. Yet the famous definitions of the reason in *The Friend* and the *Aids to Reflection* do not, if taken at face value, give us the proper clues for following the development of his positive religious position. This view is unconventional, since most studies of Coleridge's theories devote the major portion of their attention to a detailed study of the knotty problem of definition. What have the scholars uncovered, and what have they left obscure?

From the standpoint of source, Coleridge's formal distinction is a blending of elements in the seventeenth-century English Platonic tradition with others from contemporary German idealism. There is virtually no disagreement that the distinction combines Neoplatonic meaning with Kantian terminology. Differences in emphasis occur. German-orientated scholars such as René Wellek and Elisabeth Winkelmann tend more than American writers like Claud Howard or Gordon McKenzie to lay stress on the extreme degree to which Kantian terminology had permeated the original Neoplatonic basis in all Coleridge's statements of the distinction.[1] This cleavage between the two schools of critics becomes much wider in their consideration of his application of the distinction. The American writers see a consistency in the Platonic-mystical religious emphasis in Coleridge's thought, which for them quite easily compensates for, and overwhelms, the discordant critical or skeptical elements of German

1. René Wellek, *Kant in England* (Princeton, 1931), gives the most vigorous account of Coleridge's debt to the Kantian philosophy; Elisabeth Winkelmann, *Coleridge und die Kantische Philosophie* (Palaestra, 1933), assesses the relative debt of Coleridge to Kant and the other leading German idealists, Schelling, Fichte, Jacobi, and Schleiermacher; Claud Howard's *Coleridge's Idealism* (Boston, 1924) is the only specialized inquiry into the seventeenth-century English background to the reason-understanding problem; Gordon McKenzie's *Organic Unity in Coleridge* (Berkeley, 1939), takes the syncretic viewpoint in evaluating the seventeenth- and nineteenth-century sources of Coleridge's distinction.

philosophy.[2] The German critics naturally view what appears to them an unmanageable combination of mysticism and rationalism as a basic inconsistency, parallel in certain respects to similar ones in Coleridge's aesthetic and literary theories.[3]

To resolve the problem requires a basic reorientation of attitude toward the value of the distinction for the study of Coleridge's work. And perhaps a brief look at the fluctuations in the meaning of the terms "reason" and "understanding" in his writings would be a proper way to introduce the significance of the distinction for his religious thinking. If we are to appreciate the nature and breadth of the problem, the influence upon his thinking of scholastic tradition, seventeenth-century Platonism, eighteenth-century rationalism, and German idealism must be considered.

The scholastic tradition of the Middle Ages, which extended well into the seventeenth century, held, in various forms, a theory of mutual relationship between the do-

2. It is interesting to note the calmness with which the favorable critics accept the fundamental inconsistencies in the formal definition, as, for instance, McKenzie, in his *Organic Unity in Coleridge* (p. 13): "So with regard to the understanding and reason, Kant must be given credit for the formal distinction, the Platonists for the real substance. We are reminded of the line, 'A metaphysical solution that does not instantly tell you something in the heart is grievously to be suspected as apocryphal.' Coleridge's thought was always subject to approval by his emotions, and his greatest emotional need was for a real and knowable God."

3. See Wellek, *Kant in England*, p. 134: "Finally he gave up any attempts at a solution and came to take for granted the dualism of speculation and life, of the head and the heart. The monistic aim demanded precisely the solution of these dualisms. However, they resisted Coleridge's speculative powers, although he saw that they must ultimately prove unsatisfactory. At length, he seduced the struggling spirit to acquiesce in immediate knowledge and faith, he lured it to enjoy a mere feeling of mystery and to give up the labor of thinking penetration into problems." A similar view of Coleridge's dualisms in literary criticism appears in the same author's *The Romantic Age*, Vol. 2 of A History of Modern Criticism (New Haven, 1955), pp. 186–87.

mains of reason and revelation. Revelation, above man's power to achieve for himself, was the *given,* a gift from God to be accepted and believed. Reason might make clear various aspects of this revelation and supplement it with arguments of its own. Moreover, revelation was interpreted to a large extent in the light of reason, which became a negative norm controlling the possibilities and probabilities in the meaning of a given revelation. This reason was obviously not a mystic or occult quality, but a natural gift, duly constituted by God, enabling man to understand his commands.[4] The understanding as a special faculty was not recognized at all.[5] Reason and understanding were synonymous terms. In both the Platonic tradition of the Augustinians and the Aristotelian tradition of the Thomists, reason was held to be a unique power related to Divine Reason and constituted for the purpose of searching out the attributes of God which might be known by natural means. Hence there was little need for mysticism or special forms of knowledge. Only in Occamism, the medieval counterpart of modern skepticism, was the reason reduced to such an extent that some form of blind faith was needed to fill the gap.

The revival of Platonism and the increased scope given to intuition in seventeenth-century religious writers reflects the breakdown of the scholastic tradition in the Western Church. The new Age of Reason, with its vanguard in Hobbes and Locke, enforced a sharper distinction, in the seventeenth century, between the truths of reason and the truths of revelation. Coleridge's reaction

4. This is clearly stated by St. Thomas in the *Summa Theologica, 1* (Ottawa, Institute of Medieval Studies, 1941), 548–49. *Prima Pars, Quaestio* lxxxviii, *Articulus* III, *Utrum Deus Sit Primum Quod a Mente Humana Cognoscitur.*

5. Ibid., *1,* 488–89. *Prima Pars, Quaestio* lxxix, *Articulus* VIII, *Utrum Ratio Sit Alia Potentia Ab Intellectu.* The negative answer is especially interesting because Coleridge certainly knew some of St. Thomas.

to some of the numerous excursions of the emancipated reason into the area formerly sacred to revelation appears in *Aids* as his criticism of the understanding. The Cambridge Platonists, like Coleridge after them, had reacted against this rationalism in their own day by turning the formerly neglected intuition to a more general use and giving to it the title of "higher reason." [6] It is this appeal to the reason on a plane above the rationalistic view of the Enlightenment which pleased Coleridge in his reading of John Smith, Henry More, Archbishop Leighton, and others.[7] In a hazy, general way, the regular reasoning power of man, which had proved in the hands of rationalists destructive to religion, came to be viewed as the lower faculty, or the understanding.

But in all these writers the distinction between the higher function and the ordinary reason was not always clear, as is noticed by Coleridge in some of the critical notes on the works of his favorite divines. The one on Leighton is typical: "How often have I found reason to regret, that Leighton had not clearly made out to himself the diversity of the reason and the understanding." [8] The

6. For a general treatment of Neoplatonism see Thomas Whittaker, *The Neo-Platonists* (Cambridge, 1918), especially p. 199, where its influence on the English Platonists is considered. Specific treatment of individual English Platonists occurs in John Tulloch's *Rational Theology in England in the Seventeenth Century*, Vol. 2, London, 1872.

7. Coleridge quoted John Smith in *Aids*, p. 264 n.: "While we reflect on our own ideas of Reason, we know that our souls are not it, but only partake of it: and that we have it κατὰ μέθεξιν, and not κατ᾽ οὐσίην. Neither can it be called a faculty, but far rather a light, which we enjoy, but the source of which is not in ourselves, nor rightly by any individual to be denominated *mine*." In Smith's *Selected Discourses* (London, 1660) the full text of this quotation appears in *Discourse* 5, pp. 126-34. There are also numerous other treatments of the higher reason in *Discourse* 1, pp. 14, 20; *Discourse* 3, p. 62, etc. Henry More on the reason in relation to faith is quoted by Coleridge in *Aids*, pp. 199-201. In the *Notes Theological and Political, Works*, 5, 112-18, there are some comments, mostly critical, on More's *Theological Works*, London, 1708.

8. *Lit. Rem.*, p. 378.

English Platonists had not been faced with Coleridge's critical problems. They did not distinguish the functions of the reason clearly because they still accepted the prevailing notion that reason in man is an aspect of the Universal Reason. The doctrine of innate ideas implanted in the mind by God led to the notion that any contradictions arrived at by the reasoning power, used alone, should be readily superseded by faith in the higher reason.[9] Between these Platonists and Coleridge lay the eighteenth century, which, with its keen adherence to rationalism and humanism, had distinguished the truths of reason from those of revelation, and ridiculed the doctrine of innate ideas out of vogue.

This breakdown of the unity between reason and revelation in the eighteenth century required a more profound treatment of the faculties than the Cambridge Platonists, in their vague way, had been able to give.[1] The development of philosophical thought from Locke to Hume had raised new issues regarding the theory of knowledge which had not been envisioned in the dialectic of the Cambridge Platonists. On the practical side, the distinction which limited the lower reasoning faculty—the understanding—

9. The Platonists' conception of reason as an emanation of the Divine lay at the root of their whole philosophy. Reason became the ultimate ground of all permanent laws of morality and religion. Its ideas were eternal and one with God. Howard's summary of the differences betwen the Neoplatonists and Kant is substantially correct, even though he errs in minimizing these differences as they appear in Coleridge (*Coleridge's Idealism*, p. 66): "For the Platonists, on the contrary, the faculty was the means of transcending the limits of finite experience and of participating in the infinite. For Kant, freedom, God, and immortality remained assumptions incapable of proof: for the Platonists, they were ultimate realities subject to the highest form of knowledge. They could be known because they *were* reason . . . the reason in which we participate by virtue of being created in God's image."

1. Both Locke in *An Essay Concerning Human Understanding*, Bk. IV, chap. 18, and Hobbes in *Leviathan*, chap. 31, make the sharp distinction between truth of reason and truth of revelation.

was not defined sharply by the Platonists in the area of most interest to Coleridge, perhaps because the dangers of pure rationalism, which became rampant in the eighteenth century in the guise of deism and skepticism, were not so apparent to them. Coleridge was forced to consider these developments, even in his attempt to draw inspiration from the seventeenth-century idealists. In sympathy with their emphasis upon the intuition and the higher reason, he was nevertheless required to take a more critical approach to the problem.[2] This led him ultimately to the study of the great German idealists of his own period. Around 1799 Coleridge came in contact with the *Critique of Pure Reason*,[3] which engaged his intellect more strenuously than did the writings of the Neoplatonists.[4] He became, in fact, an enthusiast. Although he accepted

2. Coleridge in two important notes recognized the failings of the English Platonists, which also indicate the impact of eighteenth-century rationalism and Kant's *Critique* upon his thinking. On More's *Theological Works* he makes the following note (*Lit. Rem.*, pp. 112–13): "First and foremost,—the want of that logical προπαιδεία δοκιμαστική, that critique of the human intellect, which, previously to the weighing and measuring of this or that, begins by assaying the weights, measures, and scales themselves; that fulfillment of the heaven-descended *nosce teipsum*, in respect to the intellective part of man, which was commenced in a sort of tentative broadcast way by Lord Bacon in his *Novum Organum*, and brought to a systematic completion by Immanuel Kant in his *Kritik der reinen Vernunft, der Urtheilskraft, und der Metaphysiche Anfangsgrunde der Naturwissenschaft.*" A general note on Smith's *Discourses* gives Coleridge further occasion to criticize the entire Platonic school in much the same manner (*Lit. Rem.*, p. 267): "What they all wanted was a pre-inquisition into the mind, as part organ, part constituent, of all knowledge, and examination of the scales, weights, and measures themselves abstracted from the objects to be weighed and measured by them; in short, a transcendental aesthetic, logic, and noetic. Lord Herbert was at the entrance of, nay already some paces within, the shaft and adit of the mine, but he turned abruptly back, and the honor of establishing a complete προπαιδεία of philosophy was reserved for Immanuel Kant, a century or more afterwards."

3. *Letters, 1,* 172–73, to Thomas Poole, Feb. 13, 1801.

4. *Biog. Lit. 1,* 99–100.

for a time the entire *Critique*, it was obvious that the negative element in the Transcendental Dialectic appealed to him most fully, since that seemed to have dealt an effective death blow to the conflicts between reason and faith as they were constantly agitated in eighteenth-century religious controversy. According to Kant's antinomies, the pure speculative reason could neither prove nor disprove the existence of God. All the arguments of the deists, the Christian rationalists, the natural theologians, and the skeptics and Evidence-writers could at once be eliminated as having no essential value in regard to religious experience. Coleridge's confidence in making the criticisms recorded in the previous chapter was mainly based on the validity of Kant's negative work. It is therefore important to evaluate Coleridge's knowledge of Kant's writings, both in range and in depth.

Coleridge's writings and letters show clear evidence that he read the entire *Critique of Pure Reason* and *Critique of Practical Reason*. Echoes from the major sections of the *Critique of Pure Reason*—the "Transcendental Aesthetic," "Transcendental Analytic," and "Transcendental Dialectic"—appear in all his writings after 1799. From the "Aesthetic" he learned to dabble with the notions of space and time and derived a definition of imagination as a unifying power.[5] From the "Analytic" he took over all Kant's categories of logic and judgment for his own "Logic." The "Dialectic," as will be shown, made the most serious impression on him, influencing his thinking in metaphysics and theology for the remainder of his life.

The "Aesthetic" is the most highly technical section of the *Critique of Pure Reason*. Since the problems to which Kant addressed himself there are scientific in purpose and method, it is not surprising that this section concerned Coleridge least of all. Kant wished to show that a priori

5. *New Letters*, 2, 706, to Thomas Poole, March 16, 1801.

knowledge in science and mathematics is possible, and proved his point by demonstrating that all true knowledge is synthetic—the forms of space and time are inherent in the structure of the mind and determine the mode of apprehension of "objects" or phenomena. The imagination performs the act of synthesis, bridges the gap, as it were, between these forms of sensibility and the understanding, our power of knowing "things" and "objects" as ideas. Kant thus averred that pure mathematics and physics are possible because the "matter" of these subjects and the determining forms in the mind are intrinsically related. Coleridge accepted and understood the argument in the "Aesthetic" without becoming vitally concerned with the a priori scientific questions Kant was trying to answer. He did loosen Kant's "imagination" from its technical context in the "Aesthetic" to give it a richer creative literary meaning, but that aspect of his debt to Kant is not our concern here. The lingering impression Coleridge derived from the "Aesthetic" was that Kant had deduced and proved that a faculty, the understanding, operated legitimately to find truth in all scientific inquiry.

In the "Analytic" Kant enlarges his treatment of this faculty. He provides tables of judgment, categories of logical thought, and methods of deduction which are legitimate for this faculty. Coleridge takes over the analysis of the understanding *in toto* in his own MS Logic; his ability to reproduce Kant so clearly demonstrates the accuracy of his reading of the "Analytic." But there are differences in emphasis worth mentioning. Kant's development of the understanding in the "Analytic" is an attempt to give a metaphysical, a priori basis for Euclid's geometry and Newton's physics. He has a positive interest in scientific truth. Coleridge grasped the notion that the understanding is a faculty of the mind capable of handling sense experience and giving scientific, demonstrable truth within set limits. But his own enthusiasms were nonscientific and in the areas of metaphysics, theology, and literature. It is not surprising, then, that he emphasized the negative rather than the positive element Kant had developed concerning the understanding. The understanding by its very constitution was incapable of developing metaphysical, moral, and theological problems or establishing truth in these areas. Thus in his published writings, including *Aids to Reflection,* Coleridge employs the term understanding in a sense which is not a contradiction of Kant's deduction, yet is certainly loose and out of keeping with the spirit of Kant's own view of the understanding.

Coleridge was most vitally interested in the "Transcendental Dialectic," Kant's analysis of the pure speculative reason. In the "Aesthetic" and "Analytic" Kant had shown that the reasoning of the Understanding is synthetic; that is why scientific knowledge is possible. The "Dialectic" demonstrates that the reasoning process of the "pure speculative reason" is not synthetic—in other words, the pure speculative reason has no legitimate object of thought. The famous "Antinomies of the Pure Reason" present four sets of opposed demonstrations proving that the Pure Reason can arrive at contradictory conclusions from seemingly valid premises about the same problems. These problems are the standard metaphysical and theological questions on the nature of the Universe, Freedom, God, and so forth. The "evidence" on which the speculative reason bases its inquiry is illusory, not the synthetic evidence provided for the understanding in scientific inquiries of physics and mathematics.

In the concluding sections of his "Dialectic," however, Kant offers an avenue of escape from the seeming impasse of no knowledge in the realm of pure metaphysics and theology. This escape is his distinction between the noumenal and phenomenal order. The scientific inquiry of

the understanding is restricted to observable data, phenomena. The ideas of the pure speculative reason pertain
to the unknowable noumenal order. Yet Kant allows at
this crucial point, consistent with his view that noumena
cannot be known cognitively, that these ideas—God, Self,
Freedom, Immortality, and Moral Duty—have regulative
force; we must act as if they were true and valid ideas even
though they have no phenomenological context for the
understanding.

Kant's modern commentators of scientific and logical
positivist tendencies (such as Kemp Smith) have deplored
the introduction of regulative principles into the Critiques. Kant could not prove his regulative ideas, and did
not claim to have done so. Yet it was this section of the
Critique that naturally interested nineteenth-century
theologians and philosophers and deflected interest from
the scientific aspect of Kant's work. A host of new metaphysical and theological speculations followed, of the very
sort the Critiques were supposed to choke off.

Coleridge was immediately excited by the prospect that
such metaphysical problems as the existence of God and
immortality of the soul were no longer the proper subjects of scientific and logical inquiry. Here was an answer
to skeptics like Hume and Priestley. What difference did
it make if the problems could not be settled positively by
the speculative reason? But Coleridge, along with Hegel,
Schelling, and later-nineteenth century theologians, did
not long remain satisfied with Kant's "discipline of the
pure reason," the regulative principles, and acting "as if"
such ideas were true. Employing Kant's terminology and a
great deal of his method, Coleridge wished to assign ontological reality and validity to these (and later to other)
ideas. This "corruption" of Kant's purpose has of course
been deplored by some modern commentators, yet it cannot be doubted that Kant had left the door ajar for a

troop of theological speculators. Coleridge retained fidelity to Kant's analysis of the understanding and the pure speculative reason, and used these terms in his own writing in a strict Kantian sense. For his metaphysical and theological activity he coined the term "Higher (than merely speculative) Reason." It is this higher reason that is capable of giving validity to Kant's regulative ideas of God, immortality, freedom, the self, the soul.

Thus in general we may say that Coleridge, probably by 1818 and certainly by 1825, wanted to move beyond the limits described by Kant in the *Critique of Pure Reason* and give ontological status to the regulative ideas of God, self, and immortality. The faculty equipped to give such status Coleridge calls the "higher reason." He believed that this higher reason, in contrast to Kant's pure speculative reason, has a proper object of thought, which is itself, or simply the self (in Coleridge's terminology the subject becomes its own object). His metaphysical and theological deductions derive from this point. Our chief critical problems now become clear: to ascertain how closely the higher reason approximates the Platonic reason of the seventeenth century, to establish the relationship it bears to Kant's practical use of the pure reason, and to decide what, if anything, can be said for it as a vehicle for describing religious experience.

It has been said that Coleridge, in the *Aids to Reflection,* had recourse to the higher reason in order to provide a device for the easy maintenance of conventional orthodoxy, "a safety lamp for religious inquirers." It has also been said that in both *The Friend* and *Aids to Reflection* he exchanged Kant's definition of the reason for that of a German religious mystic, F. H. Jacobi. Now, there is an element of truth in these exaggerated views. To clarify the problem my own interpretation of his position considers first the most famous and controverted definition of the reason in Coleridge—that which appears in *Aids to Reflection* as a footnote to Appendix A. It is this definition which seems to blend Neoplatonic and Kantian elements:

> The Practical Reason alone is Reason in the full and substantive sense. It is Reason in its own sphere of perfect freedom; as the source of ideas, which ideas, in their conversion to the responsible Will, become ultimate ends. On the other hand, Theoretic Reason, as the ground of the universal and absolute in all logical conclusion, is rather the light of Reason in the Understanding, and known to be such by its contrast with the contingency and particularity which characterize all the proper and indigenous growths of the Understanding.[6]

This statement, in conjunction with another in *The Friend*[7]—which seems dangerously close to Jacobi's postulate that reason is an "eye" for perceiving objective truth[8]

6. *Aids*, p. 367.

7. *The Friend*, 144–45: "I should have no objection to define reason with Jacobi, and with his friend Hemsterhuis, as an organ bearing the same relation to spiritual objects, the universal, the eternal, and the necessary, as the eye bears to material and contingent *phenomena*. But then it must be added, that it is an organ identical with its appropriate objects. Thus God, the soul, eternal truth, &c., are the objects of reason; but they are themselves reason."

8. The passages in Coleridge which are strikingly similar to Jacobi's definition of the Reason are thoroughly studied in Winkelmann, *Coleridge und die Kantische Philosophie*, pp. 234–36. The difference between Coleridge and Jacobi in the interpretation of the light of reason is brought out in the following extract. With Coleridge "Die Erkenntnisse der Reason können denen des Understanding nicht widersprechen wenn sie auch über diese hinausgehen; ebenso ist auch Faith zwar above reason, doch nicht gegen diese gerichtet." As opposed to this moderate view stands Jacobi's irrationalism: "Im Gegensatz hierzu vertritt Jacobi den ausgesprochen mystischen Standpunkt, dass Glaubenssätze durchaus dem Verstande widersprechen können. 'Die Vernunft bejaht, was der Verstand verneint.'"

—has been looked upon as clear indication that Coleridge, in his late repentance, abandoned logic and rationality. Although that is an extreme view of the matter, it is certainly clear that there is an un-Kantian element present. Some critics have concluded that he separated the practical from the pure reason, giving extreme importance to the former, and reducing the latter to a mode of the understanding. In Kant the practical reason is substantially the same faculty as the pure reason, and has its categorical powers only by virtue of its peculiar activity in will and conscience.[9] This substantial connection ensures that the dictates of the practical reason will be only regulative, for the limitations of the pure reason are not cast aside in its activity. On the other hand, the distinction Coleridge seems to be making has been construed as giving the practical reason a dangerously free rein untrammeled by and divided from the pure reason. It has been taken as a wedge, similar in intention if not in construction, to Jacobi's "eye of reason" or to the "immediate intuitive vision of God" in Occam and the Ontologists—mysticisms

9. *Critique of Practical Reason,* trans. T. K. Abbott, 6th ed. London, 1873. Kant is extremely careful in the *Critique* to emphasize the unity between the pure and practical reason, showing that the practical reason is autonomous only by virtue of its peculiar function as will. The practical reason is still a mode of the pure reason (p. 131): "This analytic shows that pure reason can be practical, that is, can of itself determine the will independently of anything empirical; and this it proves by a fact in which pure reason in us proves itself actually practical, namely, the autonomy shown in the fundamental principle of morality, by which reason determines the will to action." Although a distinction of function is certainly made by Kant, the substantial unity of the two powers is never lost sight of (pp. 182–84): "Now practical and speculative reason are based on the same faculty, so far as both are *pure reason.* Therefore the difference in their systematic form must be determined by the comparison of both, and the ground of this must be assigned. For since it is *pure reason* that is here considered in its practical use, and consequently, as proceeding from *a priori* principles, and not from empirical principles of determination, hence the division of the analytic of pure practical reason must resemble that of a syllogism . . ."

having the same purpose of separating religious knowledge from other knowledge in order to allow the former to disregard completely the restrictions imposed on the latter.

A comparison of the Coleridgean and Kantian terminologies as to the precise wording of the various formal definitions, seems to bring out an evolution of Coleridge's thought in the direction of Jacobi and the Neoplatonists, and is the natural way to emphasize the dichotomy in his thinking. No attempt to minimize the importance of the Neoplatonic implications in the later stages of Coleridge's distinction has been convincing. Even less effective have been the efforts to eliminate the Kantian element altogether, in favor of the Neoplatonic conception of reason as the basis for faith.[1] All efforts to make anything out of these definitions have resulted in failure. Unless another approach can be found, the difficulties of Coleridge's religious phase appear to be insurmountable.

Unless one is performing the function of literary historian or is engaged entirely in the study of sources, a writer's practice is more important than his formal theories. This axiom of modern criticism can be of great advantage in aiding us to push beyond the source problem in assessing the value of Coleridge's distinction. For if a great deal of weight is placed upon his precise formulation of the distinction, with due regard for chronological order and proper sensitivity as to the exact meaning of the sources, the inevitable result seems to be that one is convinced of

1. The outstanding failure of studies sympathetic toward Coleridge's use of "reason," as, for instance, Howard's, McKenzie's, or Alice D. Snyder's earlier *The Critical Principle of the Reconciliation of Opposites as Employed by Coleridge* (Ann Arbor, 1918), is their inevitable tendency to conclude at the point where vindication ought to begin. By merely pointing out that Coleridge reached beyond Kant in an attempt to identify reason with faith, these defenders invite the verdict of contradiction in his thinking passed by the unfavorable studies.

confusion in his thinking, the "head vs. heart" conflict. If this method could be abandoned in favor of the more direct, practical approach, which takes into account his use of the distinction and its importance (or unimportance) for religious thinking, the jungle of definitions and sources might be cleared. Two writers, John Muirhead and Kathleen Coburn, have urged this method as most fruitful for assessing Coleridge's real contributions to religious and philosophical thought.[2] With their viewpoint I am in agreement, and for this reason have devoted so little space to the problem of formal agreement or diversity between Coleridge's distinction and that of Kant or Jacobi or the Neoplatonists. The ground has been covered many times by various scholars. As studies in intellectual history their efforts have pointed out what is true enough as far as it goes, that in Coleridge the tradition of seventeenth-century English and nineteenth-century German idealism merge. But we are interested in what this really meant for Coleridge as a thinker.

A meaningful analysis of the relationship between Coleridge's speculative formulas and his actual religious opinions must recognize that the relationship between reason and religious belief is very complex for any man in any age. Consequently it should not be surprising that Coleridge could not arrive at neat formulas, Kantian or Neo-

2. John Muirhead's *Coleridge as Philosopher* (London, 1930) is the most thorough study of his thinking to date. The section on the relationship between philosophy and religion (pp. 217–55) is unfortunately one of the weakest. Muirhead's method of approaching Coleridge, best expressed in his shorter work "Metaphysician or Mystic?" in *Coleridge Studies by Several Hands*, ed. Blunden and Griggs (London, 1934), seems most useful as a point of view (p. 191): ". . . if we are prepared to apply to Coleridge what surely is a sound rule in all philosophical criticism, and to interpret his meaning by the general spirit of his work and in the light of what he says in his moments of clearest insight, there can, I believe, be no doubt whatever as to what he here intended."

platonic, which might satisfactorily solve the problem.
What one ought to look for in him, a man more keenly
aware than most of his English contemporaries of the
enormous difficulties in the problem, are basic strategies
and maneuvers calculated to bring unification to the so-
called conflicting attitudes of head and heart, which really
have a basis in the fundamental dualism inherent in
Christianity. This does not imply a begging of the question. We ought not to make too large assumptions in favor
of a rationalistic monism of the intellect with which to
blind our sight to the possible soundness of the empirical,
existential method of religious thinking and experience
which Coleridge adopted. A functioning relationship between reason and faith can be worked toward; the lives
and writings of numerous sincere individuals attest to
this. Our interest is to decide to what extent Coleridge
worked toward it by examining various passages from
those of his writings devoted to theological and metaphysical problems which utilize, in one way or another, his
idea of the higher reason.

There is a very simple way to illustrate this viewpoint.
The analyses of Coleridge's religious position in Wellek's
Kant in England and H. N. Fairchild's *Religious Trends
in English Poetry* [3] rest on basic premises—in conflict, of
course, with each other, and quite different from my own.
An exposition of differences in judgment that result from
these differences in viewpoint is perhaps the surest and
most forceful way of illustrating exactly how it might be
possible to come to a closer and more sympathetic understanding of Coleridge's religious position.

From the rationalistic viewpoint Wellek concludes
"that a pernicious teaching of double truth pervades Cole-

3. H. N. Fairchild, *Romantic Faith,* Vol. 3 of his Religious Trends in
English Poetry, New York, 1949.

ridge's acquiescence in all the doctrines of the Anglican Church." [4] Our objection here is against the implication in "pernicious teaching." Measured by a strict rationalistic standard which does not take into account certain empirical evidence for faith, Wellek's conclusion would be without doubt justified, for ostensibly in *Aids to Reflection* Coleridge is endeavoring to account for all of Christian revelation by the "reason-understanding" distinction. And it appears in each case that the understanding, with its mere conceptual forms is conveniently contradicted by the higher reason whenever a doctrine or article of faith is endangered. As there seems to be nothing present in the formal descriptions of the higher reason, or faculty of ideas, which allows its workings to be made clear to an objective inquirer, the whole idea of a higher reason seems to have the status of a convenient ruse. But this rationalistic standard, which does not account in its presuppositions for the possibility of a relationship between reason and any faith not based upon some monism of the reason, becomes by its very nature unqualified to pronounce any but a negative judgment upon religious experience. This negative judgment may be consistent and valid within its own frame of reference, but it is basically an uninteresting judgment and not necessarily the whole truth. We must plainly acknowledge that an interest such as ours is neither a refutation nor a confirmation of a narrowly rationalistic analysis. Our analysis should consider whether such a charge of dualism [5] may not properly constitute the beginning rather than the end of the investigation.

Using the standard of orthodoxy, Fairchild pronounced an extremely jaundiced verdict upon Coleridge's religious phase in a comment upon his late poem "Self Knowledge":

4. *Kant in England*, p. 129.
5. See his attack on dualism, ibid., p. 134.

Here at last is the religion of IT IS, eternally opposed to the religion of I AM. We do not know to what extent he was able to make fruitful use of this glimpse of Christian objectivity. Very little time was left in which to extricate himself from the trap of self, and there is no other indication that he succeeded in doing so.[6]

This severe judgment is more serious to Coleridge's position as a religious man and thinker than is Wellek's rationalism, since Fairchild indicts Coleridge on strictly religious grounds. Also, Fairchild's conception of "objective orthodoxy" is at times difficult to follow. The standard of orthodoxy by means of which Coleridge is found wanting is sometimes naive. The relationship between reason, revelation, faith, and subjective assent, so important for Coleridge, is ignored rather than honestly evaluated. All that is forthcoming are the charges that Coleridge's empiricism is subjective, his reason an unwarranted celebration of self, and that both are opposed, it appears, to a superior kind of reason and faith which lead to the acceptance of objective truth.[7] Whereas Wellek was consistent and logical within his own frame of purely rationalistic reference, Fairchild's view of orthodoxy is open to serious question. Coleridge considered himself orthodox. If this seems to be putting the case rather strongly, one must remember that the case against Coleridge is made rather strong in Fairchild's book: nothing less than that he was self-deluded at best, or insincere at the worst.

The rejection of Coleridge's religious phase by the rationalistic approach of Wellek and the conventional orthodoxy of Fairchild confirms the point that such religious experience as Coleridge had will never be under-

6. *Romantic Faith,* p. 327.
7. Ibid., pp. 319–27.

stood by the nonreligious or the simply dogmatic mind. His was an adventure in the meaning of faith, incomprehensible alike to those for whom faith implies a retreat into fancy, and for those to whom it implies a steady objectivity. Whoever finds his experience meaningful will do so not from the naive motive of looking for an "answer" to the religious problem, for the answer, according to the method of empirical experience followed by Coleridge (TRY IT, he urged in the *Aids*) must be found by each man for himself. What he offers is an authentic example of the religious mind reporting a variety of experiences in relation to religious dogma; the validity of this experiment in the strict sense no man can judge.

In saying this much one admits automatically a certain portion of Wellek's assumption;—namely, that if Coleridge had the conscious intention of unifying faith and reason by means of the famous Kantian distinction borrowed and altered to his convenience, he failed. No honor could be done to either faith or reason by tampering with the distinction between the pure and the practical reason so as to include in the latter the intuitive "eye of reason" of some Platonists and mystics. Such tactics were apt to provide an *ignis fatuus* rather than a safety lamp for religious inquirers, as they seemed to hold out short cuts of dubious value as replacements for the legitimate paths toward faith. The question of Coleridge's intention aside, and admitting that at times he seemed to be searching for a panacea, it still seems that his religious thinking on specific issues and recorded experiences presents much sounder ground for analysis than do the few outstanding theoretical precepts. In dealing with problems peculiar to the Christian religion, Coleridge successfully reworked certain Neoplatonic notions into the acute dialectic of the critical philosophy. Such a performance required a high degree of originality. I hope to support this belief with the general tenor of his religious writings, rather than with the more famous dicta dwelt upon so frequently in the past.

In instinctively parting company with Kant in *The Friend* and *Aids to Reflection* on the issues of limiting pure reason to the realm of phenomenal reality, and making the practical reason a regulative norm only, without ontological validity, Coleridge was not merely indulging a subjective whim. But his later speculations and religious experiences do raise two questions for those interested in pointing out that his post-Kantian writings are important. There is the matter of his ability to express this new post-Kantian position coherently, important in deciding how much credit he can be given as a thinker. But more crucial is the second question, his recognition of the new orientation which the problem of reason and faith had to take after Kant. Naturally, many religious stances have been developed since Kant's Critiques produced their effects upon religious thinking. In the IT IS religion of Fairchild, for instance, the impact of the critical philosophy is largely ignored. Wellek considered the Critiques and religious belief antithetical; at least that is the implication one must draw from the arguments in *Kant in England*. Other thinkers, following the lead of Kierkegaard, advocate a kind of religious experience somewhat similar to Coleridge's existential, empirical relationship between subjective consciousness and the historical facts of Christianity. This experience takes Kant and later idealism into account but nevertheless transcends the limitations such rationalism places upon religion. My feeling is that a fairly articulate pattern can be made out of Coleridge's religious thinking, which will display its kinship to the post-Kantian phase of modern Protestantism.

Coleridge perceived clearly, even in his semirejection of Kant, what few of his Anglican contemporaries knew, and what some commentators of all religious persuasions are still unaware of today—that Kant's critique of the human reason had permanently affected the manner in which the terms "faith," "reason," "revelation" ought to be handled. Always accepting the negative element in Kant, we have seen Coleridge take his place as the first English religious thinker to criticize adequately, in *Philosophical Lectures* and *Aids,* the decayed rationalism which permeated the Established Church.

But Kant had also undercut severely the old relationship between reason and faith as it appeared in traditional Christian metaphysics, and presented to acute religious thinkers a series of new problems with which Coleridge, together with Kierkegaard, Newman, and Schleiermacher, struggled at length. The new view of the relationship between reason and religion which Coleridge proposed in his post-Kantian phase was not merely a return either to the orthodox rationalism of the seventeenth or to the emotionalism of the eighteenth century. It seems, if sensitively interpreted, to have been moving in the direction which legitimately transcends the arbitrary limits set by Kant for religious experience and belief. Thus it is not the distinction between reason and understanding, nor its sources, that would seem of greatest interest. What these terms meant for Coleridge as a religious thinker, and how he used them as a method for describing religious experience would appear of greater importance.

Coleridge's use of the understanding should be clear by now. While its definition is at times close to Kant's and thereby carries certain technical implications, more often he means the understanding to represent the reasoning faculty in a general sense. In his "Logic" Coleridge ascribes to the understanding all the traditional modes of syllogistic reasoning and judgment. These modes are legitimate and trustworthy, giving to the understanding sovereign power

as the "faculty judging according to sense." In eighteenth-
and nineteenth-century theology and philosophy, from
Locke to the deists and Paley, the understanding had been
allowed to transgress its proper bounds. Coleridge insisted
in the *Aids to Reflection* that the power of reason must
be brought to bear upon problems of morality and revelation: but reason exploited as a dynamic method, as he
used it in explaining the doctrine of Justification by Faith,
and not merely as a formal definition, as it appears in *The
Friend* [8] and other works.[9]

A clear working definition of the reason is not forthcoming from Coleridge, and those who have looked for
one have been disappointed. A German writer, Dr. Karl
Schmitt-Wendel, provides a fairly typical comment on
Coleridge's positive principle: "Von Gott, Freiheit und
Unsterblichkeit spricht Coleridge einmal (in einer Num-
mer der Wochenschrift, 'The Friend', deren Herausgeber
er war, die aber bald einging) als von dunklen Ideen,
weil sie zur sittlichen Vervollkommung der Menschenge-
schlechts unentbehrlich sind." [1] Coleridge is fairly clear
that reason is the faculty of ideas, most notably religious
ideas which are lamentably "dunklen," but a direct perusal
of definitions will not take us further than this. Yet there are
some hints, in his description of the working of the reason
in relation to the understanding which perhaps may help
to penetrate the region of dim ideas a bit more. In some
passages Coleridge tries to explain how the concepts of
the understanding lead negatively and indirectly to the
ideas of the reason; in others he grapples directly with the
"idea of an idea." These all occur in the "Logic," [2]

8. *The Friend*, pp. 138, 453.
9. *Church and State*, p. 61; *Table Talk*, pp. 265, 313, 371.
1. Karl Schmitt-Wendell, "Kants Einfluss auf die änglische Ethik,"
Kant-Studien, 25–29 (Berlin, 1912), 14.
2. This reference and page references to "Logic" are to *Coleridge on
Logic and Learning*, ed. Alice D. Snyder.

where, as we should expect, he was more severely taxed than elsewhere to make his theory clear.

Although the understanding and its functions are perfectly legitimate in many spheres, Coleridge believes there is always grave danger in ignoring the reciprocal action between these autonomous areas and the reason. He defines understanding several times as the negative "pole" by which we come to have awareness of the presence of reason, "inasmuch as the understanding is the organ of the Reason, if not directly by affirmation, yet indirectly by negation" (pp. 89–90). The chief function of the logic of the understanding is the negative one of setting the bounds of its own activity, and thus allowing for the areas of the reason which operate on a higher plane. In this way the operations of the understanding assure the existence of the reason, which cannot be proved directly:

> But though we are incompetent to give a scientific proof of any other and higher source of knowledge [than the understanding], it is equally true that no Logic requires us to assert the negative, or enables us to disprove that a position which is neither theoretically undeniable nor capable of being logically *concluded,* may nevertheless be morally *convincing* or even philosophically evident.   [p. 100]

Two examples are given of this self-limitation in the understanding by means of its own logic. Whenever the understanding, Coleridge asserts, operating by the principle of contradiction, arrives from two equally affirmable postulates at contradictory conclusions, then it must be acknowledged that a higher ground exists upon which presumably the contradictions can be reconciled (p. 119). Further, if the understanding, operating according to dichotomous logic, concludes its argument in some violation of basic moral or religious law, such as pantheism,

there again it has transgressed its bounds and must acknowledge a higher reason (pp. 128–9). But what the higher
ground is and how it manifests itself beyond the negative
stage is difficult to gather, for Coleridge admits in another
place that "we reason at all" only by conceptions, and
that it is only when conceptions and intuitions are "subsumed under some pure conception, some one of the inherent and constituent forms of the Understanding," that
they are "capable of being combined into a judgment that
has real validity and significancy" (p. 99). Manifestly, he is
guarding himself as much as possible from an illogical, or
rather arational, leap into some mode of knowing beyond
logical form, where truth might be experienced in an
intuitive, sensory way, and where the laws of thought such
as dichotomy and contradiction might be violated.

In short, he is avoiding to a large extent the charge of
mysticism. But he has not gone very far in proving that
the reason exhibits itself negatively in the understanding.
It is conceivable that someone might accept the tendency
of the understanding to involve itself in contradictions as
a puzzle inviting no further comment than that the human
understanding is limited. In other words, one might em-
brace a form of skepticism, while the moral cavil against
the reasonableness of pantheism might be considered a
begging of the question. More must be said about the
reason itself as an active principle existing in religious
thinking, in order for it to become something other than
one individual's hazy, private whim.

We find Coleridge aware that his negative norm is not
completely convincing, since he makes many attempts to
tread a narrow line between mysticism and rationalism
in dealing with the "ideas" of the higher reason. If, on the
one hand, he admits their knowability as conceptions, to
the extent that they manifest themselves through the
understanding, he removes with many qualifications what-

ever usefulness they may have as hard and fast principles. In his most usual mood he insists that their essence is inconceivability, since they exist as the ground of knowledge (p. 135), and along these lines he refused to give James MacIntosh and other rationalists an "idea of an idea." If their essence is inconceivability, then there can be no dialectic of the higher reason based upon some principle of trichotomy, synthesis, or noncontradiction. Coleridge is emphatic and consistent on this point: "This is that which cannot be *generalized*, on which the mind can exercise no modifying functions—that which can only be *contemplated*—that which is deeper than all intelligence, inasmuch as it represents the element of the Will, and it's essential indefinability" (p. 136). He does, however, slip into several dangerous generalizations about some of the ideas as they manifest themselves unessentially as conceptions in the understanding, and thereby almost seems to provide a conceptual yardstick by which to measure them. Harassed by people like James MacIntosh, he was tempted to point out mathematical propositions or Newton's Laws (pp. 136-7) as illustrations of a priori pure conceptions independent of the senses. The findings of the empirical sciences and the theory of Ptolemy—the results of understanding acting upon the material of the senses—provided an obvious and clear contrast. But this qualitative difference is merely the Kantian distinction between the speculative reason and the understanding (*Vernunft* and *Verstand*). Coleridge never retracted these dangerous examples, but when pressed for others of a similar nature he was consistent in his views: "The realities which constitute the first and last of Philosophy are not the objects of logic and therefore cannot be submitted to a discussion purely logical" (p. 87). He guards against the attempt to make a neat distinction in the higher reason according to the amount of sense evidence it involves.

Since the higher reason functions in religious experience, Coleridge insists rightly that its definition cannot, by its very nature, be purely scientific. Certain negative characteristics of the higher reason have at least emerged. By implication, it differs from Kant's pure reason in its assurance of constitutive rather than regulative principles; it is less indebted to logic and the understanding than the reason of traditional Christian philosophy. Nor is it a mystic vision, a Neoplatonic organ composed of specific, innate ideas about God, for in that case it would have been possible for Coleridge to give an "idea of an idea." The higher reason, it seems, involves both the understanding (ordinary intellect) and speculative reason (Kant's *Verstand* and *Vernunft,* with its universal laws, judgments, and conceptions), but it is intellect acting in relationship with other factors. Such mingling with other factors creates "ideas": "Those truths namely (supposing which to exist) the knowledge and acknowledgement of which require the whole man, the free will, not less than the intellect, and which are not therefore merely speculative, nor yet merely practical, but both in one" (pp. 100–1). Or again: "that which is deeper than all intelligence, inasmuch as it represents the elements of the Will, and it's essential inderivability" (p. 136). Although it might seem at first glance that the prominence of free will and practical activity in these statements leads us straight back to Kant's practical reason and the source problem, this is not what really happens. The *Critique of Practical Reason* is responsible for the introduction of the will into Coleridge's reason, as is evident from the wording of the major definitions of the distinction, but the will functions in Coleridge's higher reason in a unique relationship with the understanding and the emotions, "that which is deeper than all intelligence," in a way that distinguishes Coleridge's principle from the regulative activity of Kant's practical reason. Coleridge wanted constitutive principles, not merely regulative ones, and this introduces into his higher reason an un-Kantian element which ultimately colors his whole conception of the practical reason operating in the will and the speculative reason operating in the intellect. This element is that of emotion. His higher reason was an attempt to fuse the intellectual, volitional, and emotional elements in religious experience into one harmonious whole. On this issue he parted company with Kant.

Kant's rigorous system of religious thought based the ideas of God, freedom, and immortality upon a categorical imperative of the reason acting in its practical activity as will. The results were regulative and intended to prescribe duties. Duty alone was not enough for Coleridge, who needed emotional support and a greater amount of intellectual verification for religious convictions than Kant was able to assign. "I reject Kant's *stoic* principle as false, unnatural and even immoral, where in his *Kritik der Praktischen Vernunft,* he treats the affections as indifferent ἀδιάφορα in ethics." [3]

The emotional factor is prominent in much of Coleridge's thinking. So it is not surprising to find it playing an important role in the higher reason. One need only recall the well-known phrases about a man of deep thinking being one of deep feeling, and the conviction that great ideas are perceived dimly; or look back upon the exposition of the law of association which Coleridge gives in the *Biographia Literaria* [4] to find out what the emotions meant to him. The importance of emotion for the higher reason has not been detected by those who have been interested only in the highly theoretical phrasing of the numerous distinctions between the reason and the under-

3. *Letters,* 2, 682, to G. H. Green, Dec. 13, 1817.
4. *Biog. Lit.,* *1*, 87.

standing. Such theoretical phrasing, seeming to move in an area of pure philosophical speculation, has naturally led to comparisons between Coleridge and Kant, Schelling, the Cambridge Platonists, or others. But we have seen that in any practical attempt to work with the higher reason, to give an idea of an idea or make the idea useful in a religious context, Coleridge fell back upon a blending of emotional, intellectual, and volitional factors not derived primarily from outside metaphysics. An eclectic blending of intellect, will, and emotions is the method of the higher reason, the method Coleridge followed in religious experience.

There is an impulse in all of us, based no doubt on a pride in being logical, to scorn any eclecticism in which the parts do not seem to fit coherently. Acting upon this impulse we might now dismiss Coleridge's higher reason as private mysticism or hallucination, certainly as something useless for the serious and objective study of religious ideas. Wellek and Fairchild, for different reasons, did this. Or we might try to make a practical application of Coleridge's method of putting the objective and subjective together, since the structure of the higher reason is intimately bound up with the ideas of religious experience, such as Justification by Faith. The most important and the first of these ideas, the basis of the theology in *Aids to Reflection*, concerns the existence and nature of God.

CHAPTER 4

THE IDEA OF GOD

Fortunately, there is a concrete example of the particular blending of intellect, emotion, and will, which as a total single process constitutes Coleridge's "higher reason" in action. As early as the *Biographia Literaria* he described the process in relation to a specific religious idea, the idea of God. Appearing well before his period of sustained religious thinking and in close context with the Schellingian metaphysics of the *Biographia*, this passage is truly remarkable. For his view of the imagination in that book contradicts the religious process of the higher reason. Out of these contradictory views, the transcendental idealism of Schelling and his own religious eclecticism, arose the struggle of his later years. In the *Biographia* Coleridge entertained both views without awareness of the ultimate implications of the one for the other. Psychologically, the *Biographia* was the turning point in his career, the high-water mark of his rationalism, and also the beginning of a powerful interest in systematic religious thinking. Here is the key passage:

> The question then concerning our faith in the existence of a God, not only as the *ground* of the universe by his essence, but as its maker and judge by his wisdom and holy will, appeared to stand thus. The scien-

tial *reason,* whose objects are purely theoretical, remains neutral, as long as its name and semblance are not usurped by the opponents of the doctrine. But it *then* becomes an effective ally by exposing the false show of demonstration, or by evincing the equal demonstrability of the contrary from premises equally logical. The *understanding* mean time suggests, the analogy of *experience* facilitates, the belief. Nature excites and recalls it, as by a perpetual revelation. Our feelings almost necessitate it; and the law of conscience peremptorily demands it.[1]

A little further on we find that this demonstration of the idea is both the first step and first principle in Coleridge's religious phase:

> From these premises I proceeded to draw the following conclusions. First, that having once fully admitted the existence of an infinite yet self-conscious Creator, we are not allowed to ground the irrationality of any other article of faith on arguments which would equally prove that to be irrational, which we had allowed to be *real.* Secondly, that whatever is deducible from the admission of a *self-comprehending* and *creative* spirit may be legitimately used in proof of the *possibility* of any further mystery concerning the divine nature.[2]

From a psychological point of view these passages open for us Coleridge's religious phase. They offer a way of understanding his acceptance and defense of Christian theology in *Aids to Reflection* and other works, and also provide a method of following his movement from general religious propositions to particular dogmas. But the psychological aspect of Coleridge's religious thinking is not

1. *Biog. Lit., I,* 135.
2. Ibid., p. 136.

our only interest. More important for the present inquiry is an analysis of Coleridge's major religious idea from an objective and fuller point of view.

Our analysis can be restricted to the first passage, since the second actually concerns the method of his religious phase, how he passed from the acceptance of first principles to a construction of Christian theology. Coleridge argues, as have many others, that if the greater complexity can be made acceptable to reason, then the lesser ones inherent in the Christian scheme follow without great difficulty. This is a very large order. That is why it is best to handle the two problems separately. The first has often been called the "general religious problem" and concerns all men. The second is the province of Christians, not all of whom share Coleridge's conviction regarding the nature of its solution.

In the first passage the higher reason, a fusion of intellect, will, and emotion, functions in demonstrating the existence of God. The process perfectly illustrates an "idea" as exhibiting itself partially through the understanding with the aid of the other powers, yet remaining essentially inconceivable. The speculative reason assumes, for the sake of argument, first a positive and then a negative stance upon the question of God, and demonstrates by falling into contradictories its inability to resolve the problem one way or another. The speculative reason is the understanding acting in its higher capacity with the pure concepts of an a priori nature, and is distinguished from the lower function of the understanding, called merely the understanding, which judges upon the materials of sense evidence in a more obvious way. Thus, to this point, a certain fidelity to Kant is maintained by the division of the pure reason into a higher and lower power by Coleridge. But the sense evidence, conceived of by the "lower" understanding as the unifying factor among phenomena—

for instance, facts of nature such as change, death and natural regeneration—"facilitates" belief in a supreme cause, which now becomes the positive position of the theoretical understanding taken as a whole. Thereupon the voice of feeling and the law of conscience in the will add more evidence to this position, until belief in God's existence becomes the culmination of the simultaneous process of the higher reason, and truly an "idea."

What was just said is actually a description of the process in the "higher reason" rather than an analysis. The description is useful to show how Coleridge worked within his own terms, a valuable procedure largely ignored in most discussions of his abstract definitions. But analysis raises numerous problems. Is there any justification for limiting the "higher reason" to the religious function which it seems to have in Coleridge's usage? More important, what kind of validity or universality can be predicated of it? A further question, of definite theological importance, concerns ontological problems raised by this process. Is it that of a disguised monism in which higher reason replaces creative imagination, and therefore, as Fairchild asserts, basically inimical to Christianity?

Coleridge would probably have justified the use of the higher reason for religious matters in particular merely by referring to the terms of the reason-understanding distinction as he conceived them. Since the understanding in its lower form is capable of handling experience (the material of the senses generalized and abstracted into conceptions), and in its higher form, as the speculative reason, generates the rules and laws of the various sciences, there is obviously no need for the higher reason to operate in these areas, which include all experiences except the aesthetic, ethical, and religious. Art, bringing more of man's soul into activity, activates the emotions and the imagination, but only in religious experience are the emotions, intellect, and will united in one function. Therefore only religion activates the higher reason in the full sense of the term. Now this argument is open to the criticism of begging the question unless it can be defended or explained from a position outside the distinction itself. So in the interest of clarity and objectivity let us follow through the argument for the existence of God which Coleridge gives, with an eye toward analyzing the rational, emotional, and volitional elements in it.

For modern theists, as for Kant, Coleridge, Hegel, and St. Anselm, the ultimate rational proof for the existence of God must be some form of the ontological argument, since this argument is a presupposition of the more popular a posteriori arguments. In Coleridge's terms the ontological argument pertains to the speculative reason operating in a pure form, while the cosmological ones rely upon notices of the understanding in its lower capacity as mediator of sense knowledge. The difficulties in the argument illustrate Coleridge's position that the speculative intellect can reach, from opposed but equally valid premises, contrary conclusions about God, and thus disqualify itself as the ultimate norm. Historically we know that St. Anselm,[3] the Scholastics,[4] and Hegel [5] accepted the ontological argument, while Kant,[6] Hume,[7] and, for a time, Coleridge, de-

3. St. Anselm's argument, the basis of all ontological arguments, runs as follows in translation: "Certainly that, than which nothing greater can be thought, cannot be in the intellect alone. For even if it is in the intellect alone, it can also be thought to exist in fact: and that is greater. If then, that, than which nothing greater can be thought, is in the intellect alone; then the very thing, which is greater than anything which can be thought, can be exceeded in thought. But certainly this is impossible."

4. The traditional Thomistic arguments appear in the *Summa Theologica, Prima Pars, Quaestio* ii, *Articulus* III. These are actually "cosmological" arguments in the viewpoint of Coleridge and Kant.

5. *The Logic of Hegel*, trans. Wallace (Oxford, 1892), pp. 329–36.

6. *Kritique der Reinen Vernunft* (Berlin, 1889), pp. 475–82.

7. *A Treatise of Human Nature* (Oxford, 1888), pp. 248–49, 633.

nied it as a final speculative proof. Today some skeptics
and theists reject, while others, usually theists, accept
some form of this argument, thus illustrating Coleridge's
point that the theoretical proofs of the pure speculative
reason may be accepted by some and rejected by others.
From Hegel's criticism of Kant's attack on the ontological
argument emerges the basic issue that divides skeptics and
ontologists—whether there is some kind of necessary unity
between thought and being. For those who accept the
necessary unity—of identity, analogy, or harmony, from
St. Anselm to Hegel—some form of the ontological argument leading to an unconditioned ground of reality is not
an impossible step. But if it is postulated that accident and
chance operate in the relation between thought and being, as it was by Hume and the skeptics, or that it is impossible to make assertions about the noumenal order, as
Kant did, then any ontological assumptions become an
illogical leap. Now although there is no proof which must
be accepted as valid for the unity of thought and being on
purely theoretical grounds, the arguments concerning
"analogy of being," posed by the Scholastics,[8] or that of

8. The analogy of being, the most powerful concept in traditional the-
istic philosophy, proposes a metaphysical alternative to both pantheism
and skepticism, the two systems that plagued Coleridge constantly in his
struggle to erect a rationale of belief. Against the unity of identity in
pantheism, to preserve the notions of creation and individual personality
in creatures, the analogy argues that being in God and in created things
only allows of analogous predication (St. Thomas, De Potentia, VII, 7:
"Diversa enim habitudo ad esse impedit univocam predicationem entis").
This is true because in God essence and existence are identified, whereas
in creatures they are distinct. The analogy is one of proportionality, a relation of all being, or a "pre-established harmony," which ensures the correlation of thought and being. Late in his career Coleridge hit upon a
notion similar to this in guarding against skepticism and pantheism,
especially in regard to the interpretation of Scripture. As indications of
his interest in philosophical dualism, these similarities, with important
differences, between Coleridge and the Scholastics are significant. He mentioned reading the Schoolmen in many of his philosophical discussions.

unity of subject and object in consciousness, offered by classical idealists, are both plausible. Yet there are many forms of skepticism, ancient and modern, which maintain that the principle of contradiction is a law of thought not constitutive of being.[9]

Coleridge falls into the first group, with those who would accept the unity of thought and being, in other words the essential rationality of the world, because the idea presents plausible proofs and cannot be disproved. He did not follow further, with those who hold an absolute certainty of an ontological kind in the demonstrations of theoretical proofs for the Absolute, as do most idealists and the Scholastics. Their arguments succored him, and in the case of Schelling's deluded him for a spell, but could never permanently wean him from what he thought Kant had shown about theoretical proof. But the understanding in the lower form helped to strengthen the theoretical possibility into a practical reality. The sense experiences which understanding mediated into empirical judgments engendered belief in the rationality of the world in a pragmatic way, by means of a never-ending series of inductions indicating the correspondence of thought and being in many areas. From the crude teleological and cosmological proofs of "design" in nature to the minute findings of laboratories, practical experience lent weight to the theoretical proofs for the unity of thought and being, and hence to practical beliefs in an unconditioned ground of both thought and being, or God.

This belief, pragmatic and practical, having a plausible

9. See Paul Weiss, *Reality* (New York, 1949), pp. 141–75, for a modern presentation of the unity of thought and being which nevertheless rejects the ontological argument as a necessary part of this unity in favor of multiplicity of interrelated Beings. R. G. Collingwood, *An Essay on Metaphysics* (Oxford, 1940), pp. 34–49, 313–28, expounds the historical, relativistic, and skeptical attacks of modern science upon ontology and the unity of thought and being.

theoretical structure in reason, is a form of faith, a faith which goes beyond the reason without violating it.[1] Not based upon the heart or the emotions, it can be called the calculated faith of a practical man. Coleridge, during his Unitarian period, clearly held practical faith in reason and believed that faith and reason worked together without contradiction in the question of God's existence: "The arguments, that at all apply to it, are in its favor; and there is nothing against it, but its own sublimity. It could not be intellectually more evident without becoming morally less effective; without counteracting its own end by sacrificing the *life* of faith to the cold mechanism of a worthless because compulsory assent." [2] This rational faith in an "unconditioned" Absolute, or God, is quite common and not the least embarrassing intellectually. It is, incidentally, what Muirhead was defending in his reply to Wellek's *Kant in England*.[3] But Coleridge went beyond this point

1. *Essay on Faith* in *Works*, 5, 557: "Faith may be defined, as fidelity to our own being—so far as such being is not and cannot become an object of the senses; and hence, by clear inference or implication, to being generally, as far as the same is not the object of the senses: and again to whatever is affirmed or understood as the condition or concomitant, or consequence of the same."

2. *Biog. Lit., 1*, 135-36.

3. In answer to what he considers Wellek's charge against Coleridge to be—that is, that his position was a relapse into blind faith and logical absurdities—Muirhead in *Coleridge Studies by Several Hands* (London, 1934), p. 197 offers this: "It is on the ground of the hold he had of this essentially rational and synthetic principle that, in spite of what has been recently written by scholars for whose work I have the greatest respect, I should still claim for his philosophy, whatever its defects in detail, that it is in a true sense metaphysical rather than mystical. Coleridge was prepared (and who is not?) to admit that in the end *omnia in mysteria exeunt*. But he was also prepared to maintain that it is only by following our reason that we are able to discover when we come to that end, and to protect ourselves against the mistake, not to say the arrogance, of drawing the line where it happens to suit our prejudices or the desires of our own undisciplined hearts." Now this is surely an eloquent defense of Coleridge's metaphysical position to the point we have described it. The ontological unity of thought and being is a form of faith which transcends

to take steps criticized by Wellek and ignored in Muirhead's reply. For this rational faith is merely the operation of the understanding in its theoretical and practical activity, producing a conception of the "unconditioned," rather than an "idea" of God. To view the unconditioned as a living God required the activity of the will and the emotions, and it is the introduction of these factors into the proof which provides the real difficulties in following Coleridge's religious thinking. An unconditioned Absolute of Will, Intellect, or Substance, the product of the intellect alone, Coleridge called pantheism; but his own Living God, product of the intellect, emotions, and will operating together, some call nonsense and others an egotistical form of self-delusion. In pursuing Coleridge's "idea" of God through these difficult areas we are not merely following his psychological processes or concerning ourselves with his personal problems but are trying to discover, as with the arguments of the understanding above, what kind of validity such recourse to the will and emotions may have.

The will can enter into the conviction of God's existence in two ways, as the volitional inclination toward belief and as the grounds for a rationale of belief. As the first it might well be used to force the belief of what is absurd —*credo quia absurdum est*—regarding almost any proposition of a religious nature. This is not the use of will we find in *Aids* and Coleridge's other religious works. He argues, in the *Aids* and elsewhere, for the will as a rationale of belief, "the law of conscience" which "peremptorily commands" belief. Traditional Christian ethics held that the existence of the law of conscience argued a Lawgiver, and that the capacity of the will for infinite happiness and

---

the rational without violating it. But Wellek's charges were levied against the more active faith of *Aids to Reflection*, the specifically Christian faith which Muirhead ignored in his *Coleridge as Philosopher*. It is an exposition of the rationale of this faith which is really required.

duration indicated the necessity of immortality for the soul. Kant modified these arguments in the subtle reasoning of the *Critique of Practical Reason,* reducing their importance from normative to regulative principles. Coleridge's position is substantially the traditional one modified to a certain extent by knowledge of Kant. There are important differences between traditional, Kantian, and Coleridgean viewpoints on this subject, but the basic premise of the three is the same, that the will exists as a fact, choosing good over evil in order to conform to a law of conscience.

Coleridge also considered the religious feelings and emotions as self-evident, existential facts immediately given in consciousness and operating in a manner analogous to that of the conscience in the experience of knowing God. The specific religious emotion operating directly as a feeling that God exists for the individual, and manifesting itself now as loneliness, now as the need for communication with some Other, a personal yet spiritual Father, was a powerful factor in translating the "unconditioned" into the God of Christian tradition. Also a powerful factor in Coleridge's life, he urged that readers of *Aids* TRY IT themselves.

There is of course a grave difference between the quality of the evidence for the question of the "unconditioned" and that for the question of God as a Person. In the first a speculatively reasonable position is strengthened by means of evidence of its plausibility in the external world into a kind of faith in the "unconditioned." This assent is not required by reason, but the evidence upon which both the skeptic and the believer judge is public and objective. But the evidence of the conscience and the will, or the awareness in feeling of the God-consciousness, is subjective. One man may deny the existence of feelings held by another, and there is no outside, objective source of arbitration. The difference between the two types of evidence is not always perceived by Coleridge in his arguments for religion and morality in *Aids to Reflection*. As a basis for religious belief his TRY IT is sound for those who themselves admit the possibility of such experiences; the phrase has an exasperating sound for those who, like Wellek, feel that the argument must be confined to the sphere of the logical.

The question of the validity of Coleridge's position cannot be raised here, for obvious reasons. One need only be reminded of the claims and counterclaims which pass between the philosophers, psychologists, and theologians, or take note of the impressive list of minds that have considered the timeless question to realize that Coleridge could not solve this basic and profound issue to everyone's satisfaction. The higher reason as Coleridge defined and employed it is an organ of a special religious truth; consistent within its own premise, it does not violate the canons of logic and rationality. Yet it proposes and dares to deal with a highly controversial area of experience. Our particular problem, within the area of describing Coleridge as a religious thinker, is not to judge peremptorily in the manner of Wellek and Fairchild but rather to follow his argument through carefully in all its phases. Coleridge's idea of God must be considered as a rationale for the Christian positions in the *Aids,* not on the basis of ultimate validity, but of inner consistency. This problem is serious enough in itself. Christianity is a historical religion, among other things, and Coleridge's higher reason presents certain difficulties for Christian thinking.

The greatest difficulty is that Coleridge's idea of God does not necessarily require correlation with objectively revealed fact. This idea of God might approach the God of the Testaments, but seemingly does so by subjective means. Keeping in mind Fairchild's distinction between the religion of I AM and that of IT IS, Coleridge's reason, his doctrine of ideas, in its relationship to the doctrines of historical Christianity should be examined. Some major distinctions come to light between his position and the various subjective approaches to religious experience. There was a point in Coleridge's career, 1816–17, when he attempted to work out a synthesis of the higher reason and the imagination in the construction of religious ideas. This phase of subjective idealism was temporary, and the evidence we have suggests a falling-away from transcendental monism after 1817, carrying with it the separation of the higher reason and the creative imagination.

The definitions of primary and secondary imagination are well known; the primary is a dim analogue of creation, the secondary similar in kind but related specifically to aesthetic experience. In the *Lay Sermon* of 1816 Coleridge leaned heavily upon this conception of the imagination in one description of the higher reason of ideas: "The completing power which unites clearness with depth, the plenitude of the sense with the comprehensibility of the understanding, is the imagination, impregnated with which the understanding itself becomes intuitive, and a living power" (p. 461). In the definition of ideas the same note is struck: "but which is an educt of the imagination actuated by the pure reason, to which there neither is or can be an adequate correspondent in the world of the senses;—this and this alone—an Idea" (p. 484). From there he asserted the ability of this imagination or higher reason to create symbols of Scripture:

> In the Scriptures they (the stories) are the living educts of the imagination; of that reconciling and mediatory power, which incorporating the reason in images of the sense, and organizing (as it were) the flux of the senses by the permanence and self-circling

energies of the reason, gives birth to a system of symbols, harmonious in themselves, and consubstantial with the truths of which they are the conductors.

[p. 436]

One notices here that the terminology is similar to that of Coleridge's descriptions of aesthetic experience under the influence of Schelling. Finally, the symbol itself is described in Schellingian terms: "On the other hand a symbol (ὁ ἔστιν ἀεὶ ταυτηγόρικον) is characterized by a translucence of the special in the individual, or the general in the special" (p. 437).

This equation of the higher reason with imagination may have been the high-water mark of Coleridge's transcendentalism, but it was not the basis or rationale of his religious experience. It gave no place to the emotions or the will and was truly a monism of the understanding, based upon an exalted view of the imagination—of the symbol and of the myth-making powers of man. Had Coleridge held this view consistently, his religious direction might then justly be described in Fairchild's terms as a religion of the I AM, an attempt by man to create by intuitive imaginative experience his own God. Coleridge held confused and contradictory views in 1817, but the sudden falling-off in allusions to the myth-making power and the imagination in his later writings leads one to the belief that the role of the imagination in the higher reason was reduced by a thinker fully conscious of the implications such contradictions held for a truly Christian point of view. He never, of course, lapsed into a pre-Kantian view of psychology, so it is not surprising to find him including in the Essay On Faith (1840) the naturalistic description of the imagination as the unification of sense experience in defining the process of faith. Though idealistic in principle, his later definitions are drastic reductions of the role of the imagination from the role accorded it by Schelling, and a return to a dualism more favorable to Christianity.

In the years between the *Biographia* and *Aids to Reflection* Coleridge made some searching criticisms of his enthusiastic equation of the higher reason and the imagination. There are certain criticisms of Schelling which appear in the Notebooks [4] written after 1817 and before 1825, of which the following are the most striking (by 1818 he notices that his idol Schelling and his whipping boy Fichte were not so different after all):

> I cannot approve the choice of the proper name Nature Philosophy because it is 1 a useless Paradox 2 chosen to make the difference between his and his old Master Fichte's systems greater than it is—and 3 because the phrase has been long & universally appropriated to the knowledge which does not include the Peculia of Men, i.e. to Physiology.[5]

4. In the following sections, reference will be made to the Notebooks which Coleridge kept in the later years of his life. Some 55 in all, they are now being published by the Bollingen Foundation under the editorship of Professor Kathleen Coburn of Toronto University. Volume *1* (New York, 1959) has already appeared. Victoria University in the University of Toronto has a complete photograph collection of the Notebooks, of which I examined some twenty (21½ through 40), extending from 1817 to 1830. In the notes below I have given the usual folio references. Until the final edition of all the Notebooks is completed by Professor Coburn, the scheme of reference in those published to date cannot be employed.

In content the Notebooks vary greatly. The earlier ones I examined, 21½-24, read something like the *Anima Poetae* and show a prevailing interest in poetry, aesthetics, and literary criticism. From 26 through 35 the interest is divided almost equally between religious and scientific subjects—both coming finally under the heading of the *Logosophia*, the system Coleridge hoped to complete. The later ones, 35-40—and from cursory examination this seems to be the case with those following 40—deal more and more with the study and commentary of Scripture. Any one of these areas—science, Scripture, religious views—would easily provide enough material for an extended study. What I have given here is merely a slight sampling of the wealth of material, chosen, of course, with my own special interest in view.

5. Victoria MS 19, Vol. 2, f. 10ᵛ, commentary to p. 368 of *Ueber das*

In another, he notes the subtle monism of the Identity Philosophy in general:

Now the whole scheme of Evolution, according to the Identität-system, is grounded on the impossibility of a retrocession to Identity—the constant tendency being constantly counteracted by the equal tendency to Manifestation, and, either Neutrality or Synthesis, the Products of the composite Forces. But if it be said, that the Life $=$ Prothesis be the Life Absolute and universal, and the Life $=$ the synthesis, be Life relative, ergo finite, and particular, I again demand, by what right and in which sense the term, *Identity*, is applied to the latter? An identity subject to more or less, to this sort or that sort? A modified Identity? An Identity of $>$ and $\oplus$ under the *preponderance* of $\oplus$? And what after all does the whole amount to, but a chain of bald Truisms? [6]

This most important comment indicates Coleridge's realization that his higher reason must in some way be distinguished from creative imagination. In Schelling there is no possibility for a dualism favorable to Christianity: "In short, Schelling's System and mine stand thus: In the latter there are God and Chaos: in the former an Absolute Somewhat, which is *alternately* both, the rapid leger de main shifting of which constitutes the delusive appearance of *Poles*." [7]

Verhaltnis der bildenden Kunste zu der Natur. MS 19, Vol. 2, in the Victoria University collection is a transcript in the hand of Mrs. H. N. Coleridge. The transcripts, some dated 1819, are commentaries on Schelling's *System des Transcendentalen Idealismus* (Tubingen, 1800) and *Ueber das Verhaltnis der bildenden Kunste zu der Natur* (1807). They were transcribed at an unknown date from the margins of the books into a notebook.

6. Notebook 28, ff. 27ᵛ–28.
7. Notebook 28, ff. 30ᵛ–31.

These criticisms certainly indicate Coleridge's struggle to free himself from the pantheistic monism lurking in the identity-philosophy. He identifies Schelling's conception of the ego, or self-consciousness, with the subjectivity of Fichte and Spinoza, while trying to free his own first principle of the same difficulties. In Coleridge's attempt to combine certain methods of the identity-philosophy with traditional Christian dualism, he realized that forceful distinctions were necessary to prevent the higher reason of religious experience from falling into the traps set by Schelling and Fichte. The *Ich* in Schelling is not the living subject (intellect, emotion, will), but a lifeless abstraction defining a system of false and absolute monism. Here is Coleridge's criticism of one of Schelling's assertions in his *System des Transcendentalen Idealismus* on the nature of *das Ich*:

> But how can *das Ich* then essentially if still the same "1 AM," can yet lose its essential Power. . . . how can that be and be "Ich" the essence of which is that it *does* last? The answer must be we here involve Time inappropriately.[8]

The same ground is covered in a longer more thorough Notebook entry, beginning as follows: "In my letter to Mr. Green I detect two fundamental errors of Schelling— 1. The establishment of Polarity in the Absolute and—2. the confusion of Ideas, with Theorems on one side, and with Anticipations on the other . . ."[9]

8. Victoria MS 19, Vol. 2, f. 6, commentary to p. 103 of *System des Transcendentalen Idealismus.*

9. Notebook 27. ff. 25ᵛ–26, continuation of note in text: ". . . so as to make one and the same at once self-evident and yet dependent on empirical Proof—But these and all his other errors, together with all his failures are referable to the one the making *Nature* absolute—See p. 36 of his *Einleitung zu seinen Entwarfen* where he attempts to represent as aboriginal the same idea as I have deduced under the name Multeity—but **he makes them** *simple actions*, not as existing indeed but as necessarily so

For Coleridge, Schelling's *Ich* became a false premise and led to a lifeless system or monism excluding the possibility of a personal God. The premise was false, since it ignored the ground of the *Ich* or consciousness in an other outside the self. A spirited imaginary dialogue Coleridge held with Schelling brings out the relationship between the premise and the system, the all important difference between personal *Ichheit,* or feeling, and *Ichheit* as an abstraction taken as the first postulate of a system:

> But why, if there are many *Ichheiters,* should not No. 1 *I* act on No. 2 *I?* If *I* act on itself, it is acted on, therefore actible on by an *I.* But to assert that it can be acted on by this and no other incomprehensibly-determined in its—comprehensible-determiniteness— I, is—to assert! and no more. In short, the Attributes of the Absolute Synthesis, the I Am in that I Am, are falsely transferred to the I Am in that God is—
>
> Aye! replies Schelling, this would be *secundum Principium essendi;* but I speak only *secundum Principium sciendi.*
>
> *True,* (I rejoin), but you assert that the two Principles are one . . . What is this but to admit that the *I itself* even in its absolute Synthesis supposes an already perfected Intelligence, as the ground of the possibility of its existing as it does exist? [1]

Gradually, as a result of his detection of Schelling's monism in the epistemological premises, Coleridge began

---

to be *thought:* for so it would be if *ware die unendliche Evolution der Natur vollendet.* Now this is grund-falsch. It cannot be *thought*—the thought would destroy, annihilate,—annihilation of all reality would be the consequence. And Schelling confounds the − einfach with the + einfach or the *below* Number with the supernumeral or Monody. But with this falls his *reine Intensität:* and with that the whole of his Natur-wissenschaft."

1. Victoria MS 19, Vol. 2, f. 9, commentary to p. 118 of *System des Transcendentalen Idealismus.*

to take greater care in defining higher reason, idea, consciousness, in ways that reflect a cautious return to the more traditional dualism of Christian metaphysics. Certain comments, appearing as conclusions to extended criticism of Schelling, are also positive attempts to remedy the assumptions in monism that all Being is univocal. The first is very general:

> Now I appear to myself to obviate the inconvenience [in Schelling's system] by simply reversing the assumption that Perception is a species, of which Sensation is the genus, or that perception is only a more finely organized Sensation—with me, Perception is the *essentia prima,* and sensation = *perceptio unius:* while Perception so called is = *perceptio planum simultanea.* Or thus: single intuition is Sensation, comparative or complex Intuition—Perception. The consequences of this position are wide and endless.[2]

The second is more satisfactory, and points clearly toward the epistemology of Scholasticism and "moderate realism":

> A position which occurred to me 20 years ago as an objection to Idealism (as Berkeley's) recurs with additional weight to me as often as I think on the subject—Idealism and Materialism are both grounded in the Impossibility of inter mutual action between things altogether heterogeneous—and here again it is assumed by both parties that Perception is but a sort of, or at least an immediate derivative from, *Sensation*—so that the changes or modifications of the Percipient's own Being are exclusively the objects of his perception. But is not this gratuitous? Is not sensibility just as mysterious, equally *datum, haud intellectum,* as Percipiency? If I assume, as I have a far

2. Ibid., f. 8, commentary to page 40.

better right to do because all men do so naturally, that Percipiency *in genere* is an attribute of the Soul, and that Sensation is nothing more than a species of Perception modified by the object . . . all is clear.[3]

These definitions of perception and sensation, together with others worked out with conscious revulsion from Schelling, play a great part in Coleridge's rationale of his positive position on the higher reason and ideas, at the time of *Aids* and later. At this point at least one guiding principle should be recognized, that Coleridge's position in relation to identity-philosophy became extremely complex after 1818. He certainly agreed with its postulate of harmony between subjective and objective, for upon this postulate rested his assertion of valid personal experience in relation to objective facts or doctrines. But he also recognized that any completed identity of subject and object in consciousness, a unity of thought and being, nature and history, which recognized no Other outside itself

3. Notebook 27, ff. 35ᵛ-36. Another interesting commentary in the same vein, this time directed squarely at Berkeley, is found in the MS "Logic." Regrettably, along with other significant passages, this useful passage was omitted by Miss Snyder in her book *Coleridge on Logic and Learning* and was made available to me through the courtesy of Miss Coburn. MS "Logic," ff. 163-67: "It [Berkeley's theory of sensation] is certainly no part of our immediate consciousness, and as little is it any part of the general belief of mankind, much less is it an Universal belief, which it should be to be of any force at all in the present question. Now if instead of the assumption that the perceptions are forms of sensation we should take perception as the generic term and assume that sensation is a form or mode of Perception, viz. a simple perception, a perception confined to an object which in this case is the percipient's own being, while those involving the act of comparison and which may be called complex are perceptions commonly so called, the whole superstructure of Berkeleyianism would fall. Now we are perfectly entitled to do this, for the defect if it be such of removing the diversity which the common sense of Mankind finds between sensation and perception, feeling and seeing is common to both assumptions, while the results of the former are in direct contradiction to the Universal and involuntary faith of Man, while those of the latter must be found in perfect coincidence with it.'

(unity of *essendi* and *sciendi* in Schelling) led inexorably to absolute monism.

Coleridge's progress in defining the higher reason in a way that might reconcile his interest in both objective and subjective was carried on after 1818 in both his published and unpublished writings. In the public writings the reasoning is general and the focus is on the objective, the attempt to relate certain major ideas of the higher reason with historical facts and doctrines of Christianity. His adversaries here were the hardened dogmatists of late eighteenth and early nineteenth centuries. In the private writings the reasoning is more exact and painstaking; the purpose is to find a premise for his higher reason of ideas. The great adversary here was himself.

Besides *Aids to Reflection* the public writings of greatest interests are *Confessions* and *Essay on Faith*. The orthodox view of Scripture and objectivity of his day, which is also the IT IS religion of Fairchild's view, is clearly attacked in these writings:

> But alas! this is not sufficient; this can not but be vague and unsufficing to those, with whom the Christian Religion is wholly objective, to the exclusion of all its correspondent subjective. It must appear vague, I say, to those whose Christianity, as matter of belief, is wholly external, and, like the objects of sense, common to all alike;—altogether historical, an *opus operatum* . . .[4]

But in castigating the unthinkingly orthodox he does not negate the objective, the historical fact in *Confessions*, as he had done earlier in the *Lay Sermon* under the spell of Schelling. According to his later view the subjective—emotions and aspects of will—does not create *revelation*, but becomes the means through which revelation is recognized

4. *Essay on Faith* in *Works, 5,* 562.

as truth by the individual. Several passages make this
clear:

> Friend! The truth revealed through Christ has its
> evidence in itself, and the proof of its divine author-
> ity in its fitness to our nature and needs;—the clear-
> ness and cogency of this proof being proportioned to
> the degree of self-knowledge in each individual
> hearer . . .[5]
> What you find therein (Scriptures) coincident with
> your pre-established convictions, you will of course
> recognize as the Revealed Word, while, as you read
> the recorded workings of the Word and the Spirit in
> the minds, lives, and hearts of spiritual men, the in-
> fluence of the same Spirit on your own being, and the
> conflicts of grace and infirmity in your own soul, will
> enable you to discern and to know in and by what
> spirit they spake and acted,—as far at least as shall be
> needful for you, and in the times of your need.[6]

The subjective provides existential validity for doctrines
revealed in Scripture, as is suggested in this passage:
"Christianity is not a theory, or a speculation; but a life;
—not a philosophy of life, but a life and a living process
. . . TRY IT." [7] The entire objective-subjective process is
summed up:

> I comprise and conclude the sum of my conviction in
> this one sentence. Revealed Religion (and I know of
> no religion not revealed) is in its highest contempla-
> tion the unity that is, the identity or co-inherence, of
> Subjective and Objective. It is itself and irrelatively,
> at once inward Life and Truth, and outward Fact and
> Luminary. But as all Power manifests itself as the

5. *Confessions*, p. 605.
6. Ibid., pp. 605–6.
7. *Aids*, p. 233.

harmony of correspondent Opposites, each supposing
and supporting the other,—so has Religion its objective, or historical and ecclesiastical pole, and its
subjective, or spiritual and individual pole.[8]

The objective pole, the historical doctrine of Christianity,
is the *given*, but its reception by man is according to the
mode of recipiency, in the sense of Kant's idealistic hypothesis. But the doctrines and facts are not created by the
imagination. And recognition of truth in these doctrines
is at least partially the function of the emotions and the
will acting upon the intellect.

By accepting the ideas of the personal God and of Christianity Coleridge automatically lapsed into some kind of
dualism. But he did not replace the monistic identity of
the creative imagination by Lockean dualism of diversity,
or the traditional scholastic dualism of analogy, but rather
by the implied dualism of Kant's *Critiques*. Scripture, no
longer the living educt of the writer's imagination, remained a phenomenal reality, valid to the same degree,
and received in the same manner, as any other fact of the
manifold constructed by man, according to his synthetic
and analytic powers. This did not make of it a subjective
notion of man. It became rather a noumenal reality
phenomenally received, according to the mode of man's
psychological processes. To express this change in emphasis from idealistic creativity to idealistic receptivity, in
Aids to Reflection Coleridge hit upon the notion of analogy, which he defined once as always implying "a difference
in kind and not merely in degree." Our phenomenal reception of Scripture in words and action is analogous to
its divine origin, and no more:

> Secondly, of the language [of Scripture]. This is a
> wide subject. But the point, to which I chiefly ad-

8. *Confessions*, p. 621.

vert, is the necessity of thoroughly understanding the
distinction between analogous and metaphorical language. Analogies are used in aid of conviction: meta-
phors as means of illustration. The language is analogous, wherever a thing, power, or principle in a
higher dignity is expressed by the same thing, power,
or principle in a lower but more known form.[9]

Such analogous reception of the divine Word precludes
the construction of Divine Ontology in the strict sense.
This is a limitation imposed upon the "pure" speculative
reason:

> And in this case to confound the similarity in respect
> of the effects relatively to the recipients, with an
> identity in respect of the causes or modes of causation
> relatively to the transcendent act or the Divine Agent,
> is a confusion of metaphor with analogy, and of
> figurative with literal; and has been and continues to
> be a fruitful source of superstition or enthusiasm in
> believers, and of objections and prejudices to infidels
> and skeptics.[1]

In effect, this limitation discourages any contemplation of
the objectively given pole of Scripture facts and leads to
the possibly dangerous (for dualism) construction of a religious metaphysics of the mind. It eschews certain traditional interests of the classical theologian: "And, lastly,
add to all these the strange—in all other writings unexam-
pled—practice of bringing together into logical depend-
ency detached sentences from books composed at the
distance of centuries, nay, sometimes a millennium, from
each other, under different dispensations, and for different objects." [2] This position might be called semidualism.

9. *Aids*, p. 235.
1. Ibid., p. 236.
2. *Confessions*, p. 599.

The facts, or words of revelation, become, upon reception by the mind, the property of the mind and the emotional nature of man. The impossibility of obtaining for them theoretical validity negates the method of mere theoretical or logical interest:

> On moral subjects, the Scriptures speak in the language of the affections which they excite in us; on sensible objects, neither metaphysically as they are known by superior intelligences; nor theoretically, as they would be seen by us were we placed in the sun; but as they are represented by our human senses in our present relative position.[3]

This semidualism, or implied idealism, forced Coleridge to contemplate further the construction of the mind, which was mysteriously prepared to receive religious experience. Christian doctrine and fact were the analogous echo of the divine in the mind and life of the individual:

> Religion necessarily, as to its main and proper doctrines, consists of ideas, that is, spiritual truths that can only be spiritually discerned, and to the expression of which words are necessarily inadequate, and must be used by accommodation. Hence the absolute indispensability of a Christian life, with its conflicts and inward experiences, which alone can make a man to answer to an opponent, who charges one doctrine as contradictory to another,—"Yes! it is a contradiction in terms; but nevertheless so it is, and both are true, nay, parts of the same truth." [4]

Similar passages in *Aids* on idea and conscience, morality and sense evidence show that this was no random burst on Coleridge's part but a consciously assumed position.[5]

3. *Aids*, p. 164.
4. *Lit. Rem.*, pp. 307–8.
5. *Aids*, pp. 207–8, 210.

his public position may lead a reader to believe that Coleridge either would not or could not defend his subjective-objective relationship in a clear, rational way, or free it from indebtedness to Schelling. Such a reader is naturally unaware of Coleridge's numerous private writings, in which he gives the construction of his semidualism on a theoretical level. For although in his public utterances he wished to dramatize the value of the subjective for an age of tepid orthodoxy, he fully realized the dangers of incoherence, whimsy, and personal preference, and faced them in his Notebook speculations.

We saw earlier that study of Schelling forced upon Coleridge the necessity of making some distinction between the higher reason, or consciousness (*principium sciendi*), and God (*principium essendi*), principles which, Coleridge concluded, were one in Schelling. For Coleridge "the *I Itself* even in its absolute Synthesis supposes an already perfected Intelligence, as the ground of the possibility of its existing as it does exist." This perfected intelligence, Other, or God, cannot be known by sensation, the mode of ordinary knowing, but is intuited by perception of being. Hence in the anti-Schelling definitions perception became the genus and sensation the species, and, as Coleridge said, "the consequences of this position are wide and endless." In this little table of definitions the hierarchy in modes of knowing is made clear:

Thing = A supposed Reality existing separately from our minds, and the supposed Correspondent to the impression, of which it is the supposed cause. *Object—* The impression made or left, either that in which we perceive, the thing or by which we recall it to our imagination: in the former sense, I term it a Presentation, in the latter, a Representation.

A Sensation = Feeling referring to some *Thing*

and yet not *organized* into a definite *object,* nor
separated from the sentient Being—or abstracted from
a Perception, as we abstract matter from form.
A Perception—sensation, organized into an object,
and thus projected out of the sentient Being in real
or in Ideal Space.
A Feeling = an act of consciousness having itself
for its' only object, and not a symbol or representative
of any thing else. Thus I have a *sensation* of Heat, a
Feeling of Life—We feel what *is* in us.[6]

The definitions of *thing* and *object* show that Kant, and
not Schelling, is again guiding Coleridge's thought, while
the downgrading of sensation in favor of perception and
the calling of the perception of life a feeling, not a specific
cognition, show another attempt to get away from a rationalistic monism. Life in the full sense is not a deduction, "an affection of the sentient subject" which may reveal all the phases of its being to itself:

I now see that the I is Life in the form of Mind—
and look forward to the establishment of a twofold
I—the accidental or phantom I, and the substantial
personal I, the first being the transformation of the
Self-finding of animal life . . .
But observe, that in my system *Object* is not, as in
the Fichtean Idealism, the dead, the substanceless,
the mere Idol, but the absolutely free Productivity in
the always perfected Product—Whereas the finite *I*
is ever seeking and finding its objectivity in God. . . .
Corollary—The simplification of the distinction of
Mind, as a pure *active* and proper *Perceptivity:* thus
cleansing my system from the last adhesion of the
Berkeleian Passivity, according to which (and no less
to the transcendental Idealism of Fichte and Schel-

6. Notebook 25, ff. 118ᵛ–119.

ling) the object is an *affection* of the Sentient Subject
—thus approaching to a confusion of mind with Life.[7]

These basic distinctions between mind and life,[8] or sensation and perception—"and so far therefore Sensation:
Perception :: Life: Mind and neither can be rendered into
the other, nor can both be considered as the two Sorts or
Forms, of one Power"—all have the obvious purpose of
asserting fundamental distinctions in being, an analogy
between being as known by the mind of man and felt in
his life, and the being of the ground of this life, the intuited Other, or God.

The importance of this semidualistic metaphysic for
Coleridge's religious position cannot be overemphasized,
for his entire doctrine of the higher reason and ideas assumes the premise of harmony based upon analogy or
correspondence in being. Without this analogy his confidence in the reciprocity of Scripture and reason,[9] or his
attempt to organize the meaning of justifying faith according to its effect upon men's dispositions, would be meaningless. His final philosophical formula to replace Schelling's *I Am in that* I AM became *I Am* (think, feel, act)
in that God is.

7. Notebook 36, ff. 3–3ᵛ.
8. Notebook 39, f. 31ᵛ: ". . . according to my philosophy Mind and Life
are aboriginal Distinctities, and consequently that it could not be my intention to resolve the latter into the former, while I was combatting the
contrary extreme of Berkeley and Hartley."
9. Notebook 35, f. 27ᵛ: "Why do I ever suffer myself even for a moment
to forget, that respecting all of Christianity, in which, I or any rightly informed Believer, have any spiritual, moral, or even natural interest, my
conscience and my Reason are more than satisfied, and even my understanding is convinced. When the Ideas rise up within me, as independent
growths of my Spirit, and I then turn to the Epistles of Paul and John
and to the Gospel of the latter, these seem a looking glass to me in which
I recognize the same truths, as the reflected Images of my Ideas—and
when I begin with meditation and Reading of these divine writings, then
they become the objective completing and guaranteeing the reality of the
subjective Truth in myself.

In the Notebooks, Opus Maximum,[1] and other unpublished writings Coleridge elaborated upon his position in *Aids* and *Confessions,* that the proper relationship between subjective notions and objective fact is one of analogy. A more technical way of putting this relationship is to say that the higher reason intuits the *I Am in that God is.* The reader should regard these deductions as clarifications of the basic positions, seen thus far, and not as independent or irrefutable "proofs" of a system. Coleridge is still concerned with the same higher reason. The distinctions between life and mind, perception and sensation, were worked out in support of the view that the I AM is a bigger, deeper experience than the mere mind (understanding and sensation) alone has awareness of. This view leaves room for the will and the emotions to function together with the senses and the understanding in the intuition of an IT IS as the ground of the I AM. Actual primacy in this intuition is given to the will, not the understanding, as is made clear by the following passages from widely separated sources on conscience and consciousness:

> *From* what reason, do I believe a continuous, forever (continuable) consciousness? From conscience! Not for myself—but for my conscience—i.e. my affections and duties toward others, I should have no Self—for self is deprivation, but all boundary implies neighborhood—and is knowable only by neighborhood, or Relations.[2]

1. What is referred to here as the Opus Maximum is of course only a fragment of a work, some parts of which were never written, while others are available only in rough Notebook sketches. Our fragment includes the four Vellum MSS described by Alice Snyder in *Logic and Learning* (p. xi) as B1, B2, B3, and B Supplementary. I have followed her methodology because the original marking—Vol. *1, 2* and *3*—as Miss Snyder noted mistakenly reversed the second and third volumes.

2. Notebook 24, f. 14.

Now this consciousness being thus distinguished from all other acts of consciousness by its universality and further by the circumstance that it at the same time constitutes the only practical contradistinction (i.e. diversity or difference in kind as opposed to mere difference in degree) of good right have mankind designated it by a particular term and named it the *Conscience*.[3]

Thus conscience becomes the ground of consciousness: "the consciousness in question is not only distinguished from all others by its universality and transcendent dignity but that it is likewise the root and precondition of all other consciousness." [4]

Conscience is a perception which is "neither a sensation nor a sense." Sensation and ordinary understanding reveal the shape of external visible *objects,* but conscience perceives (the more ordinary philosophical term here is intuits) the form of *things:*

So surely is there a form, not amenable to the senses; and in this we must place the principle both of the reality and individuality of each thing that truly is; and in point of fact by the intuition of this form, and by its diversity from shape, we actually do determine the reality of the objects of our senses.[5]

The term "conscience" as here defined by Coleridge is not a new factor in the higher reason but stands as the synonym for will, which Coleridge considers the experience of conscience in the individual:

But the one assumption, the one postulate, in which all the rest may assume a scientific form, and which

3. Opus Max., *3* (B2), f. 110.
4. Ibid., f. 111.
5. Opus Max., 2 (B3), f. 84.

granted we may coercively deduce even those which we might allowably have assumed is the Existence of the *Will,* which a momentary reflection will convince us is the same as *Moral Responsibility,* and that [again] with the reality and essential difference of moral *Good* and *Evil.*[6]

Obviously these assertions, the conscience over the consciousness, the unity of conscience and will, and the primacy of will in the higher reason, are first principles or intuitions, since Coleridge holds there are no prior elements in human experience with which to deal: "But the Will is unique, belongs to no Species, or Class, and possesses no common or generic characters: nor can it receive explanation from any thing else; for it is necessarily antecedent, or it ceases to be will." [7] In brief, "The Conscience is neither reason, religion, or will, but an experience *sui generis* of the coincidence of the human will with reason and religion." [8] "It follows therefore that the conscience is the specific witness respecting the unity or harmony of the Will with the reason, effected by the self-subordination of the individual Will, as representing the Self to the reason, as representative of the Will of God." [9]

Conscience is in fact, then, a point of synthesis between the reason and the will; it is a way of expressing the priority of the will in the higher reason without destroying the unity of intellect, will, and emotions in the self, or I AM. This is a very important point, for Coleridge considered the identification of the self in conscience as the critical pivot of his religious idea. "Even so to manifest the Reason as Will or Productive Power, and the Will as Reason, and the Construction (these being Acts of Free I

6. Opus Max., *3* (B2), f. 13.
7. Notebook 26, f. 17ʳ.
8. *Lay Sermon* I, p. 459.
9. Opus Max., 2 (B3), f. 7.

Am) necessary in order to such manifestations, is *Practical Philosophy . . ."* [1]

This practical philosophy is nothing less than an attempt to make certain assertions about the IT IS, the ground of the I AM, on the basis of what is known about the I AM. These assertions are perhaps a series of bold leaps from the individual to the universal, from the higher reason to the Absolute Will, and to a peculiar conception of the Trinity. This rationale of the will, both individual and in God, has some Kantian flavor; yet the very attempt to deal with the Absolute Will as God and with the Trinity as a basis for philosophical theism is decidedly un-Kantian. Kant's notion of a categorical imperative giving support for regulative principles becomes in Coleridge's deductions a mode of cognition dealing with areas anathematized by Kant—the traditional area of Christian ontology and some natural theology.

This process invites the conclusion that Coleridge's "system" is merely a return, after all, to the goal of classical Christian theism, by a road of his own choosing. Coleridge's method isolated him from the traditional theists. This fact is important to remember now, as we become entangled in the language of the Schools which he borrowed to define God as Absolute Will.

The clearest and most sustained presentation of this phase of Coleridge's thinking occurs in the Opus Maximum. Because of the unfinished state of that work, the statement of this position is inadequate without constant reference to the late Notebooks, where a great deal of material, although remaining in unfinished condition, also was obviously intended to fill up gaps in the incompleted "system." All this material, in turn, was actually no more than a completion of intentions stated in *The Friend* and partially realized in *Aids to Reflection,* where the Spiritual

1. Notebook 25, f. 105.

Aphorisms, entitled "Elements of Religious Philosophy," provide a basic sketch of Coleridge's metaphysical premises for the Christian faith. On numerous occasions, particularly in the letters, he looked upon his early published works in the field of religion as phases of a greater aim, to be completed in the form of a philosophical theism to be called the Opus Maximum.[2]

This theism is another form of the "ontological argument," about which Coleridge agreed with Kant only in the negative aspects. In *Aids to Reflection* the break with Kant is implicit and mainly negative; the Notebooks and Opus Maximum find Coleridge boldly setting forth his own form of the argument. In a commentary Coleridge made upon the *Aids to Reflection* shortly after its publication, there is definite indication that he realized all the implications of his break with Kant, mainly in the realization that he had embraced, for better or for worse, a form of the ontological argument toward which Kant had provided the hint. But Kant had insisted that the pursuit of this hint would ignore the fundamental principles of the *Critique of Pure Reason*. Coleridge accepted the implications of the *Critique* as to the cosmological arguments (i.e. those of St. Thomas and the Scholastics generally, and the eighteenth- and nineteenth-century natural theologians, such as Paley), yet at the same time rejected Kant's challenge that the ontological argument was discredited:

> When the cosmological Proof goes farther, viz. to prove the existence of a Supreme Being: it proceeds on an analogy questionable in both its factors—First the Sceptic impugns the conclusion from things *made* to things that grow, (from a watch to a sunflower) or to things that have no known beginning, (the metals, for instance) and likewise the inference from the

2. *Unpub. Let.*, 2, 342–43, 345, 355–59, 447.

cause of the composition of a whole to the cause of the existence of its ultimate particles, as a μεταβάσις εἰς ἄλλο γένος. And again, he objects that the differences of the known from the inferred agent, viz. the finiteness of Man contrasted with the infinity of God, is the condition and co-efficient cause of that Intelligence in the former which is to constitute the *similarity:* consequently, the supposed analogy fails in the positive Ingredient i.e. the point of likeness. It is *no* analogy. You infer (Spinoza might say) pure intelligence in a finite being, as the cause of a time-space, an intelligence in an infinite being, as the cause of a world. But the very intelligence from which you draw that inference, is wholly conditioned and in part constituted by that finiteship. To *invalidate* this plea we must refer to an *Idea* of intelligence, having its evidence in itself, and which must be shown to be the necessary apposition and antecedent of the Intelligence, our conception of which is generalized from the understanding of men. We must assert an intelligence that neither supposes nor requires finiteship by imperfection—ie: Reason. But in the attempt we pass out of the cosmological Proof, the Proof *a posteriori* and from the facts, into the Ontological, or the Proof *a priori* and from the Idea.[3]

The challenge of the "Idea of God," sketched in the *Biographia* and hinted and assumed in *Aids* and elsewhere, Coleridge finally faced in the late Notebooks and Opus Maximum. Recognizing that inevitably his proof must follow some form of the ontological argument, he asserted the basic premise already cited in the discussion of conscience and will, that will is antecedent not only to reason

3. Victoria LT 56, "Notes of S.T.C. on Aids to Reflection in hand of Mrs. H. N. Coleridge." Notes dated around 1826.

but even to being itself, inasmuch as will is the source of all true being.

Where the usual form of the ontological argument proceeds from the implication of the idea of being itself to the assertion that there must be a necessary Being in whom essence and existence are one, Coleridge moves from his position on will and conscience to the idea of an Absolute Will as the source and ground of all reality. He expressed the idea of this Will in his own terminology:

> . . . we must take the Will as the absolute Will. We may then without anticipation affirm that the identity of the absolute Will and the universal Reason is peculiar to the idea of God.[4]

The superessential Will is the Root of all the ground, Source and Antecedent of all Reality—Eternal Antecedent and Co-eternal Being, the unnamable. Not to express but to indicate the transcendence to all expression, I assume as the πρό πρῶτον + o + Abysmal Fulness in ineffable Identity = the Absolute Will, *the* Good.[5]

The same idea he also expressed in the traditional terms of scholastic theism, with which, especially in the pre-Thomistic formularization of John Scotus Erigena,[6] he recognized certain affinities:

4. Opus Max., 2 (B3), f. 2.
5. Notebook 37, ff. 34–34ᵛ.
6. Coleridge's best known allusion to Scholasticism is that in the *Biographia Literaria,* the famous misattribution of Hume's theory of association to St. Thomas. There is also a great deal of St. Thomas' *Parva Naturalia* in Notebook 21½, while in Notebook 30, ff. 46ᵛ, 47, 47ᵛ, 48, appear estimates of Duns Scotus and William of Occam. Some of this material Coleridge had "gotten up" for the *Philosophical Lectures* of 1818. In connection with his philosophical and theological views of the later period, it is obvious from general reading of the Notebooks that Scholasticism becomes more and more important. It is not for the most part to the

Deus sit actus purissimus—αυτοπατηρ—Causa Sui.[7]

> For the Godhead alone in the three-fold Absolute, the
> Ipseity, the Alterity, and the Community, the Will,
> the Word, and the Spirit, are in themselves Actus
> purissimus sine ulla potentialitate—the distinctions
> only as one with the Absolute, which they *will* to
> be . . .[8]

The unity of essence and existence in the Godhead, which
provided the basis for similar unity of thought and being
in the traditional ontological argument of scholastic
theism, was translated by Coleridge into his own terms;
Absolute Will is one with its object, necessitating the
unity of Absolute Will and Universal Reason:

> . . . Supreme Reason, which is One with the Eternal
> Source the Absolute Will of the Universe.[9]

> . . . most awful on this account those truths are—if
> the Result be impregnated and actualized by the *Will*,
> *which (as concentric with the Absolute Will that is
> one with the universal Reason)* is the source or index

---

great Aristotelian Scholastics that Coleridge turns, but rather to those of
an earlier era influenced by Platonic traditions. Thus his interest in John
Scotus Erigena is really another reflection of his abiding Platonism, the
Platonism of Plotinus and Proclus Christianized by Augustine and by
Erigena. In John Scotus he found a thinker who asserted the essential
attribute of God to be Absolute Will. In Notebook 35, ff. 24, 24ᵛ, 25, 25ᵛ,
he recognized the similarity of their thinking on ideas and Absolute Will,
pays tribute to John Scotus, and acknowledges their common debt to
Plotinian theology. But with this recognition comes the equally strong
assertion that Erigena, like the Neoplatonists before him, was a pantheist,
whereas Coleridge hoped to succeed ultimately in incorporating the leading ideas of this Platonism into a basically dualistic Christian world view.

7. Opus Max., 2, (B3), ff. 224, 225.
8. Notebook 26, f. 126.
9. Opus Max., 2, (B3), f. 148.

of all reality, and thus the Objective rise up, as a celestial Birth, in and from the universal Subject.[1]

From this truth, as the drift of the quotation plainly indicates, arises the rationality of the universe, or Coleridge's explanation in terms of this "rationale of the Will" of the analogy between thought and being. Another passage makes these connections more explicit:

> What then is the ground of this coincidence between reason and experience? between the laws of the sensible world and the ideas of the pure intellect? The only answer is that both have their ultimate ground and are ultimately identified in a supersensual essence, the principle of existence in all essences and of the essences in all existence or the Supreme Reason, that constitutes the objects which it contemplates . . . gives being to the whole phenomenal universe.[2]

Does this ingenious rationale differ from the usual monisms of Absolute Will, for instance that of John Scotus Erigena, which Coleridge criticized? As an answer, first of all, we have Coleridge's assurances in the Notebooks that there is a difference:

> Now the very purpose of my system is to overthrow Pantheism, to establish the diversity of the Creator from the sum whole of his Creatures, deduce the personeity, the I Am of God, and in one and the same demonstration to demonstrate the reality and originancy of Moral Evil, and to account for the fact of a finite Nature.[3]

The method is also indirectly indicated in this passage, i.e. to establish the personeity of God, implying dualism

1. Notebook 23, f. 20ᵛ (italics mine).
2. Opus Max., 2, (B3), f. 157, f. 158.
3. Notebook 35, f. 25ᵛ.

instead of monism, and to reinforce the distinction between Creator and Created. For the first he relied unques-
tionably upon the subjective assurances of conscience and
free will, backed to a certain extent by dualistic epistemological definitions of conscience, consciousness, and
perception. The personality of the Absolute Will is proved
in the Opus Maximum by the means sketched briefly in
The Friend and *Biographia Literaria*.[4] He freely admitted
that in order to prevent his idea of Absolute Will from
becoming another pantheistic monism, a chasm must be
crossed, "a Chasm, which the *Moral* Being only, which the
Spirit and Religion of man alone can fill up, or even
bridge." Here again the objective "idea of God as Absolute Will" and the subjective "feeling of God as Father
other than self" have merged into one and the same
demonstration. If we acknowledge the subjective basis to
be valid, personeity in the Absolute Will does follow from
the idea of will as source of all personality in man, experienced in the consciousness of conscience: "We have
proved that the perfection of person is in God, and that
Personeity differing from Personality only as rejecting all
commixture of imperfection associated with the latter is
an essential constituent in the Idea of God." [5] Or in a more
exciting if somewhat oblique presentation:

> What is an Idea? Answer. The identity of object,
> Light, and Eye, the hidden God, the unutterable in
> his own super-essential Absoluteness. Jehovah is his
> *Name*, the *Name* uttered from eternity, the Word

4. *Biog. Lit. 1*, 84; *The Friend*, p. 471: "All speculative disquisition must
begin with postulates, which the conscience alone can at once authorize
and substantiate: and from whichever point the reason may start, from
the things which are seen to the one invisible, or from the idea of the
absolute one to the things that are seen, it will find a Chasm, which the
Moral being only, which the Spirit and Religion of man alone, can fill up."
5. Opus Max., 2 (B3), f. 191.

that declareth, representeth and is God. The Jehovah *Person*. In this transcendent absolutely unique Mystery, which may be the still and steadfast extacy of Adoration the Eye of the Spirit may contemple, but which, not the Tongue of Angels nor the Language of Heaven can explain.[6]

Coleridge realized that approaching the idea of God in this way, from a conception of the will as source of all being, involved the danger of entirely separating the objective Absolute Will from the subjective, personal God as Father; the tendency is evident in the tone of this second passage. While he insisted that the moral being or conscience was a necessary basis for any idea of God as Absolute Will which might evade monism and pantheism, he combatted the complete duality and subjectivity which should divide the approach from reason and the approach from feeling. His major effort in the Opus Maximum was to build upon the idea of personeity in the Absolute Will the rationality of the entire Christian dualism, conceiving God as Creator, man as creature, God as Father, mankind as God's children. And as he had adapted the ontological argument to the purposes of his own demonstration of the idea of God on a volitional basis, so neither did he hesitate to appropriate certain traditional notions about the Trinity which might strengthen the concept of personeity as the basis for a philosophical theism with its ultimate sanction in will and conscience. Once it is allowed that personeity is a necessary deduction from conscience and will, the way seems opened whereby the idea of God as Absolute Will might be accommodated within the traditional patterns: "If then personeity, by which term I mean the source of personality, be necessarily contained in the idea of the perfect Will, how is it possible

6. Notebook 36, f. 23ᵛ

that personality should not be an essential attribute of this Will, contemplated as self-realized?" [7]

Coleridge's notion of personeity in the Absolute Will determines his philosophical theism and colors his conception of the Christian Trinity. It enables the reader to follow him through the "coils of Trinitarian speculation," a term John Muirhead coined in his pioneer attempt to present this thought to the modern mind. In this Trinitarian speculation, the principle of personeity in the Absolute Will (derived, so it seems, from the notion of personality in the individual conscience) allows Coleridge to reinterpret some traditional Christian material to his own purpose. His problem was to establish the otherness of the Absolute Will, and its personeity, while at the same time admitting the humanistic basis of such a deduction. He might have been swept into a Scylla of experiential monism in his effort to avoid the more obvious lure of an excessively dualistic Charybdis. The course he charted between the two is in effect his philosophical theism.

Examination of the niceties of traditional Trinitarian theology is not of vital importance in the development of personeity and personality in his own system. This is true despite the adequate interest Coleridge gave to these questions, as preserved for us in his marginal notes to the works of Sherlock, Waterland, and Oxlee.[8] When annotating the works of others, he tended almost invariably to think and write in their terms. Only once or twice, while sifting the conventional Trinitarian controversies, did he

7. Opus Max., 2 (B3), f. 243.

8. Coleridge dealt with William Sherlock's *Vindication of the Doctrine of the Trinity* (1609) in *Lit. Rem.*, pp. 381–404; with Daniel Waterland's *Vindication of Christ's Divinity* (1719) in *Lit. Rem.*, pp. 404–26; and with John Oxlee's *Christian Doctrines of the Trinity and Incarnation* (1815) in *Lit. Rem.*, pp. 456–64. The controversies in these works are of little interest to us, but they have been mentioned since from time to time a particularly inept expression would elicit from the enraged Coleridge a statement of his own views.

melt the hard, dead language of earlier thinking; in the identification of Trinity and Idea,[9] and in the substitution of Tetractys for Trinity,[1] this happens; but in general the Opus Maximum and the Notebooks together with the scattered fragments *Essay on Faith* and MS Trinity express an outlook in volitional philosophy almost as foreign to Coleridge the commentator as it was to his contemporaries.

The distinctive feature of Coleridge's Trinity is its nomenclature: Absolute Will (Personeity), conceived as the basis for the Trinity, is expressed in the four terms: Identity, Ipseity, Alterity, Community.[2] Identity, as the ground of Absolute Will, is truly the idea of God.[3] Ipseity,

9. For example, this note to Waterland's *Vindication* (*Lit. Rem.*, pp. 407–8): "that great truth, in which are contained all treasures of all possible knowledge, was still opaque even to Bull and Waterland:—because the Idea itself—that *Idea Idearum*, the one substrative truth which is the form, manner, and involvent of all truths,—was never present to either of them in its entirety, unity and transparency . . . The self-evidence of the great Truth, as a universal of the reason,—as the reason itself—as the light which revealed itself by its own essence as light—this they had not vouchsafed to them."

1. This is a more important statement (*Lit. Rem.*, p. 416): "It can not, however, be denied that in changing the formula of the Tetractys into the Trias, by merging the Prothesis in the Thesis, the Identity in the Ipseity, the Christian Fathers subjected their exposition to many inconveniences."

2. The most convenient single expression of the Trinity formula appears in a MS now in the Toronto Collection, written on the back of six name cards belonging to Dr. Gilman. This MS was printed with minor variations in *Lit. Rem.*, pp. 18–19, as a separate item of interest. Appearing thus alone, its full significance in Coleridge's religious position has never been realized.

3. Notebook 26, ff. 108–108^v: "But this idea [of God] again is impossible without producing and expanding or completing itself in the Idea of the Tetractys (A = 3 = 1) or Trinity. Again, the $\tau o\ \alpha\gamma\alpha\theta o\nu\ \kappa\alpha\iota\ \delta\ \pi\alpha\tau\acute{\eta}\rho$ must be contemplated distinctly and severally as Prothesis & Thesis in order to the contemplating of both in the unity of the Idea. And in like manner the Idea of the Father and the Son, as Thesis and Antithesis (Ipseity ⟩⟨ Alterity) and lastly both these and the Idea of the H. Ghost, which occupies the place of Synthesis . . . in order to the contemplation of the Trinity or triune God in the unity of the Ideas . . ."

Alterity, and Community correspond by convenience of analogy to the traditional notion of Father, Son and Holy Spirit (Power, Logos, Love). This particular item of Coleridgean metaphysics and speculative theology is, to say the least, unconventional, in that the emphasis upon identity or manifestation of God as Absolute or Pure Will leads necessarily to a theology of doing and becoming, to a God of action known by events rather than as a subject to be contemplated. It is the proper correlative for the fluid or organic universe Coleridge had always valued over the static hierarchical system sanctioned by traditional theology. Coleridge was willing to stake both the rational justification of theology and a possible organization of the physical universe upon this first and greatest idea—the Absolute Will as contemplated in the "Divine Idea" of the Trinity:

> The doctrine of the Trinity (the foundation of all rational theology, no less than the pre-condition and ground of the rational possibility of the Christian Faith, that is, the Incarnation and Redemption), rests securely on the position, that in man *omni actione praeit sua propria passio; Deus autem est actus purissimus sine ulla potentialitate.*[4]

The scholastic phrase, *actus purissimus sine ulla potentialitate,* as expanded by Coleridge, becomes for him the first true idea of God: "An Absolute Will, which therefore is essentially causative of reality and therefore *in origine* causative of its own reality, the essential causativeness however abiding undiminished and indiminishable, this is our first idea."[5]

Many times, and in various ways, Coleridge insisted that

4. *Lit. Rem.,* p. 397. Note to p. 127 of Sherlock's *Vindication.*
5. Opus Max., 2 (B3), f. 242.

the idea of God (based as we have seen upon a "rationale of the will" leading to Absolute Will) by its very nature implies the idea of the Trinity,

. . . so that the Idea of God involves that of a Triunity; and as that Unity or Individuality is the intensest, and the Archetype, yea, the very substance and element of all other Unity and Union, so is that Distinction the most manifest, and indestructible of all distinctions—and Being, Intellect and Action, which in their Absoluteness are the Father, the Word, and the Spirit will and must for ever be and remain the "genera generalissima" of all knowledge.[6]

The terms Being, Intellect and Action—more usually expressed Ipseity, Alterity, Community, or Πατήρ, Λόγος, Πνεῦμα—without diminishing in any way their necessity for true perception of the idea of God are the movements in the eternal Identity. Coleridge was eager to find an expression of Identity which would include *a simultaneo* Ipseity, Alterity, and Community without lapsing into hazy definitions of the three similar to Schelling's "regression to Identity." For unity he stressed Identity, for diversity the specific functions of Πατήρ, Λόγος, Πνεῦμα.

The clearest expression of the identity in the Triunal Unity occurs in a Notebook entry, similar in meaning to the longer definition of the MS Trinity fragment, but more felicitous in indicating how unity is the source of true functional diversity. The Absolute Will manifests itself as "Absolute Essence begotten in the Form, Absolute Form coexisting in the Essence, and the Unity of Both. Or the Subject-Object in absolute Identity neither Subject or Object, or both in combination, but the Prothesis, or Unground of both = τὸ ὑπέρ ὅσιον ὁ Πατήρ." [7] The Iden-

6. *New Letters*, 2, 1196, to Thomas Clarkson, Oct. 13, 1806.
7. Notebook 21½, f. 24.

tity persists in diversity since the subject becomes its own object:

> This eternal Self-position absolutely begets itself as its own Object, in which being all, it is Object-Subject—ὁ υἱός. And again asserting the identity of the Form with the Essence, or the Essence of the Form, the υἱός affirming itself as having its Subject or Essence = God, and the Father asserting the Form identical with his Essence there proceeds from both Father and Son, the Spirit of God, or Subject-Object. God *is* One, but exists or manifests himself to himself, at once in a three fold Act, total in each and one in all.[8]

Having satisfied himself with this explanation, repeated in the Opus Maximum, of unity and diversity in Tetractys, he settles to the task of describing the relationship and nature of Father (Ipseity), Son (Alterity), and Holy Spirit (Community).

Ipseity, or the Father, ultimately connected with the Absolute Will in its function as creative act, is defined generally in terms looking toward the creation of the world: ". . . the Eternal Act, which struggling with words, the ancient theologians have named Ipseity, Aseity, Identitas, ἔνθεος, mens absoluta . . ."[9] Specifically ὁ Πατήρ is the ground of holiness and the Good: "The eternally self-affirmant self-affirmed; the 'I Am in that I Am,' or the 'I shall be that I will be'; the Father; the relatively subjective, whose attribute is, the Holy One; whose definition is, the essential finific in the form of the infinite; *dat sibi fines.*"[1]

ὁ Πατήρ becomes the rational ground for ethics by creating the distinction between good and evil. The deduction

8. Ibid.
9. Opus Max., 2 (B3), ff. 252-53.
1. *Lit. Rem.*, p. 18.

of evil itself and hence Original Sin from the goodness of will in ὁ Πατήρ, results from the relationship obtaining between Absolute Will and the individual will. That this necessarily follows is a cornerstone of Coleridge's philosophical theism; the proof in detail belongs to a later area of the present study (below, p. 153).

Alterity is by far the most significant feature in the tri-unity of Absolute Will. The vital Christian positions on redemption and creation and the very possibility of a semidualism owe their rationality in this philosophical theism to Alterity. In defining it, Coleridge struggles to show both unity and duality: "the relation itself that of an infinite fulness poured into an infinite capacity, that of a Self wholly and adequately repeated, yet so that the very repetition contains the distinction from the primary act, a Self which in both is self-subsistent, but which yet is not the same because the one only is self originated." [2] The essential paradox of duality in unity he asserts strongly: "Every reality must have its own form. When therefore we contemplate the only begotten of the Father as the Alter in the union of the alter et idem, we affirm that this, namely, the alterity, is the *form* of its own reality and though one with yet not the same as the form of the Idem." [3]

Other assertions of this relationship in more conventional Trinitarian terminology maintain the same basis.[4] There is no point, of course, in estimating the value of these definitions apart from the whole doctrine of the Absolute Will. With that doctrine the Ipseity and Alterity, along with the Community, stand or fall. But the deduction of Ipseity and Alterity, and the deductions from them in the direction of Christian theology, are legitimate

2. Opus Max., 2 (B3), f. 251.
3. Opus Max., 2 (B3), f. 265.
4. Opus Max., 2 (B3), f. 254; Notebook 37, f. 31.

within the premise we are following. Alterity is especially fruitful for theology in that two central Christian positions —existence of created being and redemption by a mediator—rise from it. And here again he is employing some concepts from traditional Christian metaphysics to his own purposes.

Coleridge has been quoted as saying that only through the Trinity can pantheism or skepticism be avoided.[5] By studying the relationship between Ipseity and Alterity we find out what he means. For on the validity of the "distinctity" granted to the Logos or Alterity within the greater unity of Identity hinges the strength of a philosophical dualism of Creator and created, Absolute and individual will, God and created finite substance. In order to safeguard the uniqueness of both the Ipseity and Alterity in this Trinity, being is predicated of the first in a different sense than of the second:

> [Alterity contains] the *form* of its own reality and though one with yet not the same as the form of the *Idem.* Instead of the words Alter and Idem let us place A = B and B = A; and we then explain our further meaning by saying that B is in A in another sense than A is in B. B is affirmed in A; A is presumed in B: or A *Being,* B co-eternally *becomes.*[6]

How strikingly similar in phrasing is this idea to the doctrine of the *analogia entis* of Scholasticism! But the phrasing is unique, which shows again how Coleridge struggled

5. Another instance of his preoccupation with this conviction occurs in a commentary to Waterland (*Lit. Rem.,* p. 406): "Now I hold it demonstrable that a consistent Socinianism, following its own consequences, must come to Pantheism, and in ungodding the Saviour must deify cats and dogs, fleas and frogs. There is, there can be, no medium between the Catholic Faith of Trinal Unity, and Atheism disguised in the self-contradicting term, Pantheism; for every thing God, and no God, are identical positions."

6. Opus Max., 2 (B3), f. 265.

with his own problems in his own characteristic manner. He also drew the scholastic corollary that this basic distinction affects the world of created being, and is indeed the ground and basis of the unity in diversity which constitutes created substance:

> But as soon as the duplication [alterity—ipseity] is presented to the mind, and with it the form of alterity we have only to learn that in this other all others are included, that in this first substantial intelligible distinction (ὁ Λόγος) all other distinctions that can subsist in the indivisible unity, (Λόγοιθειοι) or contain it, are included.[7]

Ὁ Λόγος, or Alterity, is called upon to account for the rationality of the multiplicity of things within the framework of Christian dualism—avoiding philosophical pantheism, which hallows the One at the expense of the Many, and skeptical modernism, which celebrates the Many at the price of losing the One. When Coleridge said that the Logos was rationality itself, he meant that within the Christian framework belief in the Trinity is a priori, as well as through revelation, the only possible position. Even the redemption of mankind by Christ, which certainly finds a stronger basis in revelation than in a priori reasoning, has in this philosophical theism its primary justification, derives its true authority, from the necessary connection with this Λόγος, itself bound up with Absolute Will:

> Divinely and in the fulness of Inspiration did the Evangelist affirm—In the Beginning was the Word, and the Word, God of God, became the Mediator between God and Man, and the Redeemer of Man. But as Man finds his redemption from the captivity of his

7. Opus Max., 2 (B3), ff. 265ᵛ, 266ᵛ.

own Will in the Divine Humanity, so (we are assured
by the Apostle) does the whole inferior Creation,
which fell not willingly, seek, yea, yearn and groan
. . . for Redemption in the Human Animal. In Man
is the Solution of their dark Enigma for the Word,
the Son of God, has become the Son of Man, the living Sacrifice, and the perpetual Sin-offering.[8]

Evil and sin arise from the inevitable clash between man
as individual will and Πατήρ, the Absolute Will: its solution and conquest is possible because Λόγος, Alterity, is
both of the Father and of man, the everlasting middle
term uniting the One God with created substance.

Finally there is the Community, *Spiritus Sanctus,* in
which the organic unity and mutual love of all created
things rest. To explain this, Coleridge revised the "Æolian
Harp" imagery.[9] This comes as no surprise to anyone
understanding that his period of Christian thinking is
really another manifestation of a basic craving for love,
order, and harmony in the world. Community, or Holy
Spirit, replaced the "One Life" without in the least under-
cutting the poet-philosopher's basic interest. The exchange
was really a replacement of one formulation which no
longer united his emotional and intellectual needs by
another which did. So although Coleridge adopted the
idea of God as *Actus Purissimus sine ulla potentialitate,*
there was no possibility that he might also accept the
stratified, hierarchical conception of universe which often
went with it. *Actus Purissimus,* through the mediation of
Community or Spirit, was a constant process:

Lastly . . . we approach to the perfect Idea in the
Holy Spirit, that which proceedeth from the Father to
the Son, and that which is returned from the Son to

8. Notebook 25, f. 89.
9. Note to Sherlock, *Lit. Rem.,* 397.

the Father, and which in this circulation constitutes
the eternal unity in the eternal alterity and distinction, the life of Deity in actu purissimu. This is truly
the Breath of Life indeed, the perpetual action of the
act, the perpetual intellection alike of the Intellectus
and of the Intellegibile, and the perpetual being and
existing of that which saith "I Am." [1]

In more conventional language he acknowledges a sub-
stantial diversity in unity to the Spirit equal to that be-
tween Ipseity and Alterity: "Wisdom, i.e. the Holy Ghost
is ens simplissimum, not a Synthesis of the Father and the
Son but a substantial Act proceeding from the Father and
Son and the Community of the Father and the Son." [2]
Community is the expression of love between Ipseity and
Alterity:

> But in what did we find the divine necessity of the
> co-eternal filiation or the alterity? Even in the unwith-
> holding and communicative goodness of the Supreme
> Mind. Himself being all he communicated himself to
> another as to a self: but such communication is Love,
> and in what is the re-attribution of that Self to the
> Communicator but Love? This too is Love, filial Love,
> Love is the Spirit of God, and God is Love.[3]

Of course Coleridge made the analogous extension of this
community of love to the world of created being; just as
the multiplicity of things obtains its unity in the rationality of the Logos, the Spirit of Community provides
positive sanction for mutual love and cooperation among
its members. Through this Trinity, holding in identity
the Ipseity, Alterity, and Community, and by analogy the
universe of created substances, he recreated philosophically

1. Opus Max., 2 (B3), f. 260ᵛ.
2. Notebook 36, f. 51.
3. Opus Max., 2 (B3), f. 258ᵛ.

one of his greatest and earliest imaginative utterances: "The One Life, Within us and Abroad."

With the Trinity, the a priori deduction of the idea of God comes to a close, a philosophical basis for theism and the fundamental Christian position completed. Whether the rationale proves what it asserts, namely the dualistic basis of the religious experience in the higher reason, is as has been pointed out, debatable. More certain is the observation that this method combines certain idealistic with other traditional or scholastic assumptions in a tremendous effort to provide a viable modern Christianity. There remains now the task of relating in detail the specific Christian doctrines advanced by Coleridge in *Aids* and other works. They are few and relatively simple, since Coleridge was not interested in proving every position of Anglican orthodoxy; rather his sole purpose was to provide general positions acceptable to all Christians.

CHAPTER 5

THE CHRISTIAN FAITH

I. *The Aphorisms of Spiritual Religion*

If Coleridge had been a traditional theologian, a St. Thomas or a Calvin, he would have followed his speculations on the nature of God and the Trinity with orderly treatises on the Divinity of Christ, Original Sin, Justification by Faith, the Sacraments, and the Church, including its authority. Fortunately or otherwise, he was not. His observations on Justification by Faith appeared early, in *Aids to Reflection,* where he also touched upon the sacrament of baptism. *Confessions of an Inquiring Spirit* and *Church and State* contain most of what he had to say about the structure of the Church and the problem of authority. Other important areas of Christian theology remain in notebook form or in unpublished and unfinished treatises. Coleridge's method remained essentially that of an aphorist.

Yet we must not infer lack of method in the aphoristic way. Coleridge had his own method, and it is possible to fix the relationship between the *Aids to Reflection, Confessions,* other published writings, and the "rationale of the will" which appears in the unpublished writings. Seven "Positions" appearing in Notebook 26 give us insight into his scheme for unifying the Christian faith.

Aids to Reflection in isolation was a tangential document at best, with Coleridge's characteristic enthusiasm rushing ahead of more ordinary logical presentation. He knew this, and presented his case to John Taylor Coleridge in 1825, in a letter viewed by scholars as another Coleridgean boast:

> In the Aids to Reflection I have touched on the mystery of the Trinity only in a *negative* Way—That is I have shewn the hollowness of the arguments by which it has been assailed—have demonstrated that the doctrine involves nothing contrary to reason and the nothingness and even the absurdity of a Christianity without it. In short, I have contented myself with exposing the causes of its belief. But the positive establishment of the Doctrine as involved in the Idea of God—together with . . . the origin of Evil, as distinguished from original Sin . . . and the Creation of the visible world . . . I have reserved for my large work: of which I have finished the first division, namely the Philosophy of the Christian Creed, or Christianity true in *Idea*.[1]

That this was not mere daydreaming is now clear, as we have followed "the positive establishment of the Doctrine as involved in the Idea of God" in the preceding chapter. What of the "origin of Evil, as distinguished from original Sin," and other areas of primary doctrinal concern? With remarkably few exceptions Coleridge struggled with these theological problems in the Notebooks and in the Opus Maximum, unpublished manuscripts of the years following *Aids to Reflection*.

There would doubtless be some advantage in a more orderly presentation of this area of Coleridge's thought than he himself left—a schematic organization similar to

1. *Unpub. Let.*, 2, 345, to John Taylor Coleridge, May 1825.

that given in Muirhead's *Coleridge as Philosopher*. But such organization would have the disadvantage of getting away from Coleridge's mind and essentially aphoristic methods. On the other hand, the seven positions in Notebook 26 continue Coleridge's religious thinking in his own terms, and give us some vital links needed to understand the control and organization of all his religious writings. Studied in connection with other religious fragments throughout the Notebooks, these positions reveal the superstructure of Coleridge's proposed Opus Maximum on the Christian religion.[2]

They open with a preamble which assumes as proved the a priori aspects of God's existence as Absolute Will; this preamble is a summary of the first Idea of our previous chapter:

> The attempt to solve the problem of Existence, Order, and Harmony otherwise than by an Eternal Mind—or to explain the Universe of finite and dependent Beings without assuming Will and Intelligence as its ground, and antecedent principle, is too revolting to common sense, too discrepant from our habits of thinking, feeling, and acting, offers too gross an outrage on the very instincts of humanity, and to all the principles which from the very constitution of the human mind we take for granted as the ground-work of all other Beliefs, to require any confutation . . . Taking for granted then, that the world owes its Existence to an adequately powerful Will and Reason, which being antecedent to all other Being, must itself

2. See Appendix I. Notebook 26 is the most important single source of unpublished material relating to *Aids to Reflection* and the religious phase of Coleridge's career. Many of the entries, dated in 1825 and 1826, are clearly intended as extensions of the ideas in *Aids*. The positions include ff. 28-53.

be eternal, and which we name God, we pass to our first Position.[3]

Position one, on creation, follows logically from what Coleridge said in the Opus Maximum about the nature of the Trinity. In the second proposition the existence of man, as a creature endowed with moral qualities, is related to the scheme of the Absolute Will and individual will presented in the "rationale." This relationship also includes an explanation of evil and sin as the breakdown of harmony between the Absolute and individual will. Relatively minor are positions three, four, and part of five, on the existence of external law and the importance of miracles for the scheme of redemption. The latter part of five, in conjunction with some of four, treats of the reason, will, and conscience again in a manner very similar to the "rationale" itself; the new and interesting aspect now is a definite connection established between this rationale and the Christian view of the soul, especially its responsibility and rationality. And the familiar pattern reaches its climax in the sixth position, where the personality of the Creator, previously established and now succinctly reasserted, leads to two vital conclusions, the efficacy of prayer and establishment of organized religion. In the last position the a priori phase is concluded on the assertion that subjective religious experience and objective revelation are aspects of the same truth, which subjectively appears as the feeling of need for redemption and objectively as the historical Christ of the Gospels.

In this way the final position reinforces Coleridge's stance on justifying faith and the other doctrines treated in *Aids,* and leads naturally to a discussion of all the important Christian articles. Now, in the light of the more mature Notebook speculations, we are better able to follow

3. Notebook 26, f. 27ᵛ.

the Coleridge of the earlier works. The connections between Christian doctrine and revealed religion on the one hand and the "rationale of will" and emotional ideas on the other are richer and more evident from a stance in the seven positions or middle terms than they could ever be by merely following the hit-or-miss scheme of "spiritual aphorisms" in *Aids*. Many of the charges leveled against Coleridge on the scores of inconsistency and dilettantism fade away in the light of the striking coherence of his views in their later development. It is essentially this religion of ideas and its relationship to Christian doctrine, as it was fathered by Coleridge between *Aids* and his death in 1834, that ought to be examined in more detail.

The first position, on creation, is as it stands clear enough not to require extensive commentary. Briefly, creation occurred in time, according to the revelation of the Scriptures, although a strict explanation of this paradox is manifestly impossible. There is also an attempt to make a basic distinction between God, the world, and creatures, a path for philosophy between the pantheistic and naturalistic systems of atheism. We are asked to accept some of these ideas on the basis of the reason-understanding distinction. The most difficult portion is the attempt to make Alterity the ground of creation, but this is left obscure in the passage and can be made clear only by use of other sources. The entire position, for use as a reference in dealing with the other comments which complete its meaning, appears below in Appendix I.

One Notebook passage belongs by right of logical order before the position on creation. In it we are told how the idea of Ipseity (here called Jehova) in the Trinity prepares the ground for the creation of the world: "But with this Idea of the Jehova = Word a more distinct Light arises on the origination of Minds, Spirits. Contemplated numerically, and therefore as finite, the predicate of *necessary*

Being ceases, when any one singly is spoken of, or the conception of contingency takes place, and the Idea of generation descends into that of *Creation*." [4] Coleridge continues this argument in a way that connects it with his notion of Alterity, namely that the idea of generation from Ipseity to Alterity becomes the ground and transcendent analogue for the phenomenon of creation, regarding both creatures and the universe of things. With this passage understood as a bridge between the ontological and cosmological aspects of creation, the points in the position itself are easy to understand. The words for the "capable few," "Only a positively essential unity, an I Am, can be the adequate Idea or Alterity (Deus Alter et Idem) of the Absolute Will" refer to this Trinitarian doctrine, and comprise an idea of the reason standing in contrast to the conceptions of the a posteriori argumentation and observation. Much of the position is devoted to his usual mode of arguing by means of the negative, i.e. that the world is *not* eternal, infinite multiplicity of being *cannot* be *causa sui,* cannot have sufficient reason for existence in itself. His interest, as always, is to remove obstacles in the way of "a deduction of the truth of the Christian Religion, the credibility of the Bible Creed." Whatever one may think of the logic or demonstrability of Coleridge's article on creation, there is certainly no better example of his method as a religious thinker than that which we see here. All the tendencies we have attempted to define have now come together.

In still another Notebook entry, a commentary on Genesis, a summary of position one presents in compressed form the argument just described, and in a manner which emphasizes even more strongly the method of negative proof:

4. Notebook 37, ff. 31–31ᵛ.

God the absolute beginner of all things—not of their form, and relations alone, but of their very *Being*. The Substance is not more unbeginning than the arrangement on which its existence depends. This . . . precludes the systems of Cosmotheism, Pantheism, and aprimal Elements—in short, every possible form of the eternity (i.e. unbeginningness) of the world or any part of the world. Whether there was a *first* Beginning, any thing of those that began to be, that had no thing before it, is another question, if indeed it be a possible question—i.e. if the terms do not imply a contradiction—In what time was there no time. That the matter of the Universe had no beginning is Atheism—that Beginning had no beginning may be nonsense, at least, like every form of an infinite series, utterly transcendent, but it does not alter the essential character of the dependent. Still all that has been, is, or will be, had, have, and will have, a Beginning save God alone. Yet a Beginning of the Beginning is the safer and more human doctrine.[5]

The ultimate purpose of the article on creation, whether in full or condensed form, is primarily moral; it is to ensure the distinction between the Creator and created and prepare the way for the Christian scheme of relations between God and mankind. It resembles, as was earlier noted, the scholastic "Analogy of Being." Alterity in the Trinity provides the ontological grounds for "distinctity" of beings, and creation is merely the transmission of this distinction into the cosmological order. The moral flavor and purpose of this distinction regarding creation appears in a passage from Notebook 36 which may also be considered as the culmination of Coleridge's preparation for the unique relationship between God and man:

5. Notebook 27, ff. 11ᵛ–12.

Life begins in detachment from Nature and ends in union with God. The adorable Author of our Being is likewise its ultimate End. But even this last triumphal Crown, the summit and *ne plus ultra* of our immortality, even the union with God is no mystic annihilation of individuality, no fanciful breaking of the Bottle and blending the contained water with the ocean in which it had been floating, the dreams of oriental Indolence! but on the contrary an *intension,* a perfecting of our Personality—the Attribute of Unity taken singly would lead to a Spinozistic Deity —As the Unity is Absolute, so is the distinctness— the Distinctity infinite—The force of the term, Logos, is the Distinctive Power.[6]

With the ground for the moral being of man thus established, Coleridge was free to consider in the second position the relationship between God and man created, a relationship viewed in his system under the aspects of Absolute Will and individual will.

As this relationship between the two wills presupposes a certain amount of the dialectic of will, particularly the synthesis of reason and will in conscience, it is not surprising that the first section of the second position covers much the same ground as the Opus Maximum outlined in the preceding chapter. (This familiar material appears in Appendix I, below.) What is of primary concern now is the turn the proposition takes roughly half way through, when the focus shifts from Will in the abstract and falls upon man's free will. In this way the problem of evil is introduced with the evident intention of clearing away obstacles confronting the specifically Christian doctrines of Original and actual sin:

6. Notebook 36, f. 65.

So if Reason acted *immediately* on the Life or Nature of a Creature, as one with the life or behavior it would cease to be a Law, and become a grace, a Beatitude, a perfection or Holiness. Reason contemplated severally and distinctly is a Law that supposes a Will as its subject. It cannot therefore be coercive for it requires obedience, and obedience can be required only where disobedience is *possible*. I would not say, a free will, were it only from the ambiguity and the frequent deceptive use of the word, freedom. Generally, Freedom is employed as a mere synonime of Will. To say: "it is an act of his own will" is the same as to declare it a free act or an act of freedom. But there is another less common but far more correct sense of the word, according to which Freedom expresses that highest perfection of a finite will, which it attains by its perfect self-determined subordination to Reason, "whose service is perfect Freedom." A will therefore may cease to be free and yet remain responsible: because its unfreedom has originated in its own act. A will cannot be *free* to choose evil—for in the very act it forfeits its freedom, and so far becomes a corrupt Nature self-enslaved. It is sufficient to say, that a will *can* choose evil, but in the moment of such choice ceases to be a *free* will . . . In short, Will is a primary most simple Idea, which we can only know by *being* it: and every attempt to understand it by addition of epithets is idle or worse than idle. . . . But to return: our second position then is, that [II] a creature endowed with Reason and Self-consciousness must be a responsible Agent, whose Will is amenable to a Law, and distinct from the Law. And this condition is given, where the Will is finite and individual, the Law Absolute and Universal.[7]

7. Notebook 26, ff. 32–33.

Since the primary purpose of the position is to establish man's moral duties, it rests content in asserting the
free will without delving deeply into the nature of evil
as the product of a contradiction existing between Absolute and individual will. A will is free if it avoids contradiction with the Absolute Will, "Freedom expresses that
highest perfection of a finite Will which it attains by its
perfect self-determined subordination to Reason whose
source is perfect freedom." Obviously the description is
incomplete; it invites discussion of the terms "perfect self-
determined subordination," and its opposite, "the self-
contradiction" existing in the individual will in most of
its acts. Fortunately, Coleridge provides this discussion
in another section of Notebook 26.

To remain consistent with his position on creation,
Coleridge had to account for the will in creatures having
some autonomy apart from the Absolute Will; on the
other hand any theory of individual will as a separate principle or explanation of evil apart from the doctrine of the
Trinity, would reduce his idea to some form of Manichae-
anism or materialistic atheism. By a bold synthesis of both
problems Coleridge tried to account for multiplicity as a
by-product of evil, and of evil itself as a confusion of
actual with potential being in the individual will. It was
the original destiny of individual wills, thought Coleridge,
never to become actualized:

> Each distinct Idea in the Absolute Idea is a Form of
> the Absolute Will; but there is a Will in the Form,
> grounding the reality as *that* Form, and an actual
> Will to remain a form of the *Absolute* will implies
> the possibility of willing it to be the form of its own
> Will. Otherwise it were either Absolute or not
> *Will*—the identity of All, not, as it is, a Distinctity
> in the Omniform Form Absolute of the Absolute

Identity. For the Godhead alone in the three-fold
Absolute, the Ipseity, the Alterity, and the Community, the Will, the Word, and the Spirit, are in
themselves *Actus Purissimi sine ulla potentialitate*
. . . But the *Will* to be one is the refusing to be divided. And this potential Will is eternal so indestructible, everlasting . . .[8]

The similarity in the relationship of individual will-
Absolute Will to the previously established created-Creator
juxtaposition in the realm of being is obvious; both rest
upon the original distinction between Ipseity and Alterity.
But in the order of Being the relationship is static and best
looked upon as an analogy. In the order of will it becomes
dynamic as soon as the individual will chooses not to remain in its ideal state of perfection:

The primary powers are the potential Individualities,
Individuality being the indestructible consequent of
the Absolute Will essentially causative of Reality. This
princ. Indiv. that must have been as an eternal possibility, but latent in the Idea and *willing* itself one
with its Divine Form, and offering the . . . Sacrifice
of its Idiocentricity to the universal Center, ought
never to have become actualized. The apostate act,
accursed, did take place—and the instant Birth was
the *Lie* Essential, the dark mystery of Self-contradiction.[9]

And the result of this actualization was Evil:

For pure Evil what is it but Will that would manifest
itself as Will, not in Being [Ἐτερότης] not in Intelligence (therefore formless)—not in union or Communion, the contrary therefore of Life, even eternal

8. Notebook 26, ff. 125ᵛ–126.
9. Notebook 26, f. 121.

Death. . . . It is the creaturely will which instead of
quenching itself in the Light and the Form, to be the
Warmth (of Life) and the Procession (Love); and so
resolve itself into the Will of the One, it would
quench the Light of the Form, and shrink inward, if
so it might itself remain the One, by recoiling from
the One—and find a center by centrifuge—and thus
in the Self-love, it becomes Hate and the lust full of
Hate—and in the striving to be one (instead of striving after and toward the One) it becomes the infinite
Many.[1]

Thus evil is explained as the cause of the Many without
resorting to a Manichaean explanation for the cause of
evil. It goes without saying that this speculation leaves
many facets of the problem unresolved, some of which are
extremely important for the entire "spiritual religion."
To discuss these problems we must look at Coleridge's
longest and most precise statement about the nature of
evil, from Notebook 26, which is, in essence, an elabora-
tion of his position on potency and act.

Even so is it with Evil, *materially* considered—with
the matter or substance of Evil. Regard it, as a *Potence,* or as having only potential Being, and it is the
necessary and good Involution of the Will and therein
of the Personality if all are finite Intelligences. It is
an essential perfection of their will, which without
it would cease to be a Will, as long as the *actual* Will,
or the Act of the Will, is to deny itself, to sacrifice itself, as a finite Will—and to use its' *Base* as the condition of its' own positive or + reality, which can
only be in correlation to an opposite — reality. But
what exists potentially, may become actual. This is
an interpretation of the term potential, and not an in-

1. Notebook 31, f. 33.

ference, or any thing predicated of it. Suppose this
to have taken place, and that the Will has given actual
existence or $+$ reality to the — real or the Potential
in itself. Here two cases are conceivable—both ideally
possible. Either, namely, the Evil Will avails itself of
its' actuality to will itself *absolutely* and totally,—(a
contradiction indeed; but what else can be expected
to proceed from that which is itself a contradiction to
Him who is *all* Truth, who is the Truth itself, the
source and substance of all possible truth?)—to will
no potential in itself, but to be as God, the Universal
Will, who is *Actus sine ulla potentialitate* and like
him to be self-based, having the ground of its existence in its existence. . . . What must the result be?
The evil will has no power to exclude the good: for
in itself it has no power at all, except against itself, for
its' inherent self-frustration—much less can it exert
any power over the good—It simply therefore falls
from the good, as a Precipitate. And here we have
the abysmal mystery of the Devil, the Evil One, the
Contrary of God, absolute emptiness as God is the
absolute Fullness, a mere Potence as God is a pure
Act, wherein all is that actually is—a hidden Fire,
for ever seeking a base on which it may actualize and
finding it only to convert it into its' own essence,
which is necessarily baseless: (for how can that *have*
a Base which then alone truly *is* when it is itself a
Base?)—and still, in the expressive language of Holy
Writ, roaming about, like an hungry lion, seeking
whom it may devour. For it is indeed an eternal
hunger, and the very *sting* of Famine. Eternal because
below all time even as God is eternal by transcendency
to all time—and unintelligible, because an outcast
from intelligence even as God [is] incomprehensible
as containing all intelligence. And lastly, Eternal

Death as God is eternal Life. Repent it cannot—for
the power of Repentance is potential good: and the
Evil Spirit is itself potential, and has its potentiality
in itself—and like the increase of Darkness . . .
can only be manifested by the remaining Light. Well
does the Apostle name it the Mystery of Iniquity—
the Enemy, whom Christ came not to reconcile but
to put under his feet. . . . Let us now turn to the
other possible case—that namely, in which the good
is made potential, and the Evil actual. *Tomorrow*
I will do well—only today—it is hard never to in-
dulge one-self—In all other things I will obey the
commands; but this Fruit is fair to behold, the Ser-
pent has eat it, and has become my Equal . . . But
alas! how came it to be a temptation? That it was a
temptation argues a shifting of the Poles, an Indif-
ferencing or Neutralizing of the One by the Other, to
have already taken place. Or rather, the Potential
must have no longer been the *base,* the latent *ground,*
of the Actual, the hidden center to the manifest cir-
cumference of the microcosm, but the Will has shrunk
into a radius, having the center as one of its Poles—
into a bi-polar line, the potential evil being the negative pole, and the Actual good the Positive Pole,
while the *Self* is the point of indifference between
each. In this sense we may understand and in this
alone we can justify Luther's assertion, that the *free*
will of man supposes a previous illapse and a present
co-immanence of the Evil Spirit, and that he who has
(i.e. consciously or actually) a choice, has already
chosen. But observe—this is said of Man's will, of a
Self-will, and not of the Will *in* man which prays, not
my Will but thine—let it *be* only as it knows itself
as a perpetual gift in order to a continual sacrifice—
and in this consists the [περιχωγησις?] of the Divine

Spirit in Man regenerate, and in the Spirit made perfect. Now this fault in the Will, its falling asunder, constitutes the *corruption* and here is the Mystery, and hence the correspondent Mystery of the Remedy —of which, however our Reason can comprehend this much: first, that the Fall is different from that of the Devil, and presupposes it certainly as the ground of the temptation: perhaps as a *condition,* tho' neither ground nor cause, of the temptability. Hence, fallen man may be redeemable (for tho' the actual good has disappeared, it has not been excluded, or truly fallen off from, but only sunk and if I may say so degraded into the Potential Man.) I repeat, may be the subject of Redemption, tho' the Devil was not: and he may be an object of divine compassion, and the Idea of man still contained in the Logos, or Substantial Idea of God, in this respect an object of Divine Love—tho' in this respect only— for "in him (the filial word) alone God loved the world.—" But secondly, we may see—that man tho' not absolutely unredeemable, could yet be redeemed by that power only, which could act at once *in* the Will and *on* the Will. But this is possible only for a Power *Divine*—But this is not all—Nay, compared with that which is still wanting, it is easy to be understood . . .[2]

The first section of this crucial passage clarifies the earlier suggestion that the individual will in harmony with the Absolute Will was in positive potency, while the negative potency or possibility of evil lay in its ability to act for itself. The act or evil is then distinguished as entirely realized in the Apostasy of Satan and partially in the sin of mankind. Since the meanings of the terms "po-

2. Notebook 26, ff. 14–17.

tency" and "act" shift considerably in the course of his discussion, it would be well to consider them first.

The individual will remained in harmony with the Absolute Will while it lay in negative potency toward willing itself individual, and, insofar as it had any act, this act was merely the positive potency of willing itself always in the Absolute Will. But the will realized the negative potency, willed itself individual, and fell into apostasy and Original Sin. As symbolized by the Devil (an individuality with the possibility of existing outside of the Deity), this self-contradiction or evil is absolute or total, and a complete falling away from being or the good in which there is no possible potency toward reality remaining. This, Coleridge intimates, and not Original Sin is the mystery for which no logical solution can be found that is entirely satisfactory. But the fall of man, or the creaturely will in self-contradiction can be understood, as Coleridge explains in the third paragraph, as evil insofar as it was an act and as good insofar as it remains in potency for redemption. Thus the "fortunate fall." Man's individual will, evil by means of particular bad actions, is in potency as regards good actions, and thus potentially able to be restored to its former harmony with the Absolute Will. But since this cannot, obviously, be done by the will itself—since in self-contradiction it can only will the selfish ends created by its perverse division from the Absolute—it argues the necessity of an outside help, a mediator. And at this point the "idea" of Alterity in the Trinity as the mediator between Ipseity and Community ushers in the Christian scheme of redemption.

Coleridge's scheme can be criticized on philosophical grounds, especially for reversing in his plus and minus potency scheme the usual meanings of "act" and "potency." What he is saying in bald terms is that the function (or action) of the individual will in harmony with the

Absolute Will is not to act. Professor Muirhead, who had access to this argument as it appeared in another unpublished work, stated a set of objections in his book *Coleridge as Philosopher*.[3] His purpose was not refutation, for he admits that Coleridge's brilliant juxtaposition of terms is irrefutable within his own premises. The grand assumptions behind the arguments are what he questions from his own standpoint in modern objective idealism. But since this question turns upon the basic notions of conscience and idea, there seems to be no necessity for repeating Muirhead's specific observations, which are readily available.[4] For our study of the "spiritual religion" this little treatise on evil has its own questions and interests, most important of which is that it leads directly to the consideration of Original Sin and redemption, in other words it is in the strict sense the link between the a priori philosophy of the Opus Maximum and the a posteriori theology of *Aids to Reflection*.

Original Sin, as the essential mystery, is the apostasy, for as Coleridge observed, the fall of man was secondary and explainable in terms of it: "But alas! how came it to be a temptation? . . . he who has (i.e. consciously or actually) a choice, has already chosen." Man's will is free in the commonly accepted meaning of freedom only because man, though fallen, remains potentially redeemable. If this were not the case, if the fall of man could be equated with evil as a principle, there would be no possibility for redemption. By calling Original Sin the "sin having its origin" in the will, Coleridge succeeds in shunt-

3. Professor Muirhead's *Coleridge as Philosopher*, was the first book to make use of the vast amount of unpublished material. He included the MS Logic, three Vellum MS volumes of the Opus Maximum, and, a source unavailable for this study, the Huntington Library MS on "Divine Ideas," which is another part of the Opus Maximum. The Notebooks were not drawn upon as sources of new material in *Coleridge as Philosopher*.

4. *Coleridge as Philosopher*, pp. 236–44.

ing away from his Christian theology the major problems
inherent in any explanation of evil. These are discussed
as the apostasy, or the existence of an infinitely multiplied
nature, or universe. Some implications of this theory are
important for Coleridge's later poetry. It is extremely
important to note that his emphasis on fallen Nature is
radically Calvinistic and tends to spread the taint of evil
far beyond its conventional bounds in the tradition of the
Western Church, Anglican, Roman or Greek.

The discussion of Original Sin in *Aids to Reflection*
can be equated roughly (but only roughly) with the Notebook explanation now before us. The same point is under
discussion in each case, but there is great difference in the
method. The doctrines aired in the early work are pre-
eminently practical; they are the facts of the Christian
revelation which require phenomenological explanation.
In the Opus Maximum the implications in each doctrine
are handled in an ontological context requiring strict and
logical deduction. In *Aids* Coleridge felt free, after clearing away the usual Arminian and Roman Catholic bram-
bles which had grown up around the Church article, to
define Original Sin merely by explaining the sense in
which all men, on the basis of their own experiences,
would be willing to accept its existence. Kant's influence
upon this method is obvious enough. Instead of the daring theoretical explanation which remolded the terms
"act" and "potency" in the Notebooks, *Aids* affords the
following perfectly sound but cautious conclusion:

> A moral evil is an evil that has its origin in a will.
> An evil common to all must have ground common to
> all. But the actual existence of moral evil we are
> bound in conscience to admit; and that there is an
> evil common to all is a fact; and this evil must there-
> fore have a common ground. Now this evil ground

can not originate in the Divine Will: it must therefore be referred to the will of man. And this evil
ground we call original sin. It is a mystery.[5]

Contrast this explanation with those in the Notebooks
and you sense immediately what Coleridge meant in calling *Aids* a transitional stage in his thinking. Only by making the connections between the early and later writings,
can we begin to see the whole picture, the "seamless gar-
ment" of his philosophy. The discussion of evil in the
Notebooks complements the aphorisms in *Aids*. Either
document without the other remains puzzling.

In *Aids*, at the conclusion of the long aphorism on
Original Sin Coleridge embarks immediately upon the
difficult waters of redemption, Justification by Faith, and
baptism, at all times guiding his course by the same star
of subjective fact and fidelity to the feelings and thoughts
of the phenomenal man. As an example of this method
we may refer back to the discussion of justifying faith in
Chapter 2, where the question of the validity of such a
singular procedure was also raised. I think the answer to
that question might now be given merely by saying that
we are not greatly inclined to follow Coleridge's piecemeal
reasoning in *Aids* without first returning to the five other
a priori propositions in the Notebooks. In *Aids* he presented redemption by reference to the overwhelming sense
of sin in mankind, the need to be saved, and the feeling
of rejoicing which always follows union with the Re-
deemer. His reasoning was sound enough, but becomes
much clearer and more rational if the explanation of evil
in the Notebooks is affixed. Taken in isolation, the theoretical business on act and potency might appear as mere
verbiage, and the emoting in *Aids* an escape into the irrational. But as we now see it, the Notebook materials,

5. *Aids,* pp. 287–88.

especially the seven positions and their corollaries, are
the theoretical complement to the practical doctrines in
the *Aids,* and treat the same material from a logically
prior viewpoint.

Positions three, four, and a good deal of five emphasize
again the moral nature of man, now with special reference
to the external law as the objectification of the law of
reason given by the conscience. Some familiar Coleridgean
ideas appear again, calling attention to the precedence of
conscience over consciousness and the light of reason in
the will over the same in the understanding. The external
law referred to is obviously the Ten Commandments.

The concluding portion of position five presents some
oblique observations on the nature of the soul. In conjunction with more specific statements in other Notebooks,
these provide some needed clarification of the relationship between the individual I AM and the universal IT IS
in Coleridge's philosophy. He was faced with two major
problems: to explain why the individual soul has existence apart from the Absolute, and how this existence is
preserved after death. The first question is put this way:

> The minds or Ideas subsisting distinctly in but as
> individually one with the Supreme Mind . . . are
> *so contemplated* the Divine Offspring—But the
> γένεσις of *Life,* and the Becoming of *Lives* must
> likewise be evolved, and the question determined,
> whether Life *per se* can be plurally contemplated or
> whether it must derive its plurality *ab alio*—: before
> we can hope to render the genesis of Souls intelligible,
> or attain any insight into the propriety or essential
> character of a Soul *in genere.*[6]

His early positions on generation in the Trinity, the nature of created substance, and the power of the potential

6. Notebook 37, ff. 33–33ᵛ.

will to actualize into individuality presented a basis for solution of the problem. Created substance (Soul) might be viewed as eternal in the Supreme Mind, and yet individual, in view of the analogy of being. A more exacting problem was the second, the attempt to characterize the quality of the soul in such a way as to include the immortality inferred from the Scriptures. The argument, extended and well developed (see below, Appendix II), has several familiar points. On the theoretical side, with the help of the form-shape distinction, Coleridge develops a form of the ontological argument, from necessity of thought to that of being. Very interesting in the general discussion is his open admission of circularity in his "System," dwelt upon to a surprising extent in the A and B formulas. The key passage, which develops the ontological argument, runs as follows:

> If we assume . . . a graduated scale of ascent from the minimum of consciousness . . . up to the highest imaginable perfection of consciousness that can exist in a *Creature,* there must be some first instance, in which the consciousness survives the metempsychosis of the Creature—even as there must be a first, in *which* the Consciousness becomes *individual* (i.e. proper self-consciousness). Now as this latter takes place *first* in Man, there is every reason to suppose and none to deny, Man will be the first instance of the former likewise.[7]

This argument may seem wishfully sanguine to some readers, and it is certainly not a proof in terms of facts. It suggests Coleridge's overwhelming belief in the power of the mind and of thought, a power which transforms an idea which may be believed as a logical possibility into a doctrine (immortality) of ontological necessity.

7. Notebook 26, ff. 45–45ᵛ.

A practical argument follows this theoretical one, buttressed as usual by Coleridge's definitions of conscience, the will, and the moral nature of man. The fact that man in his fallen state, cognizant of sin and the law, has a potential capacity for reunion with the Absolute Will, holds forth the possibility of an earned immortality, varying in richness with the acuteness of conscience and moral struggle in the individual soul. The idea is not dissimilar in some respects to Keats's vale of soulmaking and to certain modern theories. The following excerpt stresses the crucial relation between the conscience and earned immortality:

> This, however, we know, that both the extent and
> the distinctness of our Consciousness grows with the
> growth of the general intellect, but it is not as com
> monly considered, tho' it is equally true and a truth
> of yet higher interest, how close a connection there
> subsists between the consciousness and the conscience,
> how greatly both the quantity and the quality of our
> consciousness is affected by our moral character and
> the state of the Will. But especially the *Quality*. The
> more advanced in the Life spiritual, the more per
> fectly the will of the Individual is, self subjected to
> the Divine Light and Word (ὅ λογός ὅ φοσφόρος, ἤ το
> φῶς τὸ λογικόν) as the representative and exponent of
> the Absolute Will; the more habitually the under
> standing is submitted to the Light of Reason shining
> therein, and this light of Reason in the Understand
> ing is itself subordinated to the Reason in the Con
> science, the more does our individual consciousness
> partake of the steadfastness and identity of the per
> sonal Subsistence, which is the copula and Unity of
> all the acts and shapes of the mind, the less loose and
> detachable is the consciousness of the events and ob-

jects that make up the man's experience (τόν ἑαυταβίον) from the Self-consciousness, which is the essential and inalienable Form of his Personal Identity.[8]

The acute skill in these passages of theoretical and practical proof for the existence and immortality of the soul gives us only a partial view of Coleridge's interests in these questions. Coleridge the man bursts the rational fetters of Coleridge the theologian in several illuminating passages of intense personal feeling in the Notebooks. In all fairness these passages should be presented, if only to show again how the intellectual and emotional aspects of the dialectic merge at the highest levels in his religious thinking. The first is an ordinary outburst:

> To me therefore, and I believe to all men, the best proof of immortality is the fact, that the preassumption of it is at the bottom of every hope, fear, and action! for a moment an instinctive certainty that we should cease to be at a given time—the *whole* feeling of futurity would be extinguished at the first feeling of such a certainty—and the mind would have no motive for not dying at the same moment.[9]

The second is almost amazing in its revelation:

> Immortality! What is [it] but the impossibility of believing the contrary? The inevitable Rebounce of the I Am, itself the fearful Rebound of Life. The moment that the Soul affirms, I Am, it asserts, I cannot cease to be. For the I Am owns no antecedent, *it* is an act of Absolute Spontaneity and of absolute necessity. No cause existing why it *is* no cause can be imagined why it should cease to be. It is an impossible thought as long as the I Am is affirmed.[1]

8. Notebook 26, ff. 47ᵛ–48.
9. Notebook 25, f. 27ᵛ.
1. Notebook 39, f. 37ᵛ.

Here the emotion and the intellectual system generated by it are intertwined beyond the point where any cause and effect sequence can be distinguished. The impersonal I Am of religious philosophy is one with the I Am of personal emotion. The I Am of the ontological argument for the objective existence of God stands nakedly revealed as an individual "I," straining to assert its own immortality. Coleridge's method of playing the objective against the subjective and vice versa appears here in its fullest implication within the flash of a few lines. He more often shielded the emotional from the rationalistic devices by some of the means we have come to expect. For instance, in the next position, the Personality of God leads to the corollary on the efficacy of prayer in the ostensible logical order; but one might rejoin with equal justification that the emotional need for prayer demands the existence of a personal God.

> Position VI.   As the education of the Human Race began in Religion, so Religion began in the acknowledgement of a personal God as Creator. In an Eternal self-comprehending *One* there is the ineffable Will that created the World as well as the Adorable Might and Intelligence that gave it form and order. The Personality of the Creator, and the Creative Act of the Divine Person were the two fundamental Articles of the primeval Faith. By the first, God was the object of a Religion of Hope, Fear, Love, Communion, Thanksgiving, Prayer; by the latter involving the Unity and Absolute transcendency of the divine essence he was manifested as the object of a rational, spiritual, i.e. supersensual Religion. By virtue of the first, the conversion of the Soul to the Ground and Cause of the Universe became Religion, in contra-

distinction from Science, and Theory; by virtue of the Second, it was a Religion, as opposed to Superstition and Idolatry. "God is a spirit, and in Spirit and Truth to be worshipped." [2]

Coleridge is quite right in asserting, not proving, the existence of a personal God as creator. Hope, fear, love, communion, thanksgiving, and prayer are subjective states and needs, and we are quite free to believe, assuming again for a moment the psychological view of Coleridge's religious writings, that the necessity for a self-sufficient protective Other created in him this demand for a personal God. But to follow this line of thought would be to abandon attention to the structure of Coleridge's religious thinking.

In these terms we note that the abstract "idea of God, the Ipseity or Πατήρ" of Coleridge's deductions, has become "the object of a rational, spiritual, i.e. supersensual religion." For mankind fallen, the abstract idea of deity is not enough; there must be personal communion between the creature and its creator. In prayer alone man is able to intuit the warmth, reality, and fatherhood of this creator:

> Mere knowledge of the right we find by experience, does not suffice to ensure the performance of the Right—for mankind in general. How indeed should it, if mankind need instruction? that is, if they are sick and weak in their moral being . . . My old age is to my youth an other self *othered* by time. How then shall we act upon imperfect and enslaved man? By all together but chiefly, by setting them in action. Now what is the medium between mere conviction and resolve, and suitable action? For such a medium is absolutely necessary, since there is no *saltus* in na-

2. Notebook 26, ff. 42–42ᵛ.

ture. The medium is found in prayer, in religious intercommunion between man and his Maker. Hence the necessity of Prayer.[3]

Prayer is a function of fallen man's individual will in contradiction with itself. It is the focus of religion in that by its means man recognizes specifically that God is a Person:

> Prayer—The focus of Religion—Religion the relation of a Will to a Will, the Will in each instance being *deeper* than Reason, of a Person to a Person. The legitimate inference, that for Prayer as the realization, the Act and Product, of the Will, only a negative Rationality can be demanded. Reason must not contradict it. As it is the end and aim of Religion to unite this intuition of the Truth i.e. that God is a Person, with the *Life,* the most appropriate means of effecting this union must be religious Duty.[4]

It was easier for Coleridge to assert the connection between the personality of God and prayer than it was to find a strictly rational proof, and we note his usual resort in such difficulties to the definition and proof by negation. In several other entries he comes to closer grips with the problem. Continuing with the general notion that prayer is a personal relationship between the individual and the Absolute Will and utilizing his previous opinion that the individual fallen will is always in potency toward reunion with the Absolute, he seized upon the intuition that prayer is the only proper means, spiritual in keeping with the spirituality of will, by which the soul might bring the reunion about:

> It appears to me well worthy consideration, what occurred to me last night during prayer. viz. that on the

3. Notebook 24, ff. 27ᵛ–28.
4. Notebook 26, ff. 52ᵛ–53.

assumption of a personal Deity and a moral government of the world, that the fact of the diversity or
difference in kind, of *Man* from all the other animals,
that while *they* are what their *Nature* has made them,
Man can place himself ex oppositu to his nature, is
bound to make his Nature what he ought to be or
what the Idea of his Personality is, affords a strong
presumption in favor of a corresponding diversity in
the way, in which the conservative Providence is applied to him, and in the Law, by which the divine support, and Suppliances are administered. I have long
been of the opinion, that the terms Liberty and Necessity, are a vicious antithesis, which has diverted the
mind from the Idea which is the proper subject of
the investigation . . .

Instead of the antithesis Liberty ✳ Necessity, when in
the light of the Idea they are *absolutely* understood
the *same,* in other words, the perfection of an agent is
the Identity of Liberty and Necessity.

But when the Will determines, controlls, and gradually assimilates the Nature—this is Freedom. Now
as Freedom : Necessity :: Man to the irrational organic or inorganic Nature, and by carrying the con-
tradistinguishing constituents of Humanity and the
necessary detail, I infer a correspondent difference in
the law by which the divine conservative influences
are communicated to Man, and on this ground the rationality of Prayer and Faith—and the corollary that
they must be supernatural.[5]

A shorter and more general proof surveys the same ground
from a slightly different angle:

5. Notebook 34, ff. 7ʳ–8ᵛ.

The preservation of the world has by Divines been accounted and named a continued Creation. This supporting and sustained Spirit of the Universe we call Providence, and I conclude from the preceding Data, that as the Ways of Providence in the imparting of its influences are various because always adopted and correspondent to the capacity and distinguishing character of the various Recipients, its' Gifts, Aids, and Defenses will be bestowed on man in such manner that they shall be the product and consequent of his own Act, and Will; but from another no less indispensable Postulate we are compelled to declare them the results of the Divine Act and Will—and to reconcile both, we must affirm, however it may and does transcend the powers of our Understanding to conceive, that the gifts, aids and interventions of the Divine Power (λογος κοσμήτωρ) are consequent on an act and will of the Percipient, which yet is at the same time the Act and Will of the Divine Spirit—and vice versa, in such manner the Act and Will of the Divine Spirit as that it may nevertheless be rightly named the Act and Will of the Human Recipient. Now these conditions can be found realized only in Faith and Prayer.[6]

A justification of prayer was very dear to Coleridge's heart, especially since the master, Kant, and numerous other contemporary rationalists had established a prevailing fashion which denied its efficacy except as a psychological buttress. The emotional need for prayer was connected in Coleridge's mind with the feeling of justifying faith, and it is remarkable how similar in tone are his personal cries for both. This is the case because the proofs for prayer are actually the basis logically for the aphorism on justifying

6. Notebook 34, ff. 11–11ᵛ.

faith and redemption in the *Aids.* Grace as both the simultaneous act of the petitioner and the gift of God is only plausible in a scheme of things wherein "the gifts, aids and interventions of the Divine Power (λόγος κοσμήτωρ) are consequent on an act and will of the Percipient, which yet is at the same time the Act and Will of the Divine Spirit—and vice versa, in such a manner the Act and Will of the Divine Spirit as that it may nevertheless be rightly named the Act and Will of the Human Recipient." So it is not surprising that these two doctrines, stemming from the same rationale, should elicit similar emotional defenses. Revive again the emotional or existential assent to the doctrine of justifying faith which Coleridge had tried so hard to elicit from his readers in *Aids* and then listen for the same tone in the following quotation on prayer:

> Now this [our previous demonstration] is the Idea of Prayer; and in Prayer alone can the reality of the Idea be found . . . But these are contradictions in terms,—These are impossible conditions! It is Prayer in fact that alone enables the Christian to reply— Contradiction *in terms,* I grant you: nevertheless so it is! were it not a contradiction *in terms,* it would not be an *Idea*—not a living Truth of the whole Spiritual Man, a Ray from the convergence of the Will and the Reason . . .[7]

In this passage we find another of the many occasions in which the existential, pragmatic TRY IT of *Aids to Reflection* merges with the rational a priori *I Am in that God Is* of the Opus Maximum and the Notebooks.

The seventh position places its emphasis upon the interrelation of subjective and objective revelation, upon religion as the nexus of history and philosophy, and finally upon the historic figure of Jesus Christ as the objectifica-

7. Notebook 34, f. 13ᵛ.

tion of the eternal Logos. It is the final and culminating
position, preparing the way for the two living sources of
the Christian faith, the divinity of Christ, and the redemption of man. Indirectly, of course, it gives sanction to the
allied doctrines such as the eucharist and baptism, discussed in *Aids*. But ultimately the final position introduces in another form the perennial problem of Coleridge's system, i.e. the nature of the relationship between
the objective and subjective revelation. In the first respect
position seven brings us to the end of the entire dialectical
movement that began with the assumption of the will and
conscience as first principles; from the second, the value
of the movement as a whole comes into question. Here is
the seventh position:

> Position VII—Thus far, we have proved the fact and
> necessity of Revelation by the force of Reason, with-
> out Revelation. How to form a habit of religious
> Feelings? The first step—especially for a philosopher
> so thoroughly aware of the small value of Testimonies
> respecting Facts or Subjects above the knowledge and
> alien from the previous habits of the Attestors—must
> be—to obtain a steadfast conviction of the Truth of
> the Positions, with which the Feelings are to be as-
> sociated. The disquisition [must be] confined to man
> and in his present state and circumstances. What is
> meant by Religion generally? Is it knowable from the
> speculative Reason as a Science? From the speculations
> or Data supplied by the practical Reason, this Reason
> being taken as a faculty of the Human Mind—or
> rather as the Mind in its' highest function? No! The
> Reason and the Idea must be affirmed, as Revelation,
> as in the first chapter of John's Gospel.
>   Can Religion be grounded on a *subjective* Revela-
> tion *exclusively*? The Negative demonstrated in the

preceding VI Positions. Of the different doctrines proclaiming to be continuations of the first Teaching all may be false—but one only can be true. At all events the question for us is confined to Christianity—the System, which I call by this name and the necessity of assuming this to be Christianity. Shewn that it contains all the Articles of Faith common to all the Churches—and that the remainder are required in order to the Religion being presented as a coherent System, and must be true if the articles common to all are to be comprehended as Truths. Now then, the Question is, Has this system that Quantum of *History* requisite to give it *objective* validity, as a whole? Are the constituent *Ideas* in that connection with existing recorded Facts, which is necessary to its' being at once History and Philosophy—for this is the Definition of Religion viz. Religion is distinguished from Philosophy on the one hand and from History on the other, by being both at once. The second question is—Presuming the subjective validity and moral interest of the Ideas to be such, as to supply the necessary *a priori* probability of a historical manifestation—What Evidence ought we to expect? Assuredly no evidence precluded by the very Idea of the Religion, or excluded by its purposes—And here the Disquisition ends—re. such are the contents of the Pages devoted to the Question—What Methods should a philosopher or Thinker adopt to form or to cultivate a Habit of Religious Feeling? [8]

Coleridge said in *Aids* that "the two great moments of the Christian Religion are, Original Sin and Redemption," and held that there was a necessary connection between them. With this in mind it is easy to understand

8. Notebook 26, ff. 51ᵛ–52ᵛ.

why the aphorism on redemption relies not only upon the seventh position but upon the conclusions on evil, sin, and prayer. His theory of the potential will which clarified the nature of evil and sustained the efficacy of prayer also holds as a partial solution for the problems of redemption. The aphorist's own scheme makes the picture clear enough:

SYNOPSIS OF THE CONSTITUENT POINTS IN THE DOCTRINE OF REDEMPTION, IN FOUR QUESTIONS, WITH CORRE-SPONDENT ANSWERS.

QUESTIONS.

Who (or What) is the
1. *Agens causator?*
2. *Actus causativus?*
3. *Effectum causatum?*
4. *Consequentia ab effecto?*

ANSWERS

I. The Agent and personal Cause of the Redemp-tion of mankind is—the co-eternal Word and only begotten Son of the Living God . . .

II. The Causative Act is—a spiritual and tran-scendent mystery, *that passeth all understand-ing.*

III. The Effect Caused is—the being born anew; as before in the flesh to the world, so now born in the spirit to Christ.

IV. The Consequences from the Effect are—sanctification from sin, and liberation from the inherent and penal consequences of sin in the world to come, with all the means and processes of sanctification by the Word and the Spirit . . .[9]

9. *Aids*, p. 316.

The first question and answer involve all that the rationale of will revealed about Alterity in the Trinity existing as the eternal possibility of becoming a mediator between the Absolute Will and the fallen individual will. Thus the a priori possibility of Alterity as mediator, coupled with the necessity for one engendered by man's actual Fall, become the "two Moments" for Coleridge's belief in and defense of the revealed doctrine of Christ's divinity. That is why he was not interested in the perpetual outcry for and against the miracles in the New Testament which had agitated the eighteenth-century mind. Nor did he seem to be very much interested in historical investigations of Jesus' life.[1] The fact that Jesus lived, and the significant events in his life, confirmed objectively the eternal decree that had to *become* in time. This attitude perhaps explains the otherwise curious lack of comment upon the incarnation and the resurrection, mysteries which do not loom large in the account of "spiritual religion." That these mysteries were primary truths of Christianity he did not

1. It would be interesting to trace Coleridge's ever-changing attitude toward Christ in the chronological order in which it appears in letters to various friends from 1794 to the period of great religious interest in 1820. There are genuine expressions of unbelief in an early letter to brother George in 1794 (*New Letters, 1,* 77–78); then the Unitarian sentiments of 1797, 1801, 1802, mainly for the benefit of the Reverend John Estlin (*New Letters, 1,* 337; 2, 821, 892–93). Simultaneously with these, dubious confessions of faith were going forth to Thomas Wedgwood (Jan. 1798, *New Letters, 1,* 36) and to Reverend George Coleridge (July 1802, *New Letters, 2,* 807). Finally about 1805–06, especially in a letter to Thomas Clarkson (Oct. 13, 1806, *New Letters, 2,* 1193–99,) the language of the later Coleridge appears in somewhat hazy fashion. Now all these letters are masks between the writer and the receiver. But it does seem possible to suggest that by 1806 Coleridge was no longer using the Christian religion to facilitate a pose or to play an intellectual game for a benefactor. However, it is not likely that these early speculations were accompanied by real conviction about Christ and the sacrament of the eucharist. As a matter of fact, a Notebook entry for Christmas 1827 (36, f. 33ᵛ) tells us that Coleridge took the sacrament then for the first time since his early college days.

deny, and he accounted for them on an a priori basis satisfactory for his own needs.

The Notebook material on evil, sin, prayer, and grace
represents a great advance over the *how* of Redemption in
the *Aids* scheme. Although the *how* remains "a spiritual
and transcendent mystery," the new notions on potency
and act allowed freedom for the fallen will in its cooperation with the graces of the Divine—enough freedom so
that the mutual interaction described as "Divine Power
. . . consequent on an act and will of the Percipient,
which is yet at the same time the Act and Will of the
Divine Spirit" (in the hazy diction of the *Aids*) is somewhat clarified. The ontological possibility for redemption
in Alterity, and the logical possibility for it through the
potency and act scheme in the individual will, are assumptions which the argument in the *Aids* presumes. The insuf-
ficient discussion in *Aids* forced Coleridge to work backward to supply logically prior positions in its support.
Thus the first two questions in the *Aids* scheme are answered in the Notebooks.

In keeping with the over-all aim of the *Aids*, Coleridge
slighted the first two questions in favor of an elaborate
discussion of the third and fourth, which focus upon the
practical issues involved in Redemption. These concern
the effects of the mysterious Act and the means by which
it may become beneficial to the individual.

The explanation and defense of questions three and
four, straightforwardly presented in the *Aids*, require, in
themselves, no further reference to the rationale of the
will or the Opus Maximum. Where practical issues were
at stake Coleridge could quickly abandon abtruse reasoning and argue from the facts at hand. (The "what" of redemption, "the being born anew" and the method for
possessing "Sanctification and Liberation," were followed
through in a general way in Chapter 2 above, on Justification by Faith.) More specifically, in his elaborate analogy

of James, Peter, and Matthew, he attacked the Arminian scheme of redemption which conditioned the individual's rebirth upon his works. Following his own logic Coleridge tried to show the absurdities in the program of merits and works which arose from the Arminian position.[2] And despite his cautious attitude of respect for the practices of his mother Church, this view of the redemptive act, which he considered properly as Luther's own, led him finally, after a series of tortuous temptations toward the contrary, to admit that in essence the baptismal rite could not be taken as a sacrament: "it is neither the outward ceremony of Baptism, under any form or circumstances, nor any other ceremony, but such a faith in Christ as tends to produce a conformity to his holy doctrines and example in heart and life, and which faith is itself a declared mean and condition of our partaking of his spiritual body, and of being *clothed upon* with his righteousness . . ."[3]

Nothing more clearly differentiates him from the growing "High Church" party of his time, or from certain strains in present-day Anglican orthodoxy, than his insistence that baptism is a ceremonial and not a sacramental rite. This ceremonial rite justly belongs to the Church as a social unit, as a society of men naturally interested in preserving its own particular identity. "But it is no reason why the Church should forget that the perpetuation of a thing does not alter the nature of a thing, and that a ceremony to be perpetuated is to be perpetuated as a ceremony." In contrast with the contemporary rationalists in Germany and the extremists among the Evangelicals at home, Coleridge wished to preserve the external sign, which they contemptuously styled sentimental, because he recognized that it was deeply rooted in human nature and aided in preserving the Church as a

2. *Aids*, pp. 313–16, 306–11.
3. Ibid., p. 338.

social structure. Still, he was never prepared to travel the path of the Oxford Movement and the later Sacramentalists. In an issue so obviously beclouded by the dogmatics of extremists in both camps, he was more than willing to grant the external Church its right of establishing regulative practices, yet in a way that would not permit it to decide for the individual so personal a matter as his own justification. Again, the characteristics of Coleridge's a priori rationale which distinguish it from mere dogmatism appear, and here with heavy underscoring. In both the rational and emotional approach to religion he confined himself to the broad and recognized interests common and vital to all of Christianity, and shied away from dogmatic positions in all but the most general areas. He confined his positive positions to such fundamentals as Original Sin, redemption, and justification. If he does now and again make striking assertions about particulars of the Anglican Creed, these will almost always be in a negative spirit, directed against the conclusions of the Arminian, Evangelical, or extreme Calvinistic schools.

In a letter to his publisher Hessey, written shortly after publication of *Aids,* Coleridge outlined the areas of discussion important for the Christian faith:

> But one of my best friends is of opinion that you and Mr. Taylor hold it expedient to put to the Press immediately the Six Disquisitions—on Faith; the Eucharist; the Philosophy of Prayer; the Church as an institution of Christ and as a Constituent Estate of the State, Ecclesia ⚺ Enclesia; the prophetic character of the Hebrew Scriptures, and the nature and extent of the *Gift* of Prophecy, and in what respect peculiar to the Hebrew Seers; and, last, on the right and superstitious estimation of the Scriptures.[4]

4. *Unpub. Let.,* 2, 342, to J. A. Hessey, ca. 1825.

A remarkable thing is that, with few exceptions, the project was completed, if we take into account published and unpublished sources. The philosophical studies were yielded up by the Opus Maximum and the Notebooks, after a certain amount of reconstruction and interpretation. The disquisitions on prayer and faith were there in substance. And, of course, two items in the list, on the Church and the Scriptures, appeared separately in published form as *Confessions of an Inquiring Spirit* and *Church and State* (Lay Sermon II). The incarnation and the resurrection were subsumed by him under the article on redemption, while the other major historical facts of revelation were acknowledged in Notebook passages in the confessional spirit.[5] Hence the essay on the eucharist is the only section of the system now lost and for which we know special consideration was intended.

It was difficult for Coleridge to become too concerned over the Protestant-Catholic dispute on transubstantiation and some of the other live issues of an earlier day. In the commentaries on Jeremy Taylor transubstantiation re-

5. Notebook 21½, ff. 69, 68ᵛ:

Groundwork of the *Defensio Fidei* of an orthodox Protestant

1. I believe whatever the Catholic Church believes as Catholic.
2. The Church does not cease to be Catholic because a number or even a majority of those who name themselves Christian, dissent or differ from the sum of her doctrines.
3. Those Doctrines are not Catholic (i.e. imperative on the faith of every Christian) the unbelief or disbelief of which being deemed heretical would convict the first three centuries of the Church of Heresy.

Scholium: This is not precisely the same as, and is far safer than, the position: I hold the belief of the first three centuries of the Church. For tho' their ignorance or disbelief of a doctrine proves such a doctrine not to be Catholic, it does not necessarily follow that the contrary i.e. The un or disbelief of every point of their belief is heretical. For there is a third possible—it may have been, or it may have become, indifferent—(ex. gr. administering of Eucharistic elements to infants).

ceives only slightly more scathing treatment than do the various Protestant alternates, particularly consubstantiation.[6] His impatience appears on every page of the commentaries. To his mind both sides ignored the idea of the Second Person of the Trinity as Alterity. Transubstantiation he allowed to be logically impervious to Protestant attackers, who missed the essential point by dealing with a brainchild of the understanding in its own terms. The idea of the eucharist must be drawn from the Scriptures by the reason, and almost all parties had botched the job. Acceptance of the view of the Established Church, in a negative sense is about the extent of his deference to Anglican orthodoxy.[7] The established article on the eucharist presented the same difficulty as that on baptism, and in exactly the same way Coleridge responded to it, by rendering lip service to the orthodox viewpoint while denying it in fact.[8] Given the spirit in which he interpreted the earthly mission of Christ, it would follow that the special place of devotion and reverence for the eucharist in the general Roman and Anglican tradition must have puzzled him. He had been able to accept the formal ceremony of baptism as a symbol of the regenerative process brought about by the creative Logos or Alterity. But the eucharist, to be entertained more specifically than as a convenient token for the purification of the soul by the gradual and constant workings of the Word, required an emphasis

6. *Lit. Rem.*, pp. 140–252.

7. Ibid., p. 227: "I say again and again, that I myself greatly prefer the general doctrine of our own Church respecting the Eucharist—*rem credimus, modum nescimus*,—to either Trans- (or Con) substantiation, on the one hand, or to the mere *signum memoriae causa* of the Sacramentaries."

8. Ibid., p. 224: "The error on both sides, Roman and Protestant, originates in the confusion of sign or figure with symbol, which latter is always the essential part of that, of the whole of which it is the representative. Not seeing this, and therefore seeing no *medium* between the whole thing and the mere metaphor of the thing, the Romanists took the former or positive pole of the error, the Protestants the latter or negative pole."

upon the human life of Christ which Coleridge never gave. As far as we know, in his many confessions of faith he made no serious attempt to integrate the human nature of Christ and its many complex problems into the scheme as a whole.

Besides the confessional statements given in note 5, p. 179, some interesting Notebook comments on the nature of Christ deserve mention. Certainly they are sketchy and it would be foolish to generalize from them. Yet one of them definitely points to what may now justly be called Coleridge's tendency to minimize the human nature of Christ:

> Thus the sublime idea of the Deus Patiens, the θεός φιλάνθρωπος ἀγονισης symbolized in the crucifixion is compressed into the particular fact of the Second Person of the Godhead—suffering bodily pain on the Cross. And this second Person of the Godhead, how do they represent him to their minds? Answer—As a super-human soul superinduced on a human soul, and standing to this latter in a similar bond of sympathy as this latter stands to the organic body.[9]

Now this little piece taken alone might merely be a very ordinary sign of the antidevotional, antiritualistic, evangelical tradition which viewed with suspicion any attempt to establish a cult of the Cross. But there is a deeper problem involved here, one of religious philosophy rather than attitude. Coleridge edged away from the human nature of Christ, not so much because of emotional susceptibilities to puritanism or evangelical Protestantism as because of the enormous difficulties which the historical facts presented for his system. The general Protestant tradition had accepted the medieval dogmas on Christ's human nature, while rejecting their ritualistic implications as idolatry. Coleridge stumbled on the tradition itself. He filled Note-

9. Notebook 26, ff. 72ᵛ–73.

books 36 through 55 and passed the last years of his life assiduously attempting to absorb some of this tradition into his grand view. He even made use of the reason-understanding distinction in his attempt to reconcile the Jesus of the New Testament with the divine Alterity:

> Is not the repugnance to such a supposition [Jesus' ignorance of temporal matters] grounded in the habit of the Christian world since the Arian controversy of directing their thoughts so exclusively to the Son of God in his character of co-eternal Deity as to lose sight of the *Son of Man,* and to forget that the Son of Mary, in whom the Word ἐσκήνωσε (= tabernacled), was still *the Man,* Jesus, and that as the human understanding is in each individual united with the Reason in one and the same person, and yet cannot comprehend the Reason which shines down into it; for if it did, it would cease to be Understanding . . .[1]

He went on to make the obvious dichotomy, which served him often in his commentary on puzzling passages:

> The second Rule in the interpretation of the prophetic writings is—Distinguish the Functions of our Lord—for the different functions act, if I may so say, the part of different *Persons*—and in fact are different *Personae* personations—The Son of God becomes Son of Man, but tho' whatever we say of the latter, we may rightly affirm of the former; the converse would carry us into strange errors. Remember it is the *Son of Man,* to whom the expressions of the Psalmist refer and the Son of God is the great Being, the *Lords* most high who spoke by the Prophets of the Son of Man, the Son of David—who will dare assert that the Gospel represents *Jesus* as omniscient,

1. Notebook 35, ff. 19ᵛ–20.

in his personal consciousness as Jesus? Jesus knew
that the Son of God was the *true* and proper ground
of his Being—which was to him what our *Reason* is
to us . . .[2]

His own interpretation of Jesus allows the kind of regeneration and prayer, justification, and salvation described in *Aids,* Opus Maximum and the Notebooks. Had
he always been content to abide by his own principles
there would have been no difficulty. But he lapsed at
times, in the manner of an eighteenth-century divine, into
the hopeless attempt of reconciling to this total view every
last passage in the Scriptures. This led to difficulties and
even to incipient skepticism, which his good sense helped
overcome.[3] In the main it can be seen that he backed away
from this flirtation with literal interpretation of Scripture, just as he had slowly given up certain doctrines of
the Established Church, such as the efficacy of baptism
per se. On the basis of his better reasoning much of the
traditional Christian faith had been accommodated to the
post-Kantian period; to have reached out for more would
have been sheer folly, and would have occasioned the collapse of the entire system.

ii. *Authority*

According to the seventh position, someone might say
of Coleridge's own a priori system that no difficulty should
have arisen between the objective facts of Christianity—

---

2. Notebook 37, ff. 19ᵛ–20.

3. Notebook 39, f. 36: "But the incapability, I at present feel, to reconcile the divinity of our Lord therewith. What to be done? Walk hum-
bly and seek Light by Prayer." Notebook 35, ff. 21–21ᵛ: "God's holy
spirit, save me from having my faith shaken by these difficulties
[*Prophecies*] for I am at present utterly unable to reconcile this prophecy
. . . with the events, or rather the actual events with that sense of the
words, in which our Lord's Hearers must have understood them."

such as Jesus' humanity, the baptismal rite, and the eucharist—and their spiritual or subjective counterparts, the Logos, the spirit of regeneration, and prayer. This objection, which basically questions the relationship between theory and practice in the rationale forces us to turn again to the key portion of the position:

> Can Religion be grounded on a *Subjective* Revelation *exclusively?* The Negative demonstrated in the preceding VI Positions. Of the different doctrines proclaiming to be continuations of the first Teaching all may be false—but one only can be true. At all events the question for us is confined to Christianity—The System, which I call by this name and the necessity of assuming this to be Christianity. That it contains all the Articles of Faith common to all the Churches— and that the remainder are required in order to the Religion being presented as a coherent System, and must be true if the articles common to all are to be comprehended as Truths.

Obviously enough, this proposition does not prove the point; it is an assertion that the subjective-objective correspondence exists. The only adequate proof here, as was the case for the other six positions, would have to come out of Coleridge's own practice, and since our study of his ambiguous practice regarding the divinity of Christ has driven us back to the seventh position, perhaps there is a flaw, a flaw which confounds the system at the very end, when all the parts seemed to be coming together. There is certainly a major problem in the apparent ambiguity which clouds the issue of authority in the subjective-objective relationship. What is the final appeal in this relationship? The answer will not be found in the seven positions or *Aids to Reflection.* Other Notebook selections, in conjunction with two little-known published works, *Confessions of an Inquiring Spirit* and *On the Constitution of the Church and State,* provide the best clues.

In a large and general sense, the *Confessions* easily falls into the pattern of the spiritual religion. It assumes as its starting point the a priori positions of the rationale,[4] and repeats in the usual way the sacred dogma of objective-subjective coalescence:

> Revealed Religion (and I know of no religion not revealed) is in its highest contemplation the unity, that is, the identity or co-inherence, of Subjective and Objective. It is in itself, and irrelatively, at once inward Life and Truth, and outward Fact and Luminary. But as all Power manifests itself in the harmony of correspondent Opposites, each supposing and supporting the other,—so has Religion its objective, or historical and ecclesiastical pole, and its subjective, or spiritual and individual pole.   [p. 621]

The uniqueness of the *Confessions* derives from the fact that it attempts to deal with the objective or historical side of the coalescence, whereas the *Aids* and Opus Maximum gave almost exclusive prominence to the subjective. For Coleridge objective Christianity included the facts of the Old and New Testament along with the dogmas and doctrines gathered up in confessions of faith down the Christian centuries. Some items in each category, facts of Jesus' life and confessional proclamations such as infant baptism, stood at variance with his a priori analysis, and intractable and unaccommodated, threatened to render the "coalescence of subject and object" meaningless. On the one hand he could not ignore the weight of this two-fold Christian objectivity without joining the ranks of the other arbitrary rationalists between whose work and his

---

4. *Confessions*, pp. 578–79, states in four propositions the basic ideas of the rationale of will.

own he made such careful and elaborate distinctions; yet it seemed impossible to accept simply dogmatic positions, unless he wished to admit that the "spiritual religion" was merely a solemn farce and cover for established orthodoxy.

Writing for the early nineteenth century, and against the background outlined in our first chapter, Coleridge naturally aimed his heaviest ammunition at the hardened opinions of his fellow countrymen, even though his purpose was to save historical Christianity. He attacked the dogma of plenary inspiration, accepted the idea and some of the findings of the historical approach to the Scriptures, and hit again against the exalted and, to his mind, false position that miracles occupied in contemporary divinity.[5] These issues, no longer alive, were settled long ago in Coleridge's favor. What is really interesting about his comments on Scripture and historical confessions of faith is the positive aspect, his attempts to save them from the future disregard he (but not his contemporaries) could foresee. Dismissing both the Roman Catholic doctrine of Papal supremacy and the Protestant dogma of extreme individual interpretation of Scriptures as two forms of the same rational bankruptcy, he cautiously framed rules for preserving the objectivity of Christianity that would be in accordance with modern thought.[6] Our question is whether these rules satisfy the demands of either one or the other.

Coleridge was extremely cautious in his approach to the problem of an external or objective norm for measuring the Christian faith. Wherever he looked in the examples of the past, whether the Pope and Council, the Bible as the religion of Protestants, or the Thirty-nine Articles and authority of the early Fathers (the idolatry of the

5. Ibid., pp. 587–94.
6. Ibid., pp. 617–18, 620–21.

Established Church, in his opinion),[7] he found the twin problems of hardened dogma and sapped spiritual strength. Nor had such externalizations of doctrine served their supposed purposes, for the further fragmentation of Christianity had gone on as usual. He wanted a dynamic, subjective, and emotional approach to an irreducible minimum of beliefs which would hold all Christians together without the seemingly inevitable hardening which necessary belief had brought in the past. He suggests in the *Confessions* that the universals of the Christian faith are those doctrines common to "Greek and Latin, to Romanist, and Protestant," [8] and offered in Notebook 21½ a simple formula containing them.[9] At another juncture in *Confessions* he states a different norm, holding that certain parts of Scripture have objective validity per se—that is, if the narrator happens to be Moses or St. John claiming a direct line from heaven, his narrative should be believed on that basis.[1] Both these norms, in providing the minimum basic beliefs, would seem to cut drastically the role of subjectivity in determining a Christian's faith. Nevertheless, in the same *Confessions* we find the usual respect for the subjective element in such phrases as "the doctrine *finds* the reader," "it is the spirit of the Bible, and not the

---

7. Notebook 39, f. 35: "I am sometimes half inclined to think that the notion of the infallibility and freedom from all error of the Apostles has been as injurious to Theology as the assumption of the same by the Pope, to Faith and Christian Morals."

8. *Confessions*, p. 615.

9. Notebook 21½, f. 68: "The two factors of the Christian Religion, the one indispensable to *faith*, and the other no less to the faith of a *Christian*, are: 1. The philosophy concerning Christ = Ια περι το Λογου, το θεανθρωποι. 2. The History of Jesus Christ. The different ages of Christianity may be conveniently classed and characterized according to the due co-inherence of these, or the undue predominance of the one or the other: while the entire subtraction of either destroys Christianity altogether . . ."

1. *Confessions*, p. 583.

detached words . . . that is infallible and absolute," and "by the good Spirit were the spirits tried."

This difficult point in his theory is solved by his presentation of the principle of collective authority. Of course, not everyone can accept this solution, nor does it follow that Coleridge successfully employed collective authority in relation to all practical problems. Still, the principle had much power, and it was rooted in the same logic that produced the dialectic of the will itself.

When Coleridge calls upon us to observe the doctrines universal to all the Christian Churches, and to use them as the objective measure in our individual encounter with Scripture, he is not, in his own terms, inculcating callow deference to mere dogma, or asking us to accept as proven that which we set out to prove. For according to the principle of collective authority the doctrines of the universal Church have more than historical significance or accidental value. These beliefs and observances are the guides left for us by good men of the past who presumably brought the same conscience, and the same abilities in a priori reasoning, to the task of defining dogma. Their collective rather than individual results are therefore the objectification of the subjective spirit of Christianity, and are stages in the growth of the idea of spiritual religion. To ignore universally accepted ideas would be folly, and a deliberate severance of the branches from the roots. The idiosyncrasies of subjectivity are every bit as deadly for religion as the unthinking formalities of orthodoxy. That is why Coleridge insisted that the position of the Church on baptism should be respected even if it could not be accepted. The old principles of the universal church must always discipline the subjective spirit in its quest for new experiential meanings in doctrine. Coleridge's idea of objective-subjective coalescence did have its internal coherence; that it did not approach perfection in practice is not to say of it that it is some kind of patchwork.

The limited but powerful respect which Coleridge accords authority in his religious philosophy has all the advantages and weaknesses inherent in any dynamic conservatism. On the positive side, the locus of tradition provides a principle of order around which to build. Further, as opposed to dogmatic or static conservatism, there is the urge and willingness to grow, although this is accompanied at times, to be sure, with a certain anxiety for the discarded past. Coleridge himself attested the dynamic possibilities in his system by going against the dictates of his own branch of the universal church on several clear and important issues. Yet the tentative nature of his dissents is the sign of a man who has rejected the extreme position of individualism as a norm for religious questions.

The weaknesses can be viewed in two respects. The first is a general philosophical disposition to accept certain absolute norms, namely the conscience of Coleridge's system and the minimal but universal beliefs of the Christian religion. This means that, however palliative, flexible, and congenial to change it may be, the spiritual religion is built upon a semi-absolutist premise. One could question whether it could be otherwise and remain Christianity. For obviously, if the two-thousand-year-old conscience of the Christian, upon which Coleridge rests his system, be viewed only as one of many psychological variants, or if the doctrines and traditions of this two-thousand-year-old society be considered merely in a historically relative perspective, it may still be possible to maintain a general religious feeling and call it Christianity, but in all honesty this name would then be no more than a deferential tag. Coleridge's system provides about as broad a basis as it is possible to have and retain identification with the histori-

cal and spiritual force known as Christianity. Probably it
would be better to consider this first weakness the general
vulnerability of any position to the criticism of other systems, to the forces of cultural relativity as presented in
scientific, psychological, and historical attitudes today. As
such, this weakness is not properly an issue within the
scope of our study.

The second weakness may be a real one, and should be
cast in the form of a simple question: Can any significant
change occur in a system such as this? The question is
raised because the method of the system appears to be
circular, i.e. previous opinions mold the mind, previous
standards form the conscience, so that no truly forward
steps will ever be undertaken. One must admit, in brief,
that such a so-called system is merely a pompous and elaborate form of maintaining the status quo.

That the system can be and has been so used it would
be foolish to deny; but that this necessarily follows from
principles inherent in the system itself is not true. Two
illustrations from Coleridge's writings indicate varied uses
and results; the good example, as it happens, is in the religious sphere, and the bad in the political. Numerous
examples of good and bad in both spheres could be found,
and from writers in the conservative tradition other than
Coleridge.

The major interest in *On the Constitution of the
Church and State,* where the bad political example occurs,
is the Roman Catholic Relief Bill of 1829. In order to discuss it properly, Coleridge sets about to derive the true
idea of both the state and the church. It is his derivation
of the state which provides the illustration of his methodology in its least attractive aspect. The historical idea
of the state is juxtaposed to the existing circumstances in
1829, and on the basis of this juxtaposition some changes
are suggested. These proposed changes we might well call

the "dictates of reason based upon the past and upon present experience." But they were also inadequate to the situation and jejune—merely some minor attempts to balance the power in Parliament that had been upset by the growth of the commercial classes. They ignored the growing landless class of factory workers and missed completely the direction which the actual reforms of the nineteenth century were going to take.

Why was this so? Because Coleridge proposed his timid changes entirely on the basis of pre-established conditions —that is, upon an idea of a state composed only of barons, landed gentry, clergy, and professional and wealthy commercial interests. He drew his idea of parliamentary government from the historical growth of Parliament in the Middle Ages and the Reformation. His idea is a preconception, a closed circle in which to argue, a neat little area in which reform might occur. Thus engrossed with an idea which became a substitute for observation and thinking, he missed the central fact of the democratic process: the necessity of extending the franchise to all citizens regardless of property and rank. While others worked to achieve this goal, he was wasting his time on schemes aimed at redressing the balance of power between the obsolescent lords and the onrushing middle class. Whenever this happens, dynamic conservatism disintegrates into an intellectual farce for the promotion of existing conditions.

Merely to maintain objective, historical facts, dogmas, or constitutions as ends in themselves was not what Coleridge really intended, although, lured by the possibilities for error in his own method, that is what he sometimes seems to bring about. He intended to maintain the objective as a guide in present thinking, but the true coalescence of subject and object could not mean paralysis of thought and emotion. That is why I maintain that the

weakness of stagnation and closed-circle argumentation
does not necessarily follow from the premises within which
Coleridge worked. And it is not surprising that his more
successful excursions were in the areas of literary criticism,
aesthetics, and religion. Having greater and more permanent interests in these things, he naturally became very
acute in examining the historical idea of each, and dis-
played keen sensitivity in handling an immense amount
of knowledge about them.

Coleridge's attitude toward the Scripture truths of the
Old and New Testaments is a fine example of dynamic
conservatism at work. The situation in which he found
himself and his contemporaries viewing with concern certain advances in biblical scholarship, was not unlike similar developments regarding the British Constitution taking place at the time. The conservative upper classes of
the British public had reacted with violent disapproval of
both movements. Coleridge behaved quite differently, by
defending the possibility of radical change in attitude toward the Scriptures while holding for the status quo in
politics.

Now, consideration of the problems raised by the Scriptures and those raised by the Constitution required the
same steps: an idea for each, evaluation of contemporary
circumstances relating to this idea, and possible changes
which a juxtaposition of them might suggest. For his idea
of the parliamentary state Coleridge accepted the historical status quo; for that of the Scriptures he applied his own
delicate insight into their history. In assessing the contemporary problems there is the same vast difference, the
difference between first-hand knowledge of biblical criticism and its aims, and a mere acceptance of the middle-
class reading of contemporary events on the political scene.
Without falling into iconoclastic disregard for the past,
Coleridge's theory or idea of Scripture reverentially sees

the Testaments as living organisms. Plenary inspiration falls, the Protestant dogma of individual interpretation is discarded, and, most important, the notion that Scripture can be considered apart from historical background is discarded. The idea of sacred Scriptures which Coleridge proposes to bring to bear upon contemporary findings is one that gives fullest credence to those findings, yet preserves the Testaments from thoughtless or willful destruction. He read Eichorn and Schleiermacher without feeling the necessity of joining the worried divines of the day in their attempts to ignore or shout down the pesky Germans. As a matter of fact, his recommendations on the meaning and use of the Scriptures were far-reaching and significant enough to accommodate the later and more radical criticisms of Harnack, Renan, and Feuerbach. Scriptures were not to be considered as settled documents containing infallible proofs; they were rather the actual proofs of the faith of other men, the true authenticity of which must be looked for in the living traditions of the Churches, the collective Christian conscience, and the testimonies of the individual soul. Even if the Testaments had been criticized out of existence (a possibility he granted in theory but not in fact) on the basis of the meager conjectures of Eichorn and Schleiermacher, he would have remained steadfast in the assertion that "The worst that could happen then would be the want of any certain and authentic History of Christ according to the Flesh." The living tradition of Church and conscience would assure that "We should have the Faith and Religion of Christians without knowing the particular incidents which accompanied the Revelation further than the Creed and Tradition had preserved . . . a great loss indeed, but not a mortal injury!" [2]

2. Victoria LT 59, a transcription by Mary Coleridge of Coleridge's commentaries to Schleiermacher's *A Critical Essay on the Gospel of St. Luke,* London, 1825.

With this "idea" of Scripture firmly in hand, Coleridge considered the commentaries of the antagonists point by point, conceding here to historical criticism, denying there some dubious conjecture, and usually maintaining the same open mind and lively faith. His handling of the contemporary critics, as well as many personal observations in the spirit of the biblical criticism itself, fill many of the late Notebooks.[3] Despite a few moments of skepticism his basic position remained clear. Having preserved the principle that changes in attitude toward the two Testaments were healthy, desirable, and feasible and could be had without sacrificing the essential truths of Christianity contained within them, he followed the lead of the agnostic commentators into every daring area, and at times excelled them in discarding particular dogmatic positions. Thus he pioneered for his contemporaries, and established a standard by which religious-minded men of later days might ride the waves of the future without fear of sacrificial wreckage. In the true coalescence of subject and object an idea is a guide by means of which new areas of thought are opened; in the false coalescence either the subjectivity of irresponsible individual imagination or the objectivity of collective unthinking dogmatism distorts the operation.

When Coleridge exploits the best possibilities in his own method, whether in religion, philosophy, or politics, the result is always consistent with the premises of semidualism which we have followed from the beginning. For semidualism falls between a monism too occupied with its subjectively spun rational system and a traditional dualism of overriding and stultifying deference to authority and revelation. Subjective monism prized the imaginative

3. The amount of conjecture on the Scriptures increases in direct proportion with the dates of the Notebooks. These conjectures are too numerous to present in detail.

process by means of which man could become the measure of all things; objective dualism rested content with the constellation of facts and events beyond the power of human comprehension. Semidualism did not ignore the imagination in limiting its mode of apprehension to an analogy of the divine order, nor did it cast away the meaningful facts and events of the Christian tradition, in reference to which the emotions, feelings, and rational processes of man were to be tested. For a Coleridgean every fact and event has its own meaning, which the rational man must, as his duty, attempt to fathom. Different meanings will be assigned to the same facts by different men and ages; yet faith remains amid these changes in a set of permanent forms for things which can never be known to man inhabiting a world of sin. An explanation of this state of affairs, such as Coleridge's rich and original outgrowth of the idealistic tradition, does not alter the fact that *omnia exeunt in mysterium*. It is very significant that both the *Church and State* and the Opus Maximum are graced by the following little poem, the full implications of which shall be our interest in the concluding pages:

> Whene'er the mist that stands 'twixt God and thee
> Defacates to a pure transparency,
> That intercepts no light and adds no stain—
> There reason is, and there begins her reign!
>
> But alas!

> . . . tu stesso ti fai grosso
> Col falso immaginar, si che non vedi
> Cio che vedresti se l'avessi scosso.[4]
>
> [DANTE, *Par.* 1.88]

4. *Church and State*, p. 143.

CHAPTER 6

RELIGION AND POETRY

The little poem "Reason," which so aptly closes *Church and State* and sums up Coleridge's final epistemological position, also raises a most pertinent question about his religious thinking and his poetry: while suggesting the understandable intrusion of the philosophical and religious interests in the late poetry, it reminds us of the inferior nature of this poetry.

It seems that Coleridge in his later years was a poet who failed to relate his hard-won vision of revitalized Christianity to the experiences of daily living. His world was theoretically determinate in all the phases deduced from the "rationale of the will," but remained practically indeterminate whenever he was forced to face the facts and situations of life which constitute the hard stuff of the poetic medium. His activity and success in weaving an ever-widening web of abstract unities increased as his abilities in the concrete medium became paralyzed. He became the poet in prose of the post-Kantian Christian ontology. "Reason" is a mediocre expression in poetry of what *Aids* and Opus Maximum said in prose. Like other poems of the late period, "Reason" lacks the imaginative and structural interest of the famous early poems. An explanation of this phenomenon may help our final understanding of the religious phase.

Coleridge's earlier poems, preceding 1802, were in structure and ideas informed by the doctrines of immanence
and panentheism; [1] they reflected the breakdown in modern thought of the old beliefs about the composition of
body and soul, and the collapse of the dichotomous scholastic logic which influenced earlier English poets.[2] In the
romantic heyday—the "dialectic of mind and spirit"—the
poetry of fusion indirectly led to a reduction in strategies
of paradox, in ironies of the obvious kind, or in clashes
between the world of spirit and the world of matter.[3]

A decidedly different tone and structure appears in the
later poetry. Although an obvious pattern of opposition
between the early and late poetry does not exist, since
permanent features of Coleridge's style survive ideological
change, differences do appear in revealing areas and help
us understand the motivations of the later Coleridge. Certain poems from the early period come quickly to mind,
"The Eolian Harp," [4] "The Rime of the Ancient Mariner,"
and "Kubla Khan," as characteristic of the early Coleridge. The later poems do not come easily to mind, having been generally neglected by critics and anthologies.
"Limbo," "Ne Plus Ultra," "Constancy to an Ideal Object," "Work without Hope," "Reason" are all interesting
examples of his changes in style and thinking after 1802.

1. See Ernest Bernbaum, *Guide through the Romantic Movement*,
(New York, 1949), G. M. Harper, "Gems of Purest Ray" in *Coleridge
Studies by Several Hands*, and R. D. Havens, *The Mind of the Poet*
(Baltimore, 1941), for examples of the numerous studies which have dis-
cussed the philosophy of immanence behind the early poetry of Words-
worth and Coleridge.

2. *Letters, 1*, 73–74, to Thelwall, Dec. 17, 1796.

3. William K. Wimsatt's "The Structure of Romantic Nature Imagery,"
in *The Verbal Icon* (Lexington, Univ. of Kentucky Press, 1954), pp. 103–
16, gives a keen analysis of some imagery in which the structure of immanence is of primary importance.

4. H. J. Milley, "Some Notes on Coleridge's Eolian Harp," *Modern
Philology, 36* (1939), 359–75.

The link between the two types of poetry is the emotional basis. Coleridge's early statements, "deep thinking is attainable only by a man of deep feeling," [5] or "a passion is a state of emotion, having its immediate cause not in things, but in our thoughts of the things," [6] apply with equal force to the semidualistic religious and the imaginative or associational poetry. The differences appear in the structure and ideas which grow out of this emotional basis. In the early period, the emotions aided in the blurring of ideas and structures generally regarded as belonging to the poetry of the romantic imagination; later the emotions became the means of dramatizing the opposed ideas and dualistic conceptions of Christian paradox in poetry. If it is customary to call the early poetry that of the imagination, the later may with some justice appear as that of the higher or religious reason.

In the poetry written between 1802 and 1825 Coleridge was caught between the old and the new view. Pessimism replaced his earlier optimism about Nature, which became more and more an alien object, opposed or at best indifferent to spirit, while there was a constant recognition of the presence of sin and evil in the world. But this gradual acknowledgment and appreciation of Christian ideas never quite compensated for the spontaneous unity of the earlier "One Life." The semidualism and grudging accommodation we have noticed in his development of the doctrine of Original Sin and that of religious analogy appear throughout this poetry. There is no whole-hearted acceptance, no true modus vivendi, as earlier poets had with the great Christian theological and metaphysical systems of the seventeenth century or earlier. Intellectual acceptance of Christian dogma and metaphysics unfortunately did not carry with it the free, spontaneous com-

5. *Letters, 1,* 108, to Poole, March 23, 1801.
6. *Inquiring Spirit,* ed. Kathleen Coburn (London, 1951), p. 66.

mitment necessary for good poetry. Emotion was the driving force behind all the great early work. Given, then, the emotional failure in the late poetry, it is no surprise that Coleridge is not remembered as a great Christian poet. Our interest is now to examine the later poetry in the light of the obvious failure of emotional commitment to Christian doctrine.

The most startling development in the later poetry occurs in the relationships between spirit and Nature, and between good and evil as potent forces in the poet's world. Here, rather than in the intrusion of any obvious Christian symbols or devotional methods, the semidualism of the post-Kantian phase asserts itself. The mode of devotional or decorative religious verse was absolutely foreign to Coleridge—his separation of religious functions is mentioned in *Table Talk* in a revealing comment [7]— and it is a second attitude, that of religious speculation, which gets into the later poetry. Some of the speculations are personal, as in "Constancy to an Ideal Object" and "Work without Hope"; others are fanciful, as in "Limbo" and "Ne Plus Ultra." The display of wit muffles the tone of anguish in the later poems, but the personal, conversational poems bemoan the lost glory of the poet. Coleridge was not at home emotionally in the abstract world of spiritual Christianity into which he had thought himself. As the poetry shows, some of the major Christian consolations were denied him in the context of the religious speculation revealed in *Aids to Reflection* and other prose works.

7. *Table Talk*, p. 407, "Faith and Belief": "The sublime and abstruse doctrines of Christian belief belong to the Church; but the faith of the individual, centered in his heart, is or may be collateral to them. Faith is subjective. I throw myself in adoration before God, acknowledge myself his creature—simple, weak, lost; and pray for help and pardon through Jesus Christ; but when I rise from my knees, I discuss the doctrine of the Trinity as I would a problem in geometry; in the same temper of mind, I mean, not by the same process of reasoning, of course."

Man in these poems is primarily a spiritual being, heavily burdened with moral evil and placed in a world of physical and metaphysical evil. Nature, with which he once shared the One Life, is at worst hostile and inanimate, at best a living force across the path of which man travels by mere accident. The former dialectic of subject and object is replaced now by the agitation of spirit orphaned in an alien world. Nor can the analogical consolations of Nature in a Christian context replace the One Life. The ruined systems of medieval Catholicism and seventeenth-century Protestantism lie dead beside the recently collapsed immanential panentheism. God now inhabits a changed firmament of widened space and larger areas of unintelligible forces. It is a heroic existence which semidualism and recognition of Christian ideas such as Original Sin forced upon Coleridge as one of the first Christians with a modern sensibility. Intellectually he bore the burden well, as we have seen; emotionally, and this is reflected constantly in the poetry, he winces, cries out, and seems at times even to despair.

Everywhere in the later Coleridge pessimistic notes sound, replacing the smooth, unruffled melody of "Frost at Midnight." Sometimes they can be extremely personal, reflecting the loss of Sara Hutchinson, domestic peace, or health. At other times he turns, seriously or otherwise, to speculation upon the nature of evil, in "Limbo" and "Ne Plus Ultra." There is no doubt that his personal sorrows and losses greatly accentuated his interest in evil, expressed in the Christian framework as sin, and in the darker sides of existence generally, thus admitting elements into the poetry which had been shut out of the One Life, the monism of panentheistic benevolence. The semidualism and religious paradox traced in this book had their influence also, in such poems as "Reason" and "Coeli Enarrant." As a matter of fact, a certain group of the later poems can profitably be read in connection with Coleridge's view of Original Sin as expressed in *Aids to Reflection* and discussed in the previous chapter. The more striking differences between the early and late poetry, in the relationship between man and Nature, is partially a reflection of the importance of Original Sin in Coleridge's later thinking.

Although ultimately Original Sin and the meaning of evil remained mysteries for Coleridge, the rational explanation which he gave of them carried certain implications for his entire theological and metaphysical position. Original Sin, or the theological explanation of moral evil in the world, is only intelligible if the will is acknowledged as a spiritual faculty absolutely distinguishable from everything in the natural world, animate and inanimate alike. Coleridge clearly acknowledged this in *Aids to Reflection* (pp. 284–85). Such emphasis upon the will as spiritual principle tends to divorce man, as a spiritual being, from the undifferentiated manifold of monistic interpenetration. Secondly, his position on the extent of original depravity in man's will and intellect, which we remember turned out to be essentially Reformation doctrine midway between scholastic and Arminian interpretations, also exercises a distinct influence against the immanential One Life. The darkened intellect, having its categorical imperative in conscience and shorn of the theological assumptions of medieval Scholasticism, bears close connection with the semidualistic metaphysics of Kant, in which the world must be separated distinctly from the transcendental reality, or God. Now this attitude differs from traditional theism as well as from the optimistic Greek philosophical systems. But semidualism provides a barren outlook for a Christian poet, since Nature, either as friend or alter ego, or as the analogue of a personal Creator, can no longer play a substantial role.

In this new theology man is a spiritual being conscious of evil in himself and around him, of his darkened intellect, and above all of his position as an alien in the world of matter and sense, longing for his God whom he may know only partially, and this through the resources of the internal, the spiritual, alone.

This quest of Coleridge's speculative life is reflected constantly in the late poetry. He did not jest in avowing to a friend in 1806 that he wished "to know metaphysically, what the spirit of God is." [8] In this connection the question of God's opposite, evil, of which he knew so much through the enslavement of will to opium, became a serious matter. Difficulties in the moral order and in Nature itself, successfully shunted away in the early poems, assumed new importance after the collapse of the romantic union. Specifically, in a Christian universe the serious evil of sin must be acknowledged and explained on a far less optimistic basis than in the earlier years. The poems "Limbo" and "Ne Plus Ultra"—although not to be taken in a fully serious way—offer some interesting clues regarding Coleridge's attitudes toward evil, particularly "moral" evil.

An entry from Coleridge's *Anima Poetae* provides a good clue for the manner in which we should read these two poems:

> This remark is occasioned by my reflections on the fact that Christianity *exclusively* has asserted the *positive* being of evil or sin, "of sin the exceeding sinfulness"—and thence exclusively the *freedom* of the creature, as that, the clear intuition of which is, both, the result and the accompaniment of redemption . . . With what contempt, even in later years, have I not contemplated the doctrine of a devil! but

8. *New Letters*, 2, 1193, to Thomas Clarkson, Oct. 13, 1806.

now I see the intimate connection, if not as existent *person*, yet as essence and symbol with Christianity— and that so far from being identical with Manicheism, it is the surest antidote (that is, rightly understood).[9]

The serious element in these poems is this admission of an evil spiritual principle permitted by God, yet nevertheless functioning as a divisive, destructive force in the world. The sportive note is injected in the extravagant way in which Coleridge handles the traditional concepts of privation, positive and negative nothing, and evil as metaphysical entity. All in all, his "Limbo" and "Hell" are theologically sound, even in certain particulars strikingly similar to the presentation of Thomas Aquinas in the *Summa Theologica*.[1] But the numerous admissions of pagan or Manichaean elements—such as substance, fate-night, rod—testify that Coleridge was also frankly enjoy-

9. *Anima Poetae*, ed. E. H. Coleridge (London, 1895), pp. 259–60.
1. The conception of evil in "Limbo" and "Ne Plus Ultra" is in the main that of the Christian tradition. "A lurid thought is growthless dull Privation" corresponds to Aquinas' standard definition, *Malum . . . neque est sicut habitus, neque sicut pura negatio, sed sicut privatio.* But the final assertion, that Hell is "Positive Negation" and much in "Ne Plus Ultra" is theologically incorrect, and shows that Coleridge was straining for paradoxes. Nevertheless the general drift of "Ne Plus Ultra," that ultimate evil is a permitted opposite of God, and symbolized in the Christian tradition by Satan, is orthodox enough:

> The Dragon foul and fell, the unrevealable,
> And hidden one whose breath,
> Gives wind and fuel to the fires of Hell!

The presentation of evil in "Ne Plus Ultra" is given in images familiar in Christian theology. "Sole Positive of Night / Antipathist of light!" resembles Thomas' *Dicendum quod unum oppositorum cognoscitur per alterum, sicut per lucem tenebra.* Another interesting similarity occurs in the relationship between evil and prayer, where Coleridge's lines,

> Sole interdict of all-bedewing prayer
> The all-compassionate!

expresses in substance the thought in St. Thomas' *Quae quidem peccata sunt quasi obstacula interposita inter nos et Deus.*

ing himself in the play of paradox, ringing all possible changes on the difficult conception of evil as a privation of being, and that of the ontological good. Exploring "What God metaphysically is" was very often an intellectual game for him, as we know from *Table Talk* and the irate comments of H. N. Fairchild. Nevertheless the jocular tone, the metaphysical wit, and the freedom with theological accuracy should not blind us to the one great significance of these poems, his interest in the Christian universe of values, where evil is handled metaphysically as a permitted privation of the ontological good, and morally as sin in the will of man, separating the creature from home in the Creator:

> Sole interdict of all-bedewing prayer,
> The all-compassionate!

Such recognition forces man to view himself as a created being, of spiritual nature, separated from beatitude by the mystery of evil manifested by contradiction in intellect and will.[2] The former exuberance of the ego-exalting

2. Perhaps it would not be amiss to repeat at this point the serious discussion of evil which Coleridge undertook in his later Notebooks. The important thing to note is that many of the "orthodox" assertions in the poems reappear, while the extravagant or witty paradoxes drawn from the Manichaean tradition and the pagan world have disappeared. This indicates that while "Limbo" and "Ne Plus Ultra" cannot be taken entirely seriously, they are, to a certain extent, a barometer of Coleridge's early interest in these problems of the Christian tradition. See Notebook 26, ff. 14–15: "Even so it is with Evil, *materially* considered—with the matter or substance of Evil. Regard it, as a *Potence,* or as having only potential Being, and it is the necessary and good Involution of the Will and therein of the Personality if all are finite Intelligences. It is an essential perfection of their will, which without it would cease to be a Will, as long as the *actual* Will, or the Act of the Will, is to deny itself, to sacrifice itself, as a finite Will—and to use its' Base as the condition of its' own positive or + reality, which can only be in correlation to an opposite or − reality. . . . The evil will has no power to exclude the good: for in itself it has no power at all, except against itself, for its' inherent self-frustration—much less can it exert any power over the good—It simply

systems finds itself replaced by prostration before the evil
—physical, metaphysical, and moral—which plagues man
in his darkened world.

To point out that this interest was not merely speculative we need only turn to some short personal poems
of the later years which reflect the same viewpoint as
"Limbo" and "Ne Plus Ultra." The symbol of the
darkened world, which was always mitigated by light in
the early poems, becomes dominant in "Limbo"—"By
the mere horror of blank Naught-at-all"—and in "Ne
Plus Ultra"—"Sole Positive of Night, Antipathist of
Light." In certain other late poems this imagery of darkness is found in most extreme form.

In "Coeli Enarrant" the image of the darkened sky
divides the "groaning world" of sin and physical evil from
God. Man reads in anguish the black-letter starless sky as
an "O" corresponding to his own pain and alienation. The
stars, or light mediating between creature and Creator,
no longer "alphabet the skies." In the poem "Reason"
this image of alienation shifts from darkness to mist,

---

therefore falls from the good, as a Precipitate. And here we have the
abysmal mystery of the Devil, the Evil One, the Contrary of God, absolute
emptiness as God is the absolute Fullness, a mere Potence as God is a
pure Act, wherein all is that actually is—a hidden Fire, for ever seeking
a base on which it may actualize and finding it only to convert it into its'
own essence, which is necessarily baseless . . . Eternal because below all
time even as God is eternal by transcendency to all time—and unintelligible, because an outcast from intelligence even as God [is] incomprehensible as containing all intelligence. And lastly, Eternal Death as God
is eternal Life. Repent it cannot—for the power of Repentance is potential
good: and the Evil Spirit is itself potential, and has its potentiality in itself—and like the increase of Darkness . . . can only be manifested
by the remaining Light." Notebook 30, f. 33: "Satan, the Evil Principle,
that in division would be what alone the Absolute One can be—therefore
introfluent instead of affluent, destructive of reality instead of causative
and hence the contrary of God . . . For pure Evil what is it but Will
that would manifest itself as Will not in Being (ἑτερότης), not in Intelligence (therefore formless)—not in Union or Communion, the contrary
therefore of Life, even eternal Death."

"That stands 'twixt God and thee." This mist, like the
darkness in "Coeli Enarrant" is contrasted with the "pure
transparency" of the triumphant reign of pure reason.
Now, however, there is a pessimistic reminder of the power
of sin, evil, and error, and the words of Dante are included
as a corrective to the presumptions of the reason and the
expanding ego:

> tu stesso, ti fai grosso
> Col falso immaginar, si che non vedi
> Cio che vedresti, se l'avessi scosso.

> (Thine own false fancies make thee blind; hence
> unperceived are things thou wouldst perceive,
> hadst thou but left thy vain concepts behind.)

It is no surprise that Coleridge turned to the great poet
of the Middle Ages in his attempt to revaluate the power
of the human reason; his progress in gradual acceptance
of dualism has prepared us carefully for this step. But
there is an important difference. The chief peculiarity in
his theological reacceptance, the semidualism he inherited
from Kant, served as a force denying him the possibility of
becoming a Christian poet in the traditional sense, that of
Dante or the seventeenth century.

For a variety of reasons he was bereft as a poet of the
usual consolations of the Christian, even after he accepted
the orientation of the Christian tradition. Christianity on
such highly philosophical "spiritual" grounds deprived
him of the facility to use Nature in poetry in the traditional way provided by the analogy of being.

The communion of man and Nature which had been
so central to the early poetry broke apart completely in
his Christian thinking, leaving a wide chasm between
spirit and Nature. Once man came to be conceived of as
primarily spiritual, in the activity of will, oppressed by

the weight of Original Sin, the result was naturally a reorientation of man in Nature. But Coleridge was not able to rehabilitate Nature along the traditional Christian pattern. The shock of considering man apart from Nature was at times too great, as in the poem "Human Life or Denial of Immortality," where the breakdown of spirit and matter in the old immanential unity finds man the "Surplus of Nature's dread activity," a "Blank accident! nothing's anomaly!" From the moment Coleridge began to think of spirit or soul as an entity *sui generis,* a supernatural occurrence in the material world, the formerly genial Nature of inanimate objects and sensible things, carrying on the endless cycle of generation and decay, took on some of the horror present later in the poetry of the mid-Victorians. The following excerpt from a late Notebook expresses a feeling much more in common with Keats's "Ode to a Nightingale" or Tennyson's *In Memoriam* than with his own or Wordsworth's earlier poetry:

> O Nature! I would rather not have been—let that which is to come so soon, come now—for what is all the intermediate space, but sense of utter worthlessness? For, far below animals—for they enjoy a generic immortality having no individuation. But man is truly and solely an immortal series of conscious Mortalities, and inherent Disappointments.[3]

The close connection shown here between interest in personal immortality and alienation from Nature lends support to our general position. The sustenance which generations of earlier poets had taken from Nature considered as the handiwork of God was denied to Coleridge; his scornful comments upon the old system of "natural theology," coupled with what now we know of his extremely sophisticated semidualism tell us why. The thinking

3. *Inquiring Spirit,* op. cit., p. 142.

Christian could no longer pursue his God through the analogies of Nature. Henceforth Coleridge's poetry was to be written in two moods, one looking backward mournfully upon the days when Nature had been his friend through the interpenetration of subject and object, the other looking forward, in hope but not enthusiasm, to the time when the soul would be able to free itself from matter for union with a highly intellectualized version of Divinity.

The backward glance is expressed poignantly in "Constancy to an Ideal Object" and "Work without Hope," where the breakdown of interplay between spirit and Nature is complete. The Nature described in the Notebook entry, with its endless cycles, Coleridge now looks upon as a stranger. In "Constancy to an Ideal Object" everything in Nature except man's thought "beat about" in the now harsh, detached expression of the poet and in the cyclic process, "or veer or vanish." But here, instead of indulging in the self-pity of "Denial of Immortality" or the Notebook entry, Coleridge, with emphasis now on personal immortality, makes the puzzling difference between man and Nature the point of a paradox. A single thought, unsubstantial, immaterial, is yet "The only constant in a world of change." The poet keeps the paradox alive by prescinding from all the metaphysical and theological relationships between spirit, thought, and the world. In his over-all attitude the permanence of thought, or the idea, is grounded in the unity of the Godhead, so that the pure ideas become more intensely actual than the world of matter and individual fact.[4] But this poem does not address itself to the spiritual mode of relationships; it

4. In a letter to Thomas Clarkson, 1806 (*New Letters*, 2, 1193–99), Coleridge gives an elaborate explanation of his early understanding of immutable ideas as they exist in God.

considers man as a disaffected part of the formerly unified
Nature expressed in "Frost at Midnight." And in this
respect the constancy of the ideal object of thought in the
physical world is a paradox, because it is at once more and
less than the physical world around it. "She is not thou,
and only thou art she." The thought is a representation
which becomes more permanent than the thing, in this
case, the person, represented. The mingling of spirit with
Nature which occurred in his early poetry, for instance, the
thought of the poet with the breath of the babe in "Frost
at Midnight" no longer is able to take place:

> Fond thought! not one of all that shining swarm
> Will breathe on thee with life-enkindling breath.

The ideal, fixed mode of thought, the spiritual image,
must remain detached from the vibrant but mutable reality of Nature, through a paradox which is emotionally
enervating for the poet. It is interesting to note that the
possibility of reuniting thought with its object, man with
Nature, Coleridge with Sara Hutchinson, is expressed in
terms of the nature imagery of the early poems "The
Eolian Harp," "This Lime-Tree Bower"; the old symbols
of interpenetration and unity of being in immanential
monism recur in a backward glance:

> Home and Thou are one.
> The peacefull'st cot, the moon shall shine upon,
> Lulled by the thrush and wakened by the lark . . .

But the present alienation of man as spirit in Nature involves the same image cluster as did the spiritually isolated
Mariner in the early years:

> Without thee were but a becalmed bark,
> Whose Helmsman on an ocean waste and wide
> Sits mute and pale his mouldering helm beside.

Here the symbols of regeneration and isolation are not merged by the imaginative power as in the earlier poems. Man remains an isolated spirit in Nature, the generative security of which offers no consolation to him. The question, "And art thou nothing?" brings us back again to "Limbo," "Denial of Immortality," or "Ne Plus Ultra." Either man is a spiritual creature involved in an ontological complex with his Creator, essentially apart from Nature, or else his highest nature is only the self-generated illusion of the rustic:

> An image with a glory round its head;
> The enamoured rustic worships its fair hues,
> Nor knows he makes the shadow, he pursues!

In his present mood Coleridge is content to let the paradox generated by his dissociated sensibility remain at the center of his consciousness. But there is no poetic fecundity in the "ocean waste and wide" of spiritual isolation. The either/or cannot be bridged by the exuberance of poetic imagination. Coleridge has passed from what Kierkegaard calls the "aesthetic" to the "ethical" condition.

The furthest point of spiritual isolation he reached is "Work without Hope," where the meditation again is upon the individual estranged from the productivity and exuberance of Nature. The poem moves in a tortuous elegiac manner and in the end seems to break off in despair, when the hopelessness in the dichotomy between Nature and spirit has manifested itself completely:

> Work without Hope draws nectar in a sieve,
> And Hope without an object cannot live.

The observing subject is completely cut off from communication with the objects, the living slugs, bees, birds of fertile Nature. The key word in the first stanza is "seems." A barrier to immediacy of feeling between man and Nature relegates the poet to the role of a mere onlooker.[5] The active projection of the mind upon the objects of Nature, leading to the interpenetration and fusion of all things in "Frost at Midnight," no longer takes place. Nothing in Nature corresponds to this paralysis of the spirit, for even the winter, which might ordinarily be taken as an analogue of the torpid mind, "Wears on his smiling face a dream of Spring!" This is a further step from his position in "Denial of Immortality" or the Notebook entry, since the horror expressed there at the impersonal participation of man in Nature is now replaced by a spiritual stagnation, in relation to which even the former impersonal motions of Nature would come as a welcome release. The word "seems" instead of "is" ("All Nature seems at work") indicates clearly the poet's hesitation to attribute any spiritual meaning to Nature; he has become conscious of the "pathetic fallacy," a condition unthinkable in the mood and motion of "Frost at Midnight."

This spiritual isolation assumes a more general and universal status in the second stanza when the particular present scene is suddenly charged with symbolic values and associations drawn from Coleridge's earlier career. No longer engaged merely with a late February winter scene in 1825, the poet now views the sight of Nature gradually renewing itself as a metaphor for the entire sweep of former imaginative life, when Nature and spirit had responded to each other as reflex manifestations of the same reality. The amaranths, mystical flowers of eternal bloom, and the magic fount "whence streams of nectar flow" are drawn not from the present countryside but from the misty land of the imagination, the landscape of "Kubla Khan" and "The Ancient Mariner." The word "ken" is

5. This reminds one of the early letter to Poole, March 23, 1801 (*Letters I*, 350–52), in which Coleridge alleged that Newton made mind a mere lazy onlooker in Nature.

used here in the sense of "remember" rather than the usual "know" or "recognize," and in conjunction with the phrase "traced the founts" signifies that Coleridge is reproducing the hazy stream of ideas associated with the romantic imagination, ideas whose objects transcend the ordinary bounds of objective space and time. But now it is only in the memory of the poet that such stirrings can be awakened, as in the poem "The Garden of Boccaccio," where a backward glance awakens temporarily but artificially the creative spirit of the early years.

The lines in "Work without Hope" "Bloom o ye *aramanths!* bloom for whom ye may / For me ye bloom not! Glide, rich streams, away!" refer of course to the deadness of external nature in the present spiritual void, but primarily indicate that the mythical sources of poetic inspiration in the mind's imaginative powers have dried up. And the following line, "With lips unbrightened, wreathless brow, I stroll," has more than the usual connotations associated with the happy pagan at home in Nature. It should be read in connection with the closing lines of "Kubla Khan," with its enchanted poet,

> His flashing eyes, his floating hair . . .
> For he on honey-dew hath fed,
> And drunk the milk of Paradise.

Coleridge is referring to the sunny domes, the caves of ice, in short the lost world of pure active imagination projecting itself upon Nature. The spell cast by "streams of nectar" and honey-dew had long been broken; only in an imaginative flight of memory such as in this stanza could it be partially revived.

A baffling psychological situation appears to be that the fount of Coleridge's imaginative powers, the streams which nurtured his best poetry, the aramanths of eternal Nature for the sight of which he still longed, were all deeply and inextricably bound up with the early years, the brightened vistas of that immanential universe in which all Nature was the reflex of spirit, and spirit the conscious individual manifestation of Nature. Whereas, sad to say, the alien spirit of later years was shut out from the nectar fount and forced to pass through this world with wreathless brow instead of glittering eye. The alien spirit is the emotional counterpart of the spiritual will and conscience at war with matter and the evil principle, in a semidualistic universe under a personal God who could be recognized only in the dialogues of the still small voice, and never in the analogies of external Nature. Coleridge could not revive the analogy or sentiment of being from which Christian poets through the ages have drawn mythical and imaginative power.

Religious poems illustrative of the alien spirit are "Duty Surviving Self-Love," "Forbearance," and "Baptismal Birthday," where all the tendencies thus far mentioned come to a climax. Man is forced to look inward to the conscience which is the pure spiritual reality. The sense of sin is heavy, yet a feeling of the past glory in Nature is great enough to forestall any movement toward spiritual tension between soul and body, or man and Nature. The idea of God as purely spiritual wars against that anthropomorphic conception of deity which might lend the poem the personal human interest of seventeenth-century poetry. Even the more feeble blessings of the eighteenth-century hymnological tradition, in which Methodist and Anglican alike cautiously but joyously praised their Maker through his works and manifestation in Nature,[6] were denied to Coleridge as a result of his long

6. Sister Mary Eulogia Horning, *Evidences of Romantic Treatment of Religious Elements in Late Eighteenth-Century Minor Poetry—1771–1880* (Washington, D.C., 1932) points out that the hymnologists were able to view God as both immanent and transcendent, a way which was denied to the more sophisticated Coleridge in his later years.

war against "Natural Theology," issuing finally in the Post-Kantian semidualism we have defined. This semidualism, with its austere conception of the relationship obtaining between man and Nature, Nature and God, man and God, did not allow the doctrine of proportional analogy common to the great Catholic and Protestant theological systems until 1700, and thus denied a universe of sacramental impact and the sentiment of being. Christ remained primarily the symbolic manifestation of the "Divine Idea," or the Logos of Neoplatonic tradition. In "Baptismal Birthday" we come the closest yet to Coleridge on his knees in prayer, but the habit of poetry was much more entwined with the habit of speculation, so that "Forbearance" and "Duty Surviving Self-Love" are unfortunately more typical and genuine expressions of his awakened religious consciousness.

This combination of isolated spirit and extreme interest in the conscience as an element *sui generis* culminates in a preaching tendency, which is also noticeable in the prose. The minor religious poems each tend to be little sermons directed by the self at the self. In "Baptismal Birthday" the result is somewhat more liberating than usual, as the idea of God manifested in Christ supplies a wider background for the trial of conscience. But wherever the background narrows to the extent that conscience reflects only a form of duty, then the sermons—as "Forbearance" (on the theme "Beareth all things," I Cor. 13:7), and "Duty Surviving Self-Love"—tend to become mere vehicles of self-justification. The arrogant tone of righteousness, verging on defiance and quite uncommon in Coleridge, is a reminder that to a certain extent his cult of conscience is related, at least in part, through the common medium of Kant to the cult of will represented by Emerson's *Self-Reliance,* and to a great deal of Carlyle. The self-

satisfied, conscious moralizing directed at the desertion by
friends of the early years, in "Duty Surviving Self-Love,"

> Love them for what they are; nor love them less
> Because to thee they are not what they were.

shows that self-love has survived duty, or modified it into
self-pity. "Forbearance," riddled with the same self-pity,
advances to the further extreme of defiance, which indicates how close conscience as duty *sui generis* can approximate self-will, in "Give him the rotten timber for
his pains!" More significant than the un-Christian old-law
outlook in this poem is the deeper problem, the loss of
community of feeling, or of the sense of mutual inter-
course by analogy between man and man, or man and
objects of Nature, within the context of a transcendentally
good God. But the negative attitude of will or self-assertion
is really abortive and tenuous in Coleridge. More often,
in a poem such as "Baptismal Birthday," the movement
is toward real communication between man and God
through conscience in a more genial ontological context
in which the idea of God is manifested and made tangible
to the human heart through Christ. The curious thing
is that this positive Christian manifestation fails to make
these poems interesting as poetry.

In "Baptismal Birthday" the strident tone and somewhat hysterical straining to achieve union and immortality
through Christ breaks down almost completely the interesting tensions of Coleridge's spiritual career; here particularly the doctrine of justifying faith is abandoned in
favor of a complete surrender to the extreme Calvinistic
position. Complete surrender of personality and will,
"Christ my all," "Eternal Thou and everlasting we,"
"In Christ I live," emphasis upon personal immortality,
and alienation from nature go hand in hand.

> Let then earth, sea and sky
> Make war against me! On my heart I show
> Their mighty master's seal.

Spirit and matter are so sharply divided that in the pure
interchange or blending of spirit there is no dialectic between man and Nature, good and evil. Nature is merely
abandoned to the enemy.[7] The idea of God, which might
conceivably have challenged the poet as it did the philosopher, is presented in commonplace fashion. "Baptismal
Birthday" and "Gnothi Seauton" are good Calvinistic
Christianity but the lack of structure and tension shows
that Coleridge has not been able to turn his religious
interests into good poetry. Coleridge, on his own premises,
was shut up within a semidualistic world of spirit. Alien
to Nature and divided from God by sin,[8] this spirit did
not prove a fruitful source of great poetry.

The early poems, like "The Eolian Harp," "Frost at
Midnight," "Kubla Khan," and "The Rime of the Ancient
Mariner" are Coleridge's best poetry, although to his later
mentality they must have appeared as curious relics from
the early years of optimism, the One Life and the universe
of immanence. The real relationship between poetry and
Coleridge's attempt to construct a religious philosophy can
probably be summarized by the reminder that the little
poem "Reason" is a mediocre expression of what the *Aids*

7. Notebook 36, f. 65: "Life begins in detachment from Nature and ends
in union with God. The adorable Author of our Being is likewise its
ultimate End."

8. Notebook 37, f. 24. This entry on asceticism and numerous others of
similar character indicate Coleridge's increasing tendency in later years
to divorce man from Nature, and to consider the spiritual principle as a
thing apart: ". . . and further, on the score of consistency, I, S.T.C.
ought to have taken time to put to myself the question, whether the es-
sentials of the ascetic morality do not follow inevitably from my own views
of Nature ⚹ God, and Man like the Moon flown off, but still reclaimed
by the Sun."

to Reflection and Opus Maximum said in energetic prose. So also with the other late poems. It is no accident that a poem like "Reason" finds its way into the Opus Maximum, or that the flashing insights into the unity of being of the early poems now appear in prose.[9] "Reason" and the other little poems of the late period show the influence of the "One Life" of the fine early poems and the semi-dualistic doctrine of analogy in the remarkable late prose. The later vision was widened and deepened, and was infinitely more flexible than that of the Bard of the Susquehanna. But the principle of unity had survived the march from the Susquehanna to the Jordan, from the simple and joyous to the sad and complex.

A few final words should be said about the religious philosophy itself. While others were drifting down the lazy main stream of apologetics and natural theology, bequeathed to Christianity by the eighteenth century, Coleridge had searched out the hidden springs from which were to flow the new torrents of Christian thought, the kind of thought which has dominated Christian philosophy since Kierkegaard. Thus there is a common existential and volitional basis for Christian thinking shared by Coleridge, Kierkegaard, and the modern revival of orthodoxy in Germany.

Twentieth-century literary criticism has paid its homage to Coleridge, in some cases to the point of absurdity. It is not surprising that a gesture of similar proportions has not

9. Notebook 36, f. 66: "What the Laws of the Spiritual World are, we know not, particularly; but generally we know, that the Spiritual is likewise the *Intelligible World,* and therefore an object of the intellectual Act and intelligential energy—and surely not the less so, because the Intellectus, Intelligible, and Intellectio are distinctly *one.* If even Nature, the basis *ab intra* of our present Individuality, in its living process of superseding herself, by assumption of true Being, calls forth our faculties to only not the noblest direction, surely the depths of True Being, the Nature above all Nature, sustaining our personal life, *a supra,* will supply a still further object for our contemplation, meditation, and discovery."

been forthcoming from religious thinkers, for one must admit that Coleridge has been historically considered as a literary man standing on the periphery of the religious scene. These leaders rightly turn to Kierkegaard, Brunner, and Barth in seeking the more potent fathers of the modern spirit. Although they do, the fact remains that Coleridge was a spiritual forerunner of this movement in many ways.

Another and more persistent error, for which Fairchild is the *locus classicus,* is that of attributing primary responsibility to Coleridge for the so-called dissipating tendencies in mid-nineteenth-century Protestantism. Now for those who rejected what he rejected in the old tradition without retaining what he retained, the tendency toward dissolution was natural. A man's thought may become a great influence in some distorted form, as has happened so often in the history of ideas. But Coleridge's religious thought leads more forcefully and justly in its richness and complexity to Kierkegaard (need we repeat the TRY IT phrase?) and to the neo-orthodox movement in Germany and the United States. It may be ironic that Coleridge's influence could not stem the cleavage between the High Churchmen moving toward Anglo-Catholicism and the Low Church sinking into humanism which was going on in his day and has been completed in ours.

Would Coleridge's influence have been greater if the documents now being published had been widely known? Probably not. He could not bequeath a system of objective principles to his followers, another way of repeating an opening remark in this book, that Coleridge was no Hegel. As a matter of interest and proof one might point to the little-known work of Joseph Henry Green, Coleridge's disciple. In the *Elements of Religious Philosophy* Green systematized, to the best of his ability, the unpublished writings of Coleridge, made available to him by the Coleridge family. The impact of his work upon contemporary thought was slight. Coleridge's own writing had an infectious quality of its own, it stimulated and excited other original minds in their own quests for religious knowledge and experience. Green's effort showed how fruitless the way of a camp follower could be.

Coleridge straddled too many fences, was aware of too many contradictory trends, and lacked the profound power of integration necessary to launch a true theological movement. His "system" was really a strategy for reconciling conflicting oppositions in his own mind, and it is perfectly obvious that some of his maneuvers were less successful than others. That is why our focus has not been destructively bent upon searching out the logical difficulties, some of them insurmountable, in the "system." It was held upon the rich variety of complex philosophical and religious opinions which filtered through the mind of this genius who was literally immersed in western thought all his life. For more analytic expression of these thoughts we might turn to others. But for an aid to our own reflections, and for a sympathetic companion in our own aesthetic, moral, and religious problems, here is Coleridge in all his complexity, garrulity, and humanity. His religious musings are a monument of poetic expression in the prose medium.

APPENDIX I

(From Notebook 26, ff. 27ᵛ–43; 51ᵛ–52ᵛ)

The attempt to solve the problem of Existence, Order, and Harmony otherwise than by an Eternal Mind—or to explain the Universe of finite and dependent Beings without assuming Will and Intelligence as its ground, and antecedent Principle, is too revolting to common sense, too discrepant from our habits of thinking, feeling, and acting, offers too gross an outrage on the very instincts of humanity, and to all the principles which from the very constitution of the human mind we take for granted as the ground-work of all other Beliefs, to require any confutation. . . . Taking for granted then, that the world owes its Existence to an adequately powerful Will and Reason, which being antecedent to all other Being, must itself be eternal, and which we name God, we pass to our first Position . . .

I. and in answer to the question, was the world produced in time? Was there a *first* Finite, or is the Universe of an Eternal Cause the co-eternal Effect? In fewer words, was the world created or produced by emanation or eradiation? If there be any absurdity in the latter proposition, it must arise, not out of the supposed mode of production but out of something incompatible therewith in the conception of the Product: for we assert the former in the eternal generation of the Word, of Sire Eternal Co-eternal Son! We reply: an incompatibility does inhere in the conception of a Universe of dependent Finites, and eternal production in consequence of the succession of changes and incompleteness of the Products at every single moment, and this inadequacy is every single moment, and their inadequacy is representative of their cause in all times. Only a positively essential Unity, an I Am, can be the adequate Idea or Alterity (*Deus alter et idem*) of the Absolute Will. But waiving this profounder view of the subject, and, content with having hinted it seminatively for the capable few, it will suffice for our present purpose that we say—that in the sense in which any conclusion can be drawn for or against Religion, the hypothesis (viz. the eternity of the Universe) is contradicted by the Facts—it is demonstrably false: and in the sense, in which it is evidently and prima facie contradicted by the Fact, it is purely arbitrary and gratuitous assertion, proceeding on a transfer of the intuitions of Sense (= Forms of time & Space) to Spiritual Beings, and involving the notion of an Infinite Time, and thus an infinite Past the possibility of which for the reason is at least very doubtful.

Proof—If the assertion be, that the world has always been in the present form, the investigations of the Geologist supply the decisive negative . . .

But if this be conceded, and the advocate for the eternity of the Creation asserts only that there has been an infinite series of successive worlds—we reply as before that the assertion is groundless and gratuitous—and if he would ground it on the eternity of the divine energies, we reply—this might argue strongly for an eternal generation of infinite and adequate Being; but not necessarily for a beginningless production of an Aggregate of finite existents, each of which has begun. The assertion therefore is gratuitous—I say, yes! to which I say, no! is a fair balance but the former strikes the beam, when we add, that it involves all the inconveniences of an infinite series: that it is the *Interest* of Reason and Science to determine against it—and lastly, that the same argument from existing grades of perfection, which decided the judgement against the existence of the Human Race myriads of ages before the Mosaic Era, applies with equal force to the Planet itself, and by analogy to the whole system. It is not possible for the Mind to hold a progressive series, and yet to find the present stage of the progression proportional to an infinite period, during which it had been always ascending. The mind, that has once contemplated the Idea of God and the divine Attributes, shrinks back from the thought as a desecration.

"But still there are great difficulties attending on the idea of a Creation in time." To as many as had attained to a right use of the terms, and learnt what Reason is and what is not an Idea, I should say—the *Reason* finds none in the *Idea,* though the *understanding* makes for itself insurmountable difficulties in the *conception* of a Creation in Time . . . but they are of our own choosing, and arise out of the misapplication of a Faculty judging according to sense, and constituted for the purpose of generalizing . . . the phenomena received by the Senses in the forms of Space and Time, to a subject to which Space and Time are all together alien & untransferable. These are insuperable difficulties; but they are of our own Necromancy, conjured up by asking senseless questions that preclude all answers, such as—*when* did time begin? —that is—at *what* time was there *no* time? Only I may be permitted to remind the Assailants and Contemners of the Mosaic Narrative that their favorite question, what was God doing, the whole eternity with the exception of the last six thousand years? must carry them the whole way to Atheism: for it will apply with scarcely diminished force to any lesser point of Maturity, any inferior grade of perfection . . . Meantime, as our present object is a deduction of the truth of the Christian Religion, the credibility of the Bible Creed, we may confine our attention to the question as it respects Man and the Earth as his appointed habitation. . . . We proceed to the second position.

II. a finite rational creature, or an individual Agent endowed with Reason & self-consciousness, must be a moral and responsible creature. The proof is afforded in the idea: for Reason is a Law, that supposes a *Will* as its subject. This may be rendered evident by contrasting the Law of Reason, which is a Law only as far as it is a Light, with the *Power* of Life, which is indeed disposed and directed in its acts and products *according* to a Law of Reason, but is itself constitutive—i.e. it gives the forms, in which it acts, and acts on itself in the moment that it acts on its products, the bodily organs. For the organ must be living in order for the powers of life to act on it, which is the same thing as when I said, that Life acts on itself and is its own subject. Hence when the Light itself is a light in a creature but not for it, as an object distinguishable therefore, when the light is one and the same with the *Life,* we say that such a creature is endowed with *Instinct.* Light indistinguishable from Life is instinct, not Reason. So if Reason acted *immediately* on the Life or Nature of a Creature, as one with the life or behavior it would cease to be a Law, & become a grace, a Beatitude, a perfection or Holiness. Reason contemplated severally and distinctly is a Law that supposes a Will as its subject. It cannot therefore be coercive for it requires obedience, and obedience can be required only where disobedience is *possible.* I would not say, a free will, were it only from the ambiguity and the frequent deceptive use of the word, freedom. Generally, Freedom is employed as a mere synonime of Will. To say: "it is an act of his own free will" is the same as to declare it a free act or an act of freedom. But there is another less common but far more correct sense of the word, according to which Freedom expresses that highest perfection of a finite will, which it attains by its perfect self-determined subordination to Reason, "whose service is perfect Freedom." A will therefore may cease to be free and yet remain responsible: because its unfreedom has originated in its' own act. A will cannot be *free* to choose evil—for in the very act it forfeits its' freedom, and so far becomes a corrupt Nature self-enslaved. It is sufficient to say, that a will *can* choose evil, but in the moment of such choice ceases to be a *free* will . . . In short, Will is a primary most simple Idea, which we can only know by *being* it: and every attempt to understand it by addition of epithets is idle or worse than idle . . . It is of the last importance in the right discipline of the mind to be made fully aware, that in respect of primary Ideas, such as the Ideas, Will, Reason, Being, Act, Identity, Alterity, Unity, Multeity, etc. there is no middle state between adequate knowledge and absolute ignorance. . . .

But to return: our second position then is, that [II] a creature endowed with Reason and Self-consciousness must be a responsible Agent, whose Will is amenable to a Law, and distinct from the Law. And this condition is given, where the Will is finite and individual, the Law Absolute and Universal.

Corollary: The understanding therefore can not be the Law: for it is like the Will finite and individual, a light that guides to the means, not prescribes the ultimate ends; and which abstracted from the influence of a higher light co-present with it in the same Subject or person, would be no more than a faculty of selection and adapting means to the immediate purposes and Appetites. It would be an Instinct, one with the specific life of the creature—and the highest function of animal life. . . .

The Result is: that Man was created a rational self-conscious and responsible creature.

Position III. To account for the existence and continuance of irrational things, organic or inorganic, animate or inanimate, it is sufficient to think of God as their Creator. But this is inadequate to the solution of the problem presented to us in the preservation and continuance of man, and in the development of his proper & peculiar attributes. In the instance of the first man the Creator supplies the place of the Begetter or the Parturient in the instance of man as now born; but the newly born Babe can never become a *Man,* in contradistinction from the animal, unless the Parent, the exemplar and tutor, supervenes . . . Supposing the light of reason potentially connate as well as innate, yet to elicit or call it into actual consciousness, so that it should be a Law for mankind, it must have been outwardly propounded by a Legislator, and again, unless it were to be dormant, as a Law, some object must have been pointed out, in relation to which its' supremacy, and its' right to unconditional obedience were expressed, and the means afforded to the whole of exercising that obedience. First, its supremacy. The object of Test, therefore, must not be one, to which the will might be determined by the appetance of Life or the impulse of any lower powers, or the pride of the will itself . . . But this is not possible —for what outward object is there that does not stand in some relation to the Life, or the Sense, or the Feeling?— otherwise than by the prohibition of some object. Besides, that the supremacy of the Law is then only expressed, when it is imperative not only without aid of the lower influences but in opposition to them. Secondly, its right to unconditioned obedience—No other ground is required, but simply the Law itself—In order that the Reason might be the *Law* the Law must be obeyed as Reason. . . .

Position IV. In a finite rational Creature, such as we know man to be, Reason necessarily supposes a distinct Will, as its Correlative, or Correspondent—and to this Will the Reason stands in the relation of the Law to a Subject capable of obeying it; and for that cause capable likewise of withholding obedience. The Light and Form of life is a self-executing law *in* the living body; the Light of Reason is a Law *for* the will, not in it or is one with it. (If this latter were possible, the result would be an *Instinct*.) In order therefore to call forth and educate the moral and rational faculties of a responsible agent, a law must be imposed having the character of Supremacy and of unconditional Authority. The Law must demand obedience simply and solely because it is the Law. The Reason of the law is that it is the law of Reason. But God *is* Reason: and as every law of Reason is for *us* a law of God, so in the first calling of human rationality a law of God must have been the Law of Reason. . . .

Position V. In no auspicious hour did the spirit of speculative Theology construct or rather attempt to construct, out of the simple and universally intelligible word, Wonders or extraordinary Events and actions, a peculiar *sort,* under the denomination of *Miracles.* . . . [*An attack on miracles follows*]

For our purpose it is sufficient, that The Creator of Man was likewise his Parent and Instructor: and that he received his first human instruction, the means and condition of his *actual* humanity (i.e. rationality) in the school of Revelation. Whether the term Miracle, be defined or left indefinite, and however defined, if defined it must be, all will agree that creation is a Miracle. We may therefore lay it down as an established Position, that the Human Race began in a Miracle, and the first act of Human Reason consisted in the receiving of a Revealed Law. By this process Man was taught to know, that in the Almighty Creator Infinite Intelligence was one with Absolute Will, distinct yet indivisible omniscient Intelligence the Form of the omnipotent Will, the essence of the omniscient Intelligence; that in man there was a light of Reason, representative of the divine intelligence, and the medium through which the Supreme Mind revealed itself to him, that Reason was the universal Principle of his Being, and the indispensable *condition* of his personality; that likewise there was in man a finite Will, as the individual principle of his Being, and the *ground* of his personality, capable of determining itself to a coincidence with, or an aversion from, the universal principle—i.e. the Light of Reason; that the Divine Mind being one with the Divine Will, the representative of the former was by necessary implication the pledge and evidence of the latter, and that thus the Light of Reason became a law of God; (and by equal necessity a Light from God must be a Law of Reason). . . . Lastly, that the human will, as the capable subject of a Law, was by the Law rendered a responsible Will, and Man himself, as the personal Subject of Reason and Will, a moral & responsible agent. Moreover, as a Light from God directly and immediately such, was necessary in the past instance to actuate the Human Reason, and as it were, to induct and inaugurate it into its legislative capacity & offices, it follows likewise that the Human Reason began in *Faith;* that an insight into the reasonableness of obedience was anterior and antecedent to an insight into the reasonableness of the command to be obeyed; that therefore even from the beginning Man's moral Being had the primacy over the intellectual, and the Light of Reason in the conscience of far higher authority than the Light of Reason in the understanding.

Either the Soul or personal principle, το ΕΓΩ of the First Adam must have been intuitive of the Deity as the universal ground, in which its individual existence subsisted, and the absolute "I am in that I am," in relation to which every finite Person affirms of itself, I am in that God is—either this, I say, this exalted Power must be supposed, which however, there is no ground for supposing, but on the contrary strong grounds for believing it peculiar to the Second Adam . . . *Or in the first* Man, even as in all the descendents born of Woman, the knowledge of the *Legislator* and the conviction of his Right to be obeyed, must have been antecedent to the sense and conviction of the righteousness of the *Law,* and the *Conditio sine qua non* of the latter. And in this case, Religion must have been the Basis of Morality, and Morality of Sciential Insight. In other words, the Light from God (i.e. God's revelation of his Being and Attributes generally and of his Will relatively to Man) must have been introductory to the Light of Reason in the Conscience, and the Light of Reason in the Conscience to the Light of Reason in the understanding. Observe. This is the corner-stone of my system, ethical, metaphysical, and theological—the priority, namely, both in dignity and order of generation, of the Conscience to the Consciousness in Man—No I without a Thou, no Thou without a Law from Him, to whom I and Thou stand in the same relation. Distinct Self-knowledge begins with the Sense of Duty to our neighbor: and Duty felt to, and claimed from, my Equal supposes and implies the Right of a Third, superior to both because imposing it on both.

One most important consequence of the facts hitherto established is, that:

Position VI. As the education of the Human Race began in Religion, so Religion began in the acknowledgment of a personal God as Creator. In an Eternal self-comprehending *One* there is the ineffable Will that created the World as well as the Adorable Might and Intelligence that gave it form and order. The Personality of the Creator, and the Creative Act of the Divine Person were the two fundamental Articles

of the primeval Faith. By the first, God was the object of a
Religion of Hope, Fear, Love, Communion, Thanksgiving,
Prayer; by the latter involving the Unity and Absolute transcendency of the divine essence, he was manifested as the object of a rational, spiritual, i.e. supersensual Religion. By
virtue of the first, the conversion of the Soul to the ground
and cause of the Universe became Religion, in contradistinction from Science, and Theory; by virtue of the Second, it was
a Religion, as opposed to Superstitition and Idolatry. "God
is a Spirit, and in Spirit and Truth to be worshipped."

Position VII—Thus far, we have proved the fact & necessity
of Revelation by the force of Reason, without Revelation.
How to form a habit of religious Feelings? . . . The first step
—especially for a philosopher so thoroughly aware of the
small value of Testimonies respecting Facts or Subjects above
the knowledge and alien from the previous habits of the At-
testors—must be—to obtain a steadfast conviction of the
Truth of the Position, with which the Feelings are to be
associated.

The disquisition [*must be*] confined to man & in his present
state and circumstances. What is mean' by Religion generally?
Is it knowable from the speculative Reason as a Science? No.
From the speculations or Data supplied by the practical Reason, this Reason being taken as a faculty of the Human Mind
—or rather as the Mind in its' highest function? No! The
Reason and the Idea must be affirmed, as Revelation, as in
the first chapter of John's Gospel.

Can Religion be grounded on a Subjective Revelation *ex-
clusively?* The Negative demonstrated in the preceding VI
Positions. Of the different doctrines proclaiming to be continuations of the first Teaching all may be false—but only
one can be true. At all events the question for us is confined
to Christianity—The System, which I call by this name &
the necessity of assuming this to be Christianity. Shewn that
it contains all the Articles of Faith common to all the Churches
—and that the remainder are required in order to the Religion

being presented as a coherent System, and must be true if the articles common to all are to be comprehended as Truths. Now then, the Question is, Has this system that Quantum of *History* requisite to give it *objective* validity, as a whole? Are the constituent *Ideas* in that connection with existing recorded Facts, which is necessary to its' being at once History & Philosophy—for this is the Definition of Religion viz. Religion is distinguished from Philosophy on the one hand and from History on the other, by being both at once. The second question is—Presuming the subjective validity and moral interest of the Ideas to be such, as to supply the necessary *a priori* probability of an historical manifestation—What Evidence ought we to expect? Assuredly no evidence precluded by the very Idea of the Religion, or excluded by its' purposes— And here the Disquisition ends—re. such are the contents of the Pages devoted to the Question—What Methods should a philosopher or Thinker adopt to form or to cultivate a Habit of Religious Feeling?

APPENDIX II

(On the Soul. From Notebook 26, ff. 44-48)

The question of an ante-natal [*pre-existence of Soul*] as deduced from the assumption of a posthumous life involves or rather perhaps provokes another—viz. how far the doctrine of immortality loses or retains its moral and religious worth and interest disjoined from the continuance of a consciousness of the present state of our being? I have 30 years ago and more controverted Locke's position, that consciousness (in the sense of Memory or the definite Consciousness of having been definitely conscious) is the essence of the Personal Identity —observing that Locke might as rationally have asserted the Mile to be the essence of the Road. Now in the highest sense of consciousness, what the Germans call *unbewustsein,* I cannot deny that a great deal may be said for the deduction of a pre-existence from the immortality of the soul, after this life. But no less undeniable does it appear to me, that this (whether Idea in the Divine Mind or a Soul) is not what we mean by *us:* It is not my *I* though it may be my eye or mihi —but the source of it, not at all participating in its' crimes or their consequences and infinite above its merits of attainment, even as God is my source of Motion & animal life without partaking of them—But the main point in which I differ *toto caelo* from the newest sect of religious Philosophy in German (the School of Schleiermacher and Solger) in their charging this tenet with an unsafe sort of Pantheism on Christianity, of extolling the factor in an wholly independent or even exclusive and individual consciousness, as a Christian *Perfection*—a more exalted state of mind. On the contrary, it seems to me to have been one great & continued purpose of our Lord and of the Churches' doctrine of the Resurrection of the Body to draw the Believer's mind from all speculative notions, by asserting the resurrection of *the* Man—not of a Soul or Spirit but of the Man.

The immortality of the Soul may or may not be deducible from the New Testament. It is not expressed or enforced as an Article of Faith. But even as a philosophical theme, I see in it no universal difficulty to be grappled with. If we assume, as all the facts accumulated by the genius and industry of the constellation of great Minds, who with John Hunter as their Morning Star, have founded the science of Comparative Anatomy & Physiology, authorize us to assume, a graduated scale of ascent from the minimum of consciousness . . . up to the highest imaginable perfection of consciousness that can exist in a *Creature,* there must be some first instance, in which the consciousness survives the metempsychosis of the Creature—even as there must be a first, in which the Consciousness becomes *individual* (i.e. proper self-consciousness). Now as this latter takes place *first* in Man, there is every reason to suppose and none to deny, that Man will be the first instance of the former likewise. In the human being first we assume an immortality of the Individual, by succession instead of an immortality of the Race by a succession of Individuals: and it would be strange indeed, if the Self-consciousness which is the *Form* and indispensable Mark of the Individuality should not partake in its destiny. Only be aware of the full import of "Form" as here applied. Consciousness is not an impressed shape, as the Seal on the wax, or as the Pyriformity on a Marble Pear nor can it be compared even to the characteristic Type, or distinctive Shape resulting from the formative power of Life, in the natural fruit, or in each animal. No! It is Form, as the correlative of essence, distinct but even in thought inseparable, and co-inherent. In the same sense, that in discoursing on the Godhead, or (if that be forbidden or of doubtful right) in discoursing on the Attributes of moral and responsible creatures, we say that Intelligence is the *form* of the personal Will, and Will the essential ground of the Intelligence,—since a Will not intelligent is no Will, but a tendency or blind appetite—in this same sense must the term be understood, when I say that the consciousness is the *form* of the personal *Individuality*. N.B. The characteristic Formula of all *Spiritual* verities or Ideas is an apparent *Circle*, i.e. a proposition which if predicated of Things or conceptions, περί αἰσθητων, ἤ περί λογῶν (ἐννοιῶν τῶν λοκικῶν) would produce a vicious circle in Logic. And yet as the universal forms of Logic are for *us* the necessary forms of all discourse, the indispensable conditions of all ratiocination, we are forced into a compromise i.e. we have no other means of reconciling the contradiction, than, just by shewing that an appearance of contradiction is the necessary consequence of applying the understanding to the immediate truths of Reason, in other words, of the attempt to *conceive* what being simple & unique, is, essentially inconceivable and 2. by shewing that by admitting this circle in the first instance, and only by admitting it, we avoid all future circles, and obtain a staple of a chain logical in all its links. Now the seeming self-contradiction in which alone an Idea or Spiritual Act, can be enunciated, is contained in the following Formula—A is the Cause of B, in as far as B is the cause of A, or B is the effect of A, on condition that A is the effect of B. Or A + B = A, so B + A = B. A and B mutually constitute each the other; and yet remain distinct, A = A, B = B. Thus the essence of Self-consciousness consists in the distinction yet identity of the Subject and Object, conscientis et consciti. We may therefore confidently assume, that if the Individuality survive, the individual consciousness will likewise survive, the deposition or sloughing of its present Larva. Quite another and perhaps plainer proof may be drawn from the continuity necessarily supposed in all consciousness—an articulated continuity indeed, but yet continuous. We are self-conscious creatures, and when we speak of our consciousness after death we mean that which we now *are,* and *have.* Yet we have no memory or consciousness of our first two, three, and with few and doubtful exceptions, of our first 5 or 6 years: and Consciousness would be a burden not a blessing or perfection, were it otherwise. It is sufficient that each moment or hour is conscious of the immediate antecedent, the more or less of the past, farther back . . . This depends on the laws of association modified and determined by the character and circumstances of the individual. This, however, we know, that both the extent and the distinctness of our Consciousness grows with the growth of the general intellect, but it is not as commonly considered, tho' it is as equally true and a truth of yet higher interest, how close a connection there subsists between the consciousness and the conscience, how greatly both the quantity and quality of our consciousness is affected by our moral character and the state of the will. But especially the *Quality*. The more advanced in the Life spiritual, the more perfectly the will of the Individual is self-subjected to the Divine Light and Word (ὅ λογός ὅ φοσφόρος, ἥ το φῶς το λογικόν) as the representative and exponent of the Absolute Will; the more habitually the understanding is submitted to the Light of Reason shining therein, and this light of Reason in the understanding is itself subordinated to the Reason in the Conscience, the more does our individual consciousness partake of the steadfastness and identity of the personal Subsistence, which is the copula and Unity of all the acts and shapes of the mind, the less loose and detachable is the consciousness of the events and objects that make up the man's experience τόν ἑαυτά βίον from the Self-consciousness, which is the essential and inalienable Form of his Personal Identity.

Meantime, it must never be forgotten, that whatever the Soul, or ground of each man's individual & personal Being, may be, it must be no more than a potential entity, the *dimidium sui*, the half only of its *Actual* Being: that "the Reason in finite Beings is not the Will"—or how could the Will be ever opposed to the Reason? Yet it is *the* condition, the *sine qua non* of a free i.e. of *actual* Will. Therefore Reason and *the* Will are the co-efficients of actual personality.

INDEX

A priori knowledge, 72–73, 178
Adams, William, 28 n.
Age of Reason, 68
Aids to Reflection, 1, 15, 19, 22–25, 28 n., 32, 35, 37, 40, 42, 44, 48, 50, 51, 55, 59, 66, 69, 74, 76, 82, 85–87, 93, 95, 107, 112, 113, 116, 117, 121, 125, 176–78, 183–85, 196, 199, 201, 216; analysis of, 3–13; idea of God in, 102–4; relationship of, to Notebook speculations, 143, 144, 145 n., 147; scheme of redemption in, 159–62, 171–74
Alterity, 133–39, 141, 147, 148, 153, 175, 176, 180, 182
Anglican Church, 2, 34, 56, 160, 213. *See also* Established Church
Anglican Creed, 178
Anglican theology, 4
Anglo-Catholicism, 218
Antinomianism, 42, 61
Aphorisms, moral, prudential, and spiritual. *See* Religion, tripartite
Aristotle, Aristotelianism, 54, 55, 68
Arminianism, 37, 41, 42, 45, 50, 51, 53, 55–62, 160, 177
Arminius (James Hermann or Hermensen), 38
Association, theory of, 13 n.
Atheism, 138 n., 149; alternatives to, 12–15
Atonement, 34, 45
Authority, 183–95
Awakenings, religious, 46

Bacon, Francis, 71 n.

Bampton Lectures, Oxford, 19, 20, 43
Baptism, 184; cause of dispute within Church of England, 39 n.; symbol of redemption, 40; High Church position on, 51, 188; Justification of Faith held by, 51–52, held not by, 55; STC on, 143, 188; in seventh "position," 172; Church Article on, 180
Barth, Karl, 218
Baxter, Richard, 48
Beattie, James, 29
Behmen, Jacob. *See* Böhme
Being, analogy of, 99 n.
Berkeley, George, 22, 25, 111
Blackwood's Magazine, 5
Böhme (Behmen), Jacob, 48 n., 49
Bolingbroke, Henry St. John, Lord, 27
Boyle Lectures, 19, 20, 26
British Constitution, 192
Brown, Thomas, 43
Brunner, Emil, 218
Butler, Joseph, 22, 27

Calvin, John, 41, 56, 143
Calvinism, 37, 38, 42, 45, 50–52, 178, 215
Cambridge Platonists, 69, 70, 93
Campbell, George, 28 n., 30 n.
Cassirer, Ernst, *Philosophy of the Enlightenment*, 24
Categorical imperative, 124. *See also* Kant
Catholicism, Catholic Church, 42, 50, 51, 60, 138 n., 160, 179 n., 186

YALE STUDIES IN ENGLISH

This volume is the one hundred and fifty-first of the Yale Studies in English, founded by Albert Stanburrough Cook in 1898 and edited by him until his death in 1927. Tucker Brooke succeeded him as editor, and served until 1941, when Benjamin C. Nangle succeeded him.

The following volumes are still in print. Orders should be addressed to YALE UNIVERSITY PRESS, New Haven, Connecticut.

127. VOGEL, STANLEY M. German Literary Influences on the American Transcendentalists. $4.00.

129. BRADLEY, JOHN LEWIS. Ruskin's Letters from Venice, 1851–1852. $5.00.

130. LEYBURN, ELLEN DOUGLASS. Satiric Allegory: Mirror of Man. $3.00.

131. LORD, GEORGE DE FOREST. Homeric Renaissance. The *Odyssey* of George Chapman. $3.00.

132. BOWDEN, EDWIN T. The Themes of Henry James. $3.00.

133. NOON, WILLIAM T. Joyce and Aquinas. $3.75.

134. SCHUTTE, WILLIAM M. Joyce and Shakespeare: A Study in the Meaning of *Ulysses*. $4.00.

135. UNDERWOOD, DALE. Etherege and the Seventeenth-Century Comedy of Manners. $4.00.

136. FRANK, R. W., JR. *Piers Plowman* and the Scheme of Salvation. $4.00.

137. BERGER, H., JR. The Allegorical Temper. Vision and Reality in Book II of Spenser's *Faerie Queene*. $5.00.

138. YOUNG, RICHARD B., FURNISS, W. TODD, MADSEN, WILLIAM G. Three Studies in the Renaissance: Sidney, Jonson, Milton. $5.00.

139. HOWES, ALAN B. Yorick and the Critics. Sterne's Reputation in England, 1760–1868. $4.50.

140. TAYLOR, CHARLES H., JR. The Early Collected Editions of Shelley's Poems. $4.00.

141. BLOOM, HAROLD. Shelley's Mythmaking. $5.00.

142. KERNAN, ALVIN. The Cankered Muse. Satire of the English Renaissance. $5.00.

143. PAULSON, RONALD. Theme and Structure in Swift's *Tale of a Tub*. $4.50.

144. RIDENOUR, GEORGE M. The Style of *Don Juan*. $4.00.

145. HIRSCH, E. D., JR. Wordsworth and Schelling. $4.00.

146. SPENCER, CHRISTOPHER. Davenant's *Macbeth*. $4.50.

147. LYNEN, JOHN F. The Pastoral Art of Robert Frost. $4.50.

148. TOWNSEND, J. BENJAMIN. John Davidson, Poet of Armageddon. $6.00.

149. KNAPP, MARY E. Prologues and Epilogues of the Eighteenth Century. $6.00.

150. SALOMON, ROGER B. Twain and the Image of History. $5.00.

151. BOULGER, JAMES D. Coleridge as Religious Thinker. $5.00.

152. BORROFF, MARIE. The Style of *Sir Gawain and the Green Knight*. $7.00.